Communications
in Computer and Information Science

1493

Luca Longo · Maria Chiara Leva (Eds.)

Human Mental Workload

Models and Applications

5th International Symposium, H-WORKLOAD 2021
Virtual Event, November 24–26, 2021
Proceedings

Editors
Luca Longo (iD)
Technological University Dublin
Dublin, Ireland

Maria Chiara Leva (iD)
Technological University Dublin
Dublin, Ireland

ISSN 1865-0929   ISSN 1865-0937 (electronic)
Communications in Computer and Information Science
ISBN 978-3-030-91407-3   ISBN 978-3-030-91408-0 (eBook)
https://doi.org/10.1007/978-3-030-91408-0

This Springer imprint is published by the registered company Springer Nature Switzerland AG
The registered company address is: Gewerbestrasse 11, 6330 Cham, Switzerland

Preface

This book aggregates a collection of contributions presented at the the the 5th International Symposium on Human Mental Workload, Models and Applications (H-WORKLOAD 2021). Over the years, the symposium has become a forum to encourage discussion on mental workload, its measures, dimensions, models, applications and consequences. It is a topic that demands a multidisciplinary approach, spanning across psychology, neuroscience, human factors, computer science, statistics and cognitive sciences. This book presents recent developments in the context of theoretical models of mental workload and practical applications.

H-WORKLOAD 2021 was supported by the organizing committee within Technological University Dublin and M-Brain Train; It was also endorsed by the Irish Human Factors Society, the Federation of European Ergonomics societies and Apergo, (Associação Portuguesa de Ergonomia). It contains a revision of the best papers presented at the symposium that were selected through a strict peer-review process. From the content of these research contributions, it is evident that a single, clear definition of mental workload applicable across all sectors and applications is still to be reached, demonstrating how the field is in a continuous state of evolution. This is confirmed by the different modeling approaches employed across contributions and the methodologies deployed for measuring it. However, one thing that can be confirmed across selected articles is that the ultimate goal of assessing mental workload is to predict its influence on human performance, and to find a way to support it in its several facets. For example, the keynote talk by Mark S. Young, is related to the problem of information underload and the search for a possible threshold in determining when the underload creates the issue of disconnecting from a task. The contribution highlights the difficulty of defining mental workload as a construct, and consequently also identifying critical states for underload and overload conditions.

The capacity to assess human mental workload is a key element in designing and implementing processes capable of monitoring interactions between automated systems and the humans destined to use them. Similarly, mental workload assessment is key for designing instructions and learning tools aligned to the limitations of the human mind. This last point is also confirmed by a number of selected research contributions devoted to mental workload and connectionism, instructional efficiency, information overload and mental fatigue in online learning. Some of the articles published in this book applied psychological subjective self-reporting measures; others made use of physiological or primary task measures and some a combination of these. Increasingly, although still in its infancy, the role of machine learning and deep learning has been explored to inductively model mental workload from EEG data. This area is a field in which traditional psychological approaches and novel data-driven modeling approaches can cross-paths, and perhaps trace a new direction in research that should be further explored and promoted. The field is fostering multidisciplinary contributions and it is likely to affect different sectors in which the problem of assessing and managing mental workload for human performance is crucial such as rail, aviation, healthcare, and manufacturing.

We wish to thank all the people who helped in the organizing committee for H-WORKLOAD 2021. A special thank goes to the researchers and practitioners who submitted their work and committed to attend the event, turning it into an opportunity to meet and share our experiences on this fascinating topic.

November 2021   Luca Longo
                                                                   M. Chiara Leva

Organization

Organizing Committee

General Chairs and Programme Committee Chairs

Luca Longo	Technological University Dublin, Ireland
Maria Chiara Leva	Technological University Dublin, Ireland

Local Chair

Bujar Raufi	Technological University Dublin, Ireland

Finance Chair

Bridget Masterson	Irish Ergonomics Society, Ireland

Program Committee

Julie Albentosa	French Armed Forces Biomedical Research Institute, France
Aidan Byrne	Swansea University, UK
Alessia Vozzi	BrainSigns, Italy
Andrew Smith	Cardiff University, UK
Anneloes Maij	National Aerospace Laboratory (NLR), The Netherlands
Audrey Reinert	The University of Oklahoma, USA
Bojana Bjegojevic	Technological University Dublin, Ireland
Bridget Kane	Karlstad University, Sweden
Bujar Raufi	Technological University Dublin, Ireland
Dick De Waard	University of Groningen, The Netherlands
Enrique Muñoz de Escalona Fernández	University of Granada. Spain
Fiona Kenvyn	Metro Trains Melbourne, Australia
Gianluca Borghini	Sapienza University of Rome, Italy
Giulia Cartocci	Sapienza University of Rome, Italy
Glauco Maria Genga	Istituto Medicina Aerospaziale Aeronautica Militare, Italy
Hector Diego Estrada Lugo	Technological University Dublin, Ireland
Jialin Fan	Cardiff University, UK
Jose Cañas	University of Granada, Spain

K. Tara Smith	Human Factors Engineering Solutions Ltd., UK
Karel Brookhuis	University of Groningen, The Netherlands
Lisa Jeanson	Coganalyse, France
Loredana Cerrato	Nuance Communications, USA
Maria Gabriella Pediconi	Istituto Medicina Aerospaziale Aeronautica Militare, Italy
Mark Young	Loughborough University, UK
Martin Castor	GEISTT AB Human System Effectiveness R&D Lab, Sweden
Matjaz Galicic	Mott MacDonald, Ireland
Patricia Lopez de Frutos	CRIDA – ATM R&D and Innovation Reference Centre, Spain
Pedro Ferreira	IST-CENTEC, Portugal
Philippe Rauffet	Université Bretagne-Sud, France
Vincenzo Ronca	BrainSigns, Italy

Contents

Models

In Search of the Redline: Perspectives on Mental Workload and the 'Underload Problem'

Mark S. Young[✉]

Human Factors and Complex Systems Group, School of Design and Creative Arts,
Loughborough University, Loughborough, UK
m.young@lboro.ac.uk

Abstract. For human factors researchers and practitioners, mental workload remains both a crucial concept and a nebulous one. After decades of work in this field, there is still no real consensus on the construct of mental workload, although there is wide agreement about its multidimensional nature and the main ways to measure it. With increasing automation in many domains, the issue of underload has attracted a considerable proportion of research effort. This paper summarises work to propose a theory of underload based on the notion of malleable attentional resources, but also raises challenges that this theory – and, perhaps, underload in general – may be specific to automation. The paper goes on to discuss the elusive 'redlines' of overload and underload, and concludes by considering both theoretical and applied challenges for current research into mental workload.

Keywords: Human mental workload · Underload · Redline · Attention

1 Tackling Mental Workload

Mental workload presents human factors researchers with something of a paradox. It is certainly a crucial factor in determining performance (e.g., Hancock and Caird 1993; Wilson and Rajan 1995), particularly as complex systems are increasingly technological and, therefore, present users with more mental demands than physical demands (Singleton 1989). Despite its intuitive appeal and a wealth of both theoretical and applied research dedicated to it (see e.g., Longo and Leva 2017), mental workload remains something of a nebulous concept, for which a consistent definition and approach to measurement has eluded researchers for decades (Hancock et al. 2021; Young et al. 2015).

Given the various definitions that abound in the literature, we can be reasonably confident in saying that mental workload involves attentional resource capacity; more specifically, the balance between objective demand of the task or situation against the resource supply of the operator or user (Welford 1978). Whilst the concept of objective demand may be difficult to elaborate in some circumstances, the matter is complicated further by the suggestion that 'true' mental workload is subjective, being the workload as experienced by the operator (e.g., Hart and Staveland 1988). Moreover, mental workload might not necessarily be an individual factor, since it can be influenced by interactions

L. Longo and M. C. Leva (Eds.): H-WORKLOAD 2021, CCIS 1493, pp. 3–10, 2021.
https://doi.org/10.1007/978-3-030-91408-0_1

with other elements in the system, be they human or machine (i.e., automation) (see e.g., Young et al. 2007). While not wanting to muddy the waters further with yet another definition, Young and Stanton (2001a; p. 507) pooled all of these various factors to offer an amalgamated, overall definition of mental workload as follows:

> *"The mental workload of a task represents the level of attentional resources required to meet both objective and subjective performance criteria, which may be mediated by task demands, external support, and past experience."*

In this definition, the level of attentional resources is assumed to have a finite capacity, beyond which any further increases in demand are manifest in performance degradation. Performance criteria can be imposed by external authorities, or may represent the internal goals of the individual. Examples of task demands are time pressure, or complexity. Support may be in the form of peer assistance or technological aids. Finally, past experience can influence mental workload via changes in skill or knowledge. Owing to this multidimensional nature of mental workload as a construct, its measurement is equally diverse. This is by no means surprising; if it is difficult to define a concept, it is going to be difficult to measure. The four main classes of mental workload measurement technique (primary task, secondary task, subjective, physiological) have been well documented elsewhere (e.g., Hancock et al. 2021; Young et al. 2015), so there is no need to rehearse them here. Suffice it to say, there is an argument that the dissociation often observed between these measures means that each technique taps into a different aspect of the mental workload construct (Hancock 2017). In recent years there have also been promising developments in neuro-ergonomic techniques such as near infrared spectroscopy (NIRS; see e.g., Mehta and Parasuraman 2013) which, it could be optimistically argued, might help us reach some of the holy grails of mental workload research. But more on that later.

2 Automation and/or Underload

Over the years, a great deal of research effort has been invested in understanding, predicting and managing the problem of underload with automated systems. Many researchers assert that underload is just as detrimental to performance as overload (Wilson and Rajan 1995), pointing to classical 'inverted-U' shaped curves of performance against demand (Fig. 1; cf. Lee et al. 2020; Yerkes and Dodson 1908) by way of demonstration that optimal performance will result from optimal demands. But the reasoning behind this has been more difficult to explain. If we adopt a capacity theory of mental workload, then overload is simply a matter of demand outstripping supply. However, it is less easy to explain the other end of the curve, where supply far outweighs demand.

In our work, we proposed Malleable Attentional Resources Theory (MART; Young and Stanton 2002a) to account for this. Based on some of the original ideas behind the capacity model of attention (Kahneman 1973), MART suggests that the size of attentional resource capacity can shrink when workload is too low, perhaps because of some cognitive efficiency (whether the 'lost' capacity truly disappears or is merely allocated elsewhere is perhaps moot; the point is, these resources are no longer dedicated to the task in hand). A theoretical depression of the resource capacity limit (and, by definition,

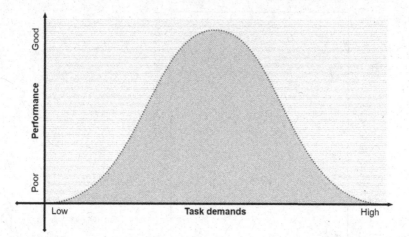

Fig. 1. Inverted-U relationship between task demand and performance.

the performance ceiling) predicts the inverted-U relationship between performance and demand (Fig. 2; Young and Stanton 2002a).

The underload problem typically manifests itself in an automation failure scenario: an operator, having been using a highly automated system for some length of time (and, hence, facing an underload situation), is suddenly faced with a sharp increase in demand in the form of an automation failure. Many studies demonstrate that this situation is difficult to cope with (see e.g., de Winter et al. 2014, and Victor et al. 2018 for reviews), offering support to this aspect of underload. MART explains these observations by recourse to the shrunken capacity limit in the underload scenario. If attentional resources are shrinking to 'meet' the workload, then any remaining demand in the task should be within the capacity of the operator to cope. However, when the operator needs to take over control, this sudden increase in demand is beyond their (reduced) ability to cope, even if it would ordinarily have been a manageable level of demand (Fig. 3; Young and Stanton 2002a). By that token, of course, the underload problem is actually an overload problem, since the task demands are more than the resource availability.

A series of studies in our driving simulator laboratory set out to provide support for MART. Firstly, drivers faced four levels of automation (manual, adaptive cruise control – ACC, lane centering – LC, and ACC+LC) while we measured mental workload and performance (Young and Stanton 2002b). Using a visuospatial secondary task as a measure of workload during the drive, we also recorded the amount of time drivers spent visually attending to the secondary task and compared that with the performance on it. This 'attention ratio' notionally reflected the efficiency in participants' performance, and so we used it as a proxy for attentional capacity. We found that, as workload decreased across the automation conditions, so too did this metric of attentional capacity – in other words, the size of attentional resources shrank directly with reductions in mental workload, as predicted by MART. Further analysis on these data (Young and Stanton 2006) showed that this shrinkage occurred relatively quickly, within the first minute of the experimental trial.

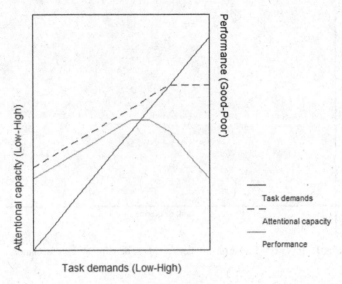

Fig. 2. Relation between task demands and performance under MART

It could be argued that the attention ratio was a confounded metric, since it relied on the same measure as mental workload itself (i.e., the secondary task). It also rests on the assumption that both the direction and duration of visual gaze represents the allocation of attentional resources. Whilst there is good evidence that the direction of gaze reflects attention (Underwood and Everatt 1996), it is less clear whether the amount of time spent looking at a task indicates the amount of resources being invested in that task.

However, mitigating against these arguments are two other key aspects in our series of studies. Firstly, we also measured subjective mental workload using the NASA- TLX (Hart and Staveland 1988), which generally revealed the same patterns of reduced mental workload with automation as shown by the secondary task. More convincingly, though, we replicated the study but, this time, with an unexpected failure in one of the automation systems towards the end of the trial (Young and Stanton 2001b). Whilst the results were by no means clear cut and depended on driver skill level, evidence of poorer responses in lower workload conditions was, in our view, consistent with the idea that participants did not have the resources to cope with what would ordinarily be a manageable situation.

3   Underload and Redlines

Reflecting on this research, one notable absence is any definition of underload – or, for that matter, overload – in their own right. Whilst we have pontificated at length about defining the core concept of mental workload, less effort has been directed at elaborating on what we mean by underload and overload. As with workload, the terms have intuitive appeal but, as with workload, if we are to measure them and determine when an individual is underloaded or overloaded, we need to understand what we are talking about.

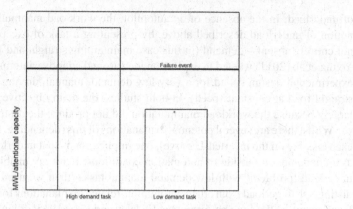

Fig. 3. Hypothetical representation of performance differences under MART

Young et al. (2015) acknowledged this in a discussion of so-called 'redlines' – that is, those theoretical points on the inverted-U performance/workload curve when one can be said to have transitioned into underload or overload. Their paper interpreted these redlines in terms of the supply-demand relationship of attentional resources, workload and performance. Whilst practically useful, such a definition is still outcome-based – we can only recognise underload by its detrimental effect on performance which, by definition, occurs after the redline has been passed. The holy grail would be to define and identify these redlines in advance.

One area of promise, touched on earlier, lies in the development of metrics in neuro-ergonomics; specifically, measures of brain oxygenation using near infrared spectroscopy. It has been suggested that these could essentially represent a quantitative measure of attentional resources (Perrey et al. 2010; Shaw et al. 2013).

If so, they offer exciting potential to properly validate MART and quantify the redlines of underload and overload. But this still does not give us a qualitative definition of underload. In much of the research on underload, the tasks that participants are faced with involve doing very little (typically some supervisory control of automation), but it is not about doing nothing (when parallel concerns of boredom might come to the fore). There still has to be some task engagement, even if that engagement is not very stimulating. Current levels of automated driving systems exemplify this kind of task – the technology is not yet mature enough for drivers to completely disengage (although it soon will be), but it can take over vast swathes of the driving task, leaving the person in the driving seat as little more than a supervisor. As we have already seen in the research summarised above (not to mention a large body of similar research), such a situation can lead to problems when the human is required to assume control.

The inexorable development of automation in many applied domains has provided an imperative for research in this area. However, there are far fewer studies investigating 'pure' underload, as a phenomenon in the absence of automation. Two of our experiments (Young and Clynick 2005; Young et al. 2011) attempted to do just that, by presenting varying levels of workload. Young and Clynick (2005) used a flight simulator in an effort to quantify the recovery curve of attentional resources after a period of underload. In the absence of an autopilot, the workload manipulation followed the notion of underload described above, by presenting a task of exceptionally low – but not entirely absent – demand (in this case maintaining straight and level flight). Later, Young et al. (2011) wanted to explore an idea around adaptive automation, but again the experimental design called for a very low demand, manual, driving task (driving on a straight road at constant speed). In both studies, the main objective was unsuccessful, largely because the workload manipulation did not produce the desired effect.

Whilst there are several potential explanations of this (depending, for instance, where each task lay on the inverted-U curve), one implication is that underload might not exist as a phenomenon outside of automation conditions. If we are unable to reproduce the underload 'problem' with low demand manual tasks, then we need to work harder to distinguish underload from other, automation-related, explanations for such performance (such as out-of-the-loop performance; Endsley and Kiris 1995; or vigilance; Molloy and Parasuraman 1996). This is not just a matter of academic debate; the practical solutions for these problems can differ depending on which explanation proves to be true.

4 Conclusions

The title of this paper was an homage to Lashley's (1950) classic paper on memory, 'In search of the engram'. Where Lashley concluded that there was no evidence for such a notion of a physiological memory trace in the brain, we might also question whether the same is true for underload? Such a conclusion may be premature and excessive, but as it stands there is good reason to suggest that underload might be automation-specific. Irrespective of the outcome of this debate, the practical implications of underload are likely to remain. Following the MART model, one natural response to counteract underload is to give the individual more to do, in order to maintain levels of attentional resources (cf. Gershon et al. 2009). This could be used as an argument to allow non-driving secondary tasks in the car, such as using a mobile phone. Whilst this is inadvisable given the weight of evidence showing it is dangerous (e.g., Collet et al. 2010; Haigney et al. 2000), it does put into context some findings that mobile phone use may facilitate performance in certain conditions, when workload is otherwise low or manageable (Liu 2003). It also forebodes the coming step up in automated driving systems, which will allow drivers to disengage from the driving task in limited circumstances. Nevertheless, a more palatable approach would be to engage in a task-related activity, such as that advocated in the study by Young et al. (2011), with the aim not just of maintaining attention, but also of directing it appropriately.

The corollary of this is the suggestion that underload might not be undesirable in all situations either. A clear example is to support older drivers (Young and Bunce 2011), for whom reduced cognitive functioning can make every day driving tasks difficult to cope with. In those situations, an automated system that otherwise might cause underload, can instead make the task manageable again. What this discourse really highlights is the problem of individual differences, which is not unique to mental workload research but is certainly applicable. Differences in attentional capacity, experience, arousal or health – both between and within individuals – can all impact on whether a task presents underload, overload or optimal workload. It is little wonder that mental workload research still grapples with problems that were identified decades ago (see Young et al. 2015). Nevertheless, the strength of research in this field and continued developments in measurement (e.g., Longo and Leva 2017) are grounds for optimism. With mental work being predominant in the modern world, this research is more important than ever.

References

Collet, C., Guillot, A., Petit, C.: Phoning while driving I: a review of epidemiological, psychological, behavioural and physiological studies. Ergonomics **53**(5), 589–601 (2010)

de Winter, J.C.F., Happee, R., Martens, M.H., Stanton, N.A.: Effects of adaptive cruise control and highly automated driving on workload and situation awareness: a review of the empirical evidence. Transp. Res. Part F **27**, 196–217 (2014)

Endsley, M.R., Kiris, E.O.: The out-of-the-loop performance problem and level of control in automation. Hum. Factors **37**(2), 381–394 (1995)

Gershon, P., Ronen, A., Oron-Gilad, T., Shinar, D.: The effects of an interactive cognitive task (ICT) in suppressing fatigue symptoms in driving. Transp. Res. Part F **12**, 21–28 (2009)

Haigney, D.E., Taylor, R.G., Westerman, S.J.: Concurrent mobile (cellular) phone use and driving performance: task demand characteristics and compensatory processes. Transp. Res. Part F Traffic Psychol. Behav. **3**(3), 113–121 (2000)

Hancock, P. A.: Whither workload? Mapping a path for its future development. In: Longo, L., Leva, M.C. (eds.) H-WORKLOAD 2017. CCIS, vol. 726, pp. 3–17. Springer, Cham (2017). https://doi.org/10.1007/978-3-319-61061-0_1

Hancock, P.A., Caird, J.K.: Experimental evaluation of a model of mental workload. Hum. Factors **35**, 413–429 (1993)

Hancock, G.M., Longo, L., Young, M.S., Hancock, P.A.: Mental workload. In: Handbook of Human Factors and Ergonomics, pp. 203–226 (2021)

Hart, S.G., Staveland, L.E.: Development of NASA-TLX (Task Load Index): results of empirical and theoretical research. In: Hancock, P.A., Meshkati, N. (eds.) Human Mental Workload, pp. 138–183. North-Holland, Amsterdam (1988)

Kahneman, D.: Attention and Effort. Prentice-Hall, Englewood Cliffs (1973)

Lashley, K.S.: In search of the engram. In: Symposium of the Society of Experimental Biology, vol. 4, pp. 454–482. Academic Press (1950)

Lee, J.D., Regan, M.A., Horrey, W.J.: Workload, distraction, and automation. In: Fisher, D.L., Horrey, W.J., Lee, J.D., Regan, M.A. (eds.) Handbook of Human Factors for Automated, Connected, and Intelligent Vehicles, pp. 107–125. CRC Press, Boca Raton (2020)

Liu, Y.: Effects of Taiwan in-vehicle cellular audio phone system on driving performance. Saf. Sci. **41**, 531–542 (2003)

Longo, L., Leva, M.C.: Human Mental Workload: Models and Applications: First International Symposium, H-WORKLOAD 2017, Dublin, Ireland, 28–30 June 2017, Revised Selected Papers, vol. 726. Springer, Cham (2017). https://doi.org/10.1007/978-3-319-61061-0

Mehta, R.K., Parasuraman, R.: Neuroergonomics: a review of applications to physical and cognitive work. Front. Hum. Neurosci. **7**, 889 (2013)

Molloy, R., Parasuraman, R.: Monitoring an automated system for a single failure: vigilance and task complexity effects. Hum. Factors **38**(2), 311–322 (1996)

Perrey, S., Thedon, T., Rupp, T.: NIRS in ergonomics: its application in industry for promotion of health and human performance at work. Int. J. Ind. Ergon. **40**(2), 185–189 (2010)

Singleton, W.T.: The Mind at Work: Psychological Ergonomics. Cambridge University Press, Cambridge (1989)

Shaw, T.H., Satterfield, K., Ramirez, R., Finomore, V.: Using cerebral hemovelocity to measure workload during a spatialised auditory vigilance task in novice and experienced observers. Ergonomics **56**(8), 1251–1263 (2013)

Underwood, G., Everatt, J.: Automatic and controlled information processing: the role of attention in the processing of novelty. In: Neumann, O., Sanders, A.F. (eds.) Handbook of Perception and Action, pp. 185–227. Academic Press, London (1996)

Victor, T.W., Tivesten, E., Gustavsson, P., Johansson, J., Sangberg, F., Ljung Aust, M.: Automation expectation mismatch: Incorrect prediction despite eyes on threat and hands on wheel. Hum. Factors **60**(8), 1095–1116 (2018)

Welford, A.T.: Mental work-load as a function of demand, capacity, strategy and skill. Ergonomics **21**, 151–167 (1978)

Wilson, J.R., Rajan, J.A.: Human-machine interfaces for systems control. In: Wilson, J.R., Corlett, E.N. (eds.) Evaluation of Human Work: A Practical Ergonomics Methodology, pp. 357–405. Taylor & Francis, London (1995)

Yerkes, R.M., Dodson, J.D.: The relation of strength of stimulus to rapidity of habit formation. J. Comp. Neurol. Psychol. **18**, 459–482 (1908)

Young, M.S., Birrell, S.A., Davidsson, S.: Task pre-loading: designing adaptive systems to counteract mental underload. In: Anderson, M. (ed.) Contemporary Ergonomics and Human Factors 2011, pp. 168–175. Taylor & Francis, London (2011)

Young, M.S., Brookhuis, K.A., Wickens, C.D., Hancock, P.A.: State of science: mental workload in ergonomics. Ergonomics **58**(1), 1–17 (2015)

Young, M.S., Bunce, D.: Driving into the sunset: supporting cognitive functioning in older drivers. J. Aging Res. **2011**, 6 pages (2011). Article ID 918782

Young, M.S., Clynick, G.F.: A test flight for malleable attentional resources theory. In: Bust, P., McCabe, P. (eds.) Contemporary Ergonomics 2005, pp. 548–552. Taylor & Francis, London (2005)

Young, M.S., Stanton, N.A.: Mental workload: theory, measurement, and application. In: Karwowski, W. (ed.) International Encyclopedia of Ergonomics and Human Factors, vol. 1, pp. 507–509. Taylor & Francis, London (2001)

Young, M.S., Stanton, N.A.: Size matters. the role of attentional capacity in explaining the effects of mental underload on performance. In: Harris, D. (ed.) Engineering Psychology and Cognitive Ergonomics: Vol. 5 – Aerospace and Transportation Systems (Proceedings of the Third International Conference on Engineering Psychology and Cognitive Ergonomics, Edinburgh, 25–27 October 2000), pp. 357–364. Ashgate, Aldershot (2001b)

Young, M.S., Stanton, N.A.: Attention and automation: new perspectives on mental underload and performance. Theor. Issues Ergon. Sci. **3**(2), 178–194 (2002)

Young, M.S., Stanton, N.A.: Malleable Attentional Resources Theory: a new explanation for the effects of mental underload on performance. Hum. Factors **44**(3), 365–375 (2002)

Young, M.S., Stanton, N.A.: The decay of Malleable Attentional Resources Theory. In: Bust, P.D. (ed.) Contemporary Ergonomics 2006, pp. 253–257. Taylor & Francis, London (2006)

Young, M.S., Stanton, N.A., Walker, G.H., Jenkins, D.P., Salmon, P.M.: Mental workload in command and control teams: musings on the outputs of EAST and WESTT. In: Harris, D. (ed.) Engineering Psychology and Cognitive Ergonomics – HCII2007, pp. 455–464. Springer, Berlin (2007). https://doi.org/10.1007/978-3-540-73331-7_50

A Novel Parabolic Model of Instructional Efficiency Grounded on Ideal Mental Workload and Performance

Luca Longo[✉] and Murali Rajendran

Applied Intelligence Research Centre, School of Computer Science, City Campus, Technological University Dublin, Dublin, Ireland
luca.longo@tudublin.ie

Abstract. Instructional efficiency within education is a measurable concept and models have been proposed to assess it. The main assumption behind these models is that efficiency is the capacity to achieve established goals at the minimal expense of resources. This article challenges this assumption by contributing to the body of Knowledge with a novel model that is grounded on ideal mental workload and performance, namely the *parabolic model* of instructional efficiency. A comparative empirical investigation has been constructed to demonstrate the potential of this model for instructional design evaluation. Evidence demonstrated that this model achieved a good concurrent validity with the well-known likelihood model of instructional efficiency, treated as baseline, but a better discriminant validity for the evaluation of the training and learning phases. Additionally, the inferences produced by this novel model have led to a superior information gain when compared to the baseline.

1 Introduction

The construct of efficiency, within the field of learning and instruction, is assumed to be the capacity to achieve established goals with minimal expenditure of effort or resources [12]. Models exist for assessing instructional efficiency, and they are based upon a measure of mental effort or workload exerted during a learning task, and a measure of test performance [36,46,47]. Ideally, any instructional activity conducted should be as efficient as possible and it is important to understand how particular approaches to learning influence the performance of learners. The above assumption that underpins efficiency is that low mental effort, with high performance, provides the best efficiency, whereas, high mental effort, with low performance, provides the worst efficiency. However, this article challenges this assumption by arguing that there are cases where it does not hold. Through the illustration of counter-examples, and by using the terminology brought forward in the years by Cognitive Load Theory, and its cognitive load types, this article proposes a novel model of instructional efficiency, named *the parabolic model*. This is inspired by the well-known assumption, within mental workload research, focused on the parabolic relationship between experienced mental workload and

L. Longo and M. C. Leva (Eds.): H-WORKLOAD 2021, CCIS 1493, pp. 11–36, 2021.
https://doi.org/10.1007/978-3-030-91408-0_2

performance, inspired by the seminal Yerkes-Dodson law, an inverted-U shaped model that links stress and performance [49].

The aim of this research is to propose and describe this novel model, by stating its main assumptions, contextualising it in the wider framework of instructional efficiency and cognitive load theory, as well as evaluating its effectiveness with a comparative empirical experiment. For these purposes, the reminded of this article focuses on presenting related work on cognitive load theory and on the construct of instructional efficiency, respectively in Sects. 2.1 and 2.2. The terminology, extracted from related work, is coupled with an introduction of the concepts of mental effort and mental workload in Sect. 2.3, serving as necessary information for discussing, in Sect. 2.4, the issues behind the main assumption of current instructional efficiency models. The article continues with the presentation of the novel *parabolic model* of instructional efficiency, in Sect. 3, along with its main assumption and formalities. Subsequently, a comparative quantitative empirical research experiment is designed and illustrated in Sect. 6, along with a research hypothesis aimed at testing this one of its kind model of instructional efficiency, with a set of evaluation criteria described in Sect. 3.2. Empirical resulting evidence is presented in Sect. 4 followed by a summary of this research, the implications for teaching and learning, and a delineation, in Sect. 5, of future work.

2   Related Work

2.1   Cognitive Load and Its Theory

Cognitive Load Theory (CLT) is a widely known theory in educational psychology which is used to enhance the learning phase by developing instructional material and applying instructional teaching techniques based on the limitations of the human cognitive architecture [33]. CLT provides an effective framework for designing and delivering work to learners of any standard. It is backed by empirical research supporting different amounts and types of instruction according to the level of learners and it enables instructors to provide well-crafted guidance in their topics. It states that effective learning can only take place where the cognitive capacity of an individual in a particular domain is not exceeded. The human cognitive architecture (HCA) provides a generic framework of the information-processing stages that learners use to encode, store, and modify information for the purposes of reasoning and decision making [1,38]. It describes the necessary and sufficient conditions for a human to input, process and store information which in turn becomes knowledge. Cognitive load includes units of knowledge and elements of relationship. The cognitive load associated to a task is created when the units of knowledge interact with the relationship elements [44].

Sensory memory, short-term memory, also known as working memory, and long-term memory are three essential dimensions of HCA. Atkinson and Shiffrin (1968) proposed that the input of the information entered via sensory memory is processed in the working memory and then proceeds to be stored in the long-term memory [1]. Working memory is limited and it processes incoming information from sensory memory, long term memory instead is unlimited, highly structured and it stores relevant information as acquired knowledge [2,28]. Short-term memory, as described by Miller (1956), has the capacity to hold seven plus or minus two chunks of information at any given time [28]. It is not specified whether the chunks of information were novel or familiar, interrelated or discrete, but rather that a chunk is a unit of knowledge. Long-term memory is a permanent store of experience, knowledge and process, all of which is held outside the conscious awareness until recalled in the working memory. It does not have an executive function [2]. The information stored in the long-term memory in knowledge structures of varying complexity is called 'schemata' [44]. A schemata makes the construction and transfer of knowledge possible, which equates to learning. The more schemata an individual holds for a particular topic, the more advanced they become in learning. Schema construction is believed to reduce the load in working memory. Leaving sufficient cognitive resources in the working memory to process new information is one of the core objectives of educational instructional design [33]. Explicit instructions are required to process information and build schemata of knowledge in working memory. Cognitive Load Theory distinguish three types of load, whose definitions have evolved over time: intrinsic, extraneous and germane loads [33]. Traditionally, CLT has focused on instructional methods aimed at decreasing the cognitive load experienced by learners so that their available resources can be fully devoted to learning. However, these have been redefined over time, and the latest belief, as shown in Fig. 1, is that:

- *intrinsic load* depends on the number of elements to be processed in working memory and on the characteristics of the learning task, which are believed to be fixed and immutable;
- *extraneous load* depends on the characteristic of the instructional material, and the characteristics on the instructional design, and on the prior knowledge of learners;
- *germane load* depends on the characteristics of the learner and the resources allocated to deal with the intrinsic load.

These definitions and terminology will be useful for a subsequent discussion on the limitations of current instructional efficiency models, as described in the following section, as well as the design of a novel model.

2.2   Instructional Efficiency

Efficiency of instructional designs in education is a measurable concept. Efficiency in the context of problem-solving, learning and instruction is the capacity to achieve established goals at the minimal expense of resources [12]. Pass and colleagues suggest that combining performance and mental effort measures allows the calculation of an index of mental efficiencies [35,36]. Studies that investigated processing instructional efficiency made use of uni-variate scores to compare the impact of an experimental condition in respect to a control condition. Sweller (2010) argues that instructional effectiveness will be compromised

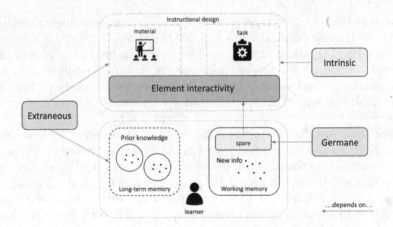

Fig. 1. Latest definition of the cognitive load types of Cognitive Load Theory [31], including intrinsic, extraneous and germane loads.

by the extent that instructional choices require learners to devote working memory resources to dealing with elements imposed by extraneous cognitive load [45]. It is also believed that, at a basic level, understanding efficiency is an essential precursor to assessing educational effectiveness and improvement. Various studies that propose measures of efficiency have been conducted in the past. The most common and widely used models of efficiency are discussed below.

Deviational Model - In search of a single measure to determine the relative efficiency of instructional conditions in terms of learning outcomes, Paas and Van Merrienboer developed a computational approach for combining a measure of performance with a measure of mental effort to attain efficiency [36]. This was characterised as the instructional condition efficiency. This is referred to as the Deviational model of efficiency by Hoffman and Schraw because this model computes the difference between a standardised score of performance and a standardised score of effort [12]. The reasoning behind this formula is based on the assumption that the resulting efficiency is high when an individual experiences high performance and low effort. Conversely, the resulting efficiency is low when an individual experiences low performance and high effort [36]. The deviational model of efficiency computes a measure of efficiency based on how the participant performs relative to the group [12]. It measures the distance from the observed score to the ideal efficiency slope. The deviational model provides a group-referenced score representing an individual efficiency that requires scores to be converted to a common scale. Formally, $Efficiency = \frac{(ZP-ZR)}{\sqrt{2}}$, where ZP is the standardised performance score and ZR the standardised effort score. If $ZP - ZR > 0$, then efficiency is positive. If $ZP - ZR < 0$, then efficiency is negative. According to the authors, the highest efficiency condition occurs when performance is maximal and effort is minimal. The lowest efficiency corresponds to the lowest performance and highest effort [36]. There are concerns expressed by Hoffman and Schraw that the efficiency score computed by the deviational model is problematic because the standardised scores are affected by variability and performance of others within the group [12]. They also suggested that resulting scores should be interpreted cautiously as they may be conceptually incommensurate even if they can be mathematically identical in magnitude and direction. Additionally, the original deviational model was believed to assess only learning efficiency. However, over the years, a differentiation between various types of efficiency was made [47]. In particular, for the reminded or this article, in line with [46], training efficiency is referred to that measure computed with effort/mental workload obtained prior test performance, while learning efficiency with effort/mental workload obtained after it.

Likelihood Model - Another measure of efficiency widely employed within education is based upon the likelihood model put forward by Hoffman and Schraw [12]. Efficiency in this model is computed as a ratio of work output to input. In other words, a ratio of performance to perceived mental effort. Output is identified with learning and input is identified with time, work or effort [43]. Formally $Efficiency = \frac{P}{R}$, where P is the raw score of performance and R is the raw score of perceived effort. An estimation of the rate of change of performance is calculated by dividing P by R and the resulting ratio represents the individual efficiency based on individual scores of performance and effort [12]. The ratio ranges from zero to extensive positive values; it goes towards zero when performance is low and effort is high (low efficiency) and conversely, it goes towards the extensive positive value when performance is high and effort is low (high efficiency). The authors argue that, compared to the deviational model of efficiency, the likelihood model provides an unambiguous measure because the inputs are not standardised scores, and there is no restrictions in the range of efficiency scores. However, the resulting efficiency here is always going to be positive. It must be interpreted with caution because the formula assumes that the work input is not zero [11]. It is also acknowledged that efficiency scores based on this model is supposedly more reliable and sensitive to minor effect size changes compared to the deviational model. An extension of this model has been proposed by Kalyuga and Sweller where an extra reference to a *critical value* is used, under or above which the efficiency can be considered negative or positive [14]. The authors suggest to obtain the critical value by dividing the maximum performance score by the maximum effort exertable by a learner in order to establish whether that learner is competent or not. The ratio of the critical value is based on the underlying assumption that an instructional design is inefficient if a learner invests maximal effort in a task without reaching maximal performance and vice-versa [14]. Through this extended formula, the model evolves from one being able to define only positive efficiency scores to one capable of defining a positive or negative efficiencies.

2.3   Mental Effort and Mental Workload

Despite all the years of empirical research, no proven measure of the three cognitive load types of the Cognitive Load Theory have emerged. Similarly, no single measure of mental effort or workload exist, and many models have been proposed, each employing different techniques [19–21,24,40,41]. The concept of cognitive load is mainly employed in the educational field, whereas the concept of mental workload, a psychological construct strictly connected to cognitive load, is employed mainly within ergonomics and human factors [7,25]. Although very similar, some difference exists. Among them, the former relates mainly to working memory resources, whereas the latter takes into account other factors such as the level of motivation, stress and the physical demand experienced by humans as a consequence of a learning task. Despite of their different fields of research, they both assume that working memory limits, or a limited pool of resources and their capacity must be considered to predict performance while accomplishing an underlying task. Although the field of educational psychology is struggling to find ways of measuring cognitive load of learning tasks [27], there is an entire field within Ergonomics devoted to the design, development and validation of reliable measures of mental workload. Intuitively, mental workload (MWL) can be defined as the volume of cognitive work necessary for an individual to accomplish a task over time [22,39]. However, many other definitions exists, making its formalisation a non-trivial goal. The measurement of cognitive load is of crucial importance for instructional research. The few efforts to measure it are almost exclusively concerned with performance measures [35]. Different techniques, with different advantages and disadvantages, have been proposed in education to measure cognitive load and they can be clustered in two main groups: subjective and objective measures [37]. Subjective measures are more suitable to be applied in an educational context and in general are easy to administer and analyse, in contrast to objective measures. Subjective measures, also referred to as self-reported measures, rely on the individual's perceived experience of the interaction with a learning task. They are based on the assumption that only the individual involved in the task can provide an accurate and precise judgement about the experienced load, as employed in a number of studies [13,30]. The perception of the individual can be gathered through means of a survey or questionnaire. Subjective measures include both uni-dimensional and multidimensional approaches, which have been conceptualised, applied and validated. On one hand, the most commonly used subjective measures are uni-dimensional, for example the Rating Scale of Mental Effort (RSME) and its modifications [51]. They provide an index of overall workload/effort, but provide no information about its temporal variation. On the other hand, multidimensional measures, such as the NASA Task Load Index [9] and its raw version [3,8,10,18], can determine the source of mental workload, as based upon different factors. They seem to be the most appropriate types of measures for assessing mental workload because they have demonstrated high levels of sensitivity and diagnosticity [42]. However, it was argued that their use is exceptional within education [4], with only a few studies investigating its validity and sensitivity [5,6,17].

2.4   Discussion on Instructional Efficiency Models and Assumptions

The deviational and likelihood models of instructional efficiency, as described in Sect. 2.2, have their own advantages and limitations. The deviational model is group-referenced, and although is good to consistently investigate the variations of efficiency scores of learners within the same instructional design, it does not allow comparison across different instructional designs. In fact, the procedure that converts raw scores to standardised scores affects the variability and performance of learners within a group. Thus scores may be mathematically identical in magnitude and direction across different instructional designs, but they may be conceptually incommensurate. For example, a very difficult instructional design can generate the same distribution of standardised scores when compared to a very easy instructional design. The likelihood model aims at solving some of the problems associated to the deviational model, as it provides an unambiguous measure since the inputs are not standardised scores. Unfortunately, with null effort, the formula cannot work, as dividing performance by zero is mathematically not possible. This technical issue is rather minor since it is reasonable to assume that the plausibility of performance with no reported effort is improbable, and in practice, the scale for effort assessment always starts with values higher than zero. However, a major issue is that, since there are no restrictions in the range of efficiency scores - from greater than zero to infinite - it still makes comparison across different instructional designs difficult. In fact, the efficiency scores obtainable by a group of learners associated to a particular instructional design, can be totally the same when compared to a totally different instructional design, even if the magnitude of performance and effort are different. In other words, an efficiency score of 2 can be achieved both with a performance of 10 and an effort of 5, or with a performance of 20 and an effort of 10 ($10/5 = 20/10$), assuming performance and effort are assessed using the same scale across the two instructional conditions. Eventually, given the definition of efficiency as the capacity to achieve established goals at the minimal expense of resources [12], it is here argued that negative efficiency scores do not make sense. In fact, the achievement of established goals, regardless if with a minimal of maximal expenses of resources, can be null, or equates to some positive extent, but can never be negative. In short, the opposite of achieving, which is not achieving, cannot be measured. Additionally, the fact that a model of instructional efficiency has infinite values can make comparisons across instructional designs more cumbersome. Therefore, it is argued that a measure of efficiency with a positive bounded range is ideal to tackled the above consideration. The deviational and likelihood models of efficiency share the same assumption of other models often employed in education, as synthesised below:

ASSUMPTION 1 (likelihood model)

Instructional efficiency is higher if similar degrees of performance are achieved with less effort, or similarly, if higher degree of performance are achieved with the same expenditure of resources.

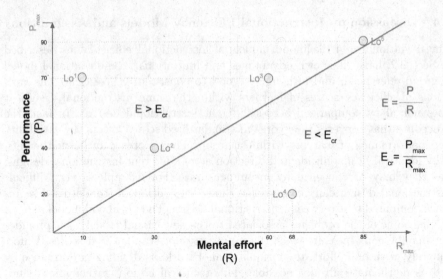

Fig. 2. The likelihood model of efficiency with a critical value, and five learners who achieved different levels of performance, exerting different degrees of effort.

This assumption is the starting point of a critical discussion and a number of considerations aimed at challenging its validity. In order to elaborate on this, consider Fig. 2 where 5 learners ($Lo^1 - Lo^5$) are depicted at the intersection of performance and experienced effort, with efficiency scores computed with the likelihood model (Table 1).

Table 1. An illustrative example with 5 learners who exerted different degrees of effort achieving different levels of performance, thus leading to different instructional efficiency scores as computed by the likelihood model [12] with a critical value $P_{max}/R_{max} = 100/100 = 1$.

Learner	Performance (P)	Effort (R)	Efficiency (E)
Lo^1	70	10	+7.00
Lo^2	40	30	+1.33
Lo^3	70	60	+1.16
Lo^4	20	68	− 0.29
Lo^5	90	85	+1.06

According to the likelihood model, by employing the critical value, four learners obtained positive instructional efficiency (Lo^1, Lo^2, Lo^3, Lo^5) and one negative efficiency (Lo^4), as per Table 1. Through the use of the terminology associated to the latest definition of the cognitive load types of the Cognitive Load

Theory [31] (Sect. 2.1), these learners had various experiences when exposed to a certain instructional design, and these are analysed below.

1. Lo^1 - a learner who exerted very low germane load but achieved good performance. Intuitively, this could be a skilled learner with good prior knowledge. As a consequence, the very high efficiency score computed by the likelihood model (+7.0) is not fully justifiable and correctly reflecting the fact that the instructional design might have been probably of low utility for this learner, because of the low intrinsic load. Additionally, the extraneous load was probably intermediate, not influential nor redundant, as the learner achieved good performance anyway.

2. Lo^2 - a learner who exerted minimal germane load and achieved medium performance. This is probably due to the medium extraneous load that means the instructional material might have not been fully engaging and stimulating and the intrinsic load was probably not optimal and not fully influential. Therefore, the efficiency score of the likelihood model (+1.33) is positive and close to the critical line (1). However, it is hard to establish to what extent the instructional design was efficient.

3. Lo^3 - a learner who exerted medium germane load but achieved good performance. The extraneous load was probably optimal, either because of the good prior knowledge of the learner or because of the moderately efficient instructional material. Additionally, the intrinsic load might have been good as the learning task might have moderately and positively engaged the learner. Therefore, the efficiency score of the likelihood model (+1.16) is positive and close to the critical line (1). However, as for learner Lo^2, it is hard to establish to what extent the instructional design was efficient.

4. Lo^4 - a learner who exerted a good portion of germane load but achieved poor performance. The extraneous load might have been low as the instructional material failed to promote learning and was probably not engaging, or the learner's prior knowledge was almost absent, not allowing to follow the material itself for the formation of knowledge. Also, the intrinsic load might have been probably high and the learner could not cope fully with the learning task. The likelihood model led to an efficiency score of -0.29 which is very close to the critical line (1). Additionally, for the same level of effort 68, but with a lower level of performance, let's say 5, the likelihood model would have led to an efficiency score of $5/68 = 0.073$, which would have been deemed negative as below the critical value of 1, thus becoming -0.073. However, the latter case was clearly worse in term of efficiency than the former case, but its efficiency value is closer to 1 that the former, suggesting a slightly better efficiency (less negative) when in reality should have been deemed worse (more negative). Clearly, this is counter-intuitive, generating confusion during interpretations.

5. Lo^5 - a learner who exerted high germane load and achieved good performance. The extraneous load might have been probably optimal as it might have motivated the learner to exert high germane load for coping with an high intrinsic load and thus correctly promoting the formation of knowledge. This

case might be seen as a situation in which a learner had high perseveration in exerting effort, despite the difficulty of the instructional design exposed to, but eventually achieved high performance. This can be regarded as a positive outcome, in terms of instructional efficiency. However, according to the likelihood model, this learner achieved a positive efficiency score of +1.06, very similar to those of learners Lo^2 and Lo^3, which is clearly counter-intuitive since they either exerted significant lower effort or achieved significant lower performance.

According to the above considerations, examples, interpretations and discussion, a novel model of instructional efficiency is proposed in the next section. This model, grounded on measures of test performance and cognitive load, is aimed at tackling the above problems by providing scholars with instructional efficiency scores that should support higher interpretation of behavioural performance of learners and facilitate comparisons among instructional designs.

3   Design and Methodology

The discussion of Sect. 2.4 serves as the main motivation for the design of a novel model of instructional efficiency that is referred to as the *parabolic model of instructional efficiency*. The word 'parabolic' originates from a well-known assumption within mental workload research. This assumption focuses on the parabolic relationship between experienced mental workload and performance, as depicted in Fig. 3 (right). This relationship has been theorised by many scholars within mental workload research over the last 50 years [15,16,29,48,50], and originally motivated by the Yerkes-Dodson law, as depicted in Fig. 3 (left), whereby the relationship between pressure and performance was formulated from empirical research [49], the well-known inverted U-model. Starting from this reasonable assumption, a novel model of instructional efficiency is proposed, as depicted in Fig. 4.

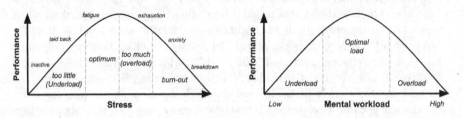

Fig. 3. The Yerkes-Dodson inverted U-model of stress and performance (left) and the assumed relationship between mental workload and performance (right)

This new model expects that performance, intended as test performance of learners, achieves maximality when experienced mental workload and expenditure of resources or effort is moderate, and it achieves minimality when mental workload is either too little (underload) or too much (overload). The optimal point for performance is depicted with the label *ideal* in Fig. 4, which equates to the top of the inverted parabola (black) that models the expectation itself. This is the first difference with state-of-the-art models of instructional efficiency, as discussed in Sect. 2.4, whereby efficiency is the linear capacity to achieve established goals with minimum expenditure of effort or resources [12], while in the parabolic model, it is the non-linear capacity to achieve established goals with moderate expenditure of effort or mental workload.

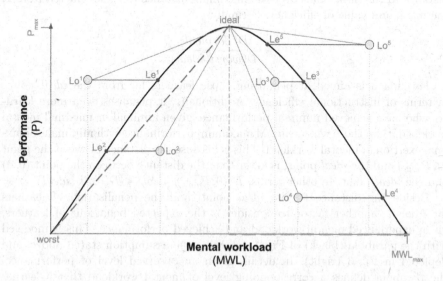

Fig. 4. A novel parabolic model of instructional efficiency based on ideal mental workload and performance, with 5 illustrative learners. (Color figure online)

Secondly, it is argued that the efficiency associated to a learner depends on the distance between a point at the intersection of exerted mental workload (MWL) and observed test performance (P) to the *ideal* point. Formally:

$$D(Lo^x, ideal) \tag{1}$$

with D is the function of the euclidean distance between two points, which is the length of the line segment between the point Lo^x (the observed intersection of mental workload and performance for a learner L) and the *ideal* point ($MWL_{max}/2, P_{max}$). The yellow segments of Fig. 4 depict these distances for five illustrative learners. The goal of this measure of distance is to penalise learners far from the *ideal* point, in terms of efficiency, and award those close to it. Consequently, the *worst* performing learner is one who exerts minimal mental workload, the closer available point to zero on the x axis, with null performance. Therefore, the longest distance from the *ideal* point equates to the red dashed line in Fig. 4. Formally:

$$D(worst, ideal) \tag{2}$$

with D is the function of the euclidean distance between two points, which is the length of the line segment between the point $worst$ $(0,0)$ and the $ideal$ point $(MWL_{max}/2, P_{max})$. Thus, the proportional distance associable to a learner, is the ratio between the formula 1, the observed distance, and the formula 2, the maximum distance to the $ideal$ point. Such ratio is inversely proportional to instructional efficiency, which, in this model is set in the range $[0,1] \in \Re$. In other words, the higher the ratio, the lower the efficiency, and vice-versa. Thus, the instructional efficiency associable to a learner is the ratio between the distance to the $ideal$ point over the maximum distance to it, subtracted from 1, the maximum value of efficiency. Formally:

$$1 - \frac{D(Lo, ideal)}{D(worst, ideal)} \tag{3}$$

Formula 3 is aimed at penalising those learners far from the $ideal$ point, in terms of instructional efficiency. Additionally, it penalises even more learners who have achieved minimal performance, given minimal or maximal mental workload, than those who achieved maximum performance with minimal or maximal exertion of mental workload. This is because the distance between the point $(0, P_{max})$ and the $ideal$ point, is lower than the distance between the point $(0,0)$ and the $ideal$ point. In other terms, $D((0, P_{max}), ideal) < D((0,0), ideal)$.

Beside the distance to the $ideal$ point, and the penalisation of learners far from it, another factor to consider is the expected behaviour of learners, given experienced mental workload and achieved performance. This is modeled with the parabola (black) of Fig. 4, following the assumption stated above, and depicted in Fig. 3 (right). In detail, given an observed level of performance, the parabola defines a corresponding level of mental workload that a learner is expected to exert for reaching such performance. Departures from such an expected point on the parabola equates to penalisations, in terms of instructional efficiency. This can be modelled with another measure of distance between the $observed$ behaviour (o), the actual point at the intersection of actual mental workload and actual performance, and the $expected$ behaviour (e), the point at the intersection between expected mental workload and actual performance on the parabola, which defines a straight horizontal segment (blue segments in Fig. 4. Formally,

$$D(Lo, Le) \tag{4}$$

with D is the function of the euclidean distance between two points, which is the length of the line segment between the observed point at the intersection between observed mental workload and performance of learner L (Lo), and the point at intersection of expected mental workload given a certain level of experienced performance (Le). The longest straight segment that can be drawn from the parabola equates to the half of the mental workload range $MWL_{max}/2$ (green segment). This is the maximum distance from the parabola that models a learner who achieved null or maximal performance, with either minimal or maximal mental workload (the four corners of the diagram of Fig. 4), the farthest points from the expected points on the parabola. Thus, the proportional distance associable to a learner is the ratio between the formula 4, the distance to the expected point on the parabola, and $MWL_{max}/2$, the maximal distance achievable from the parabola. Such ratio is inversely proportional to instructional efficiency, which, as mentioned above, is set in the range $[0,1] \in \Re$. Thus, the instructional efficiency associable to a learner, in this case, is the ratio between the distance to the expected point on the parabola, over the maximal distance to it, subtracted from 1, the maximal value of efficiency. Formally:

$$1 - \frac{D(Lo, Le)}{MWL_{max}/2} \tag{5}$$

Formulas 3 and 5 are two terms of instructional efficiency, and since they are percent proportions, they are bounded in the same range $[0,1] \in \Re$. They are treated with equal priority, thus have the same importance. Eventually, averaging them give a combined measure of instructional efficiency, also bounded in $[0,1] \in \Re$. Formally:

$$E : [0,1] \in \Re$$

$$E = \frac{1}{2}\left(1 - \frac{D(Lo, ideal)}{D(worst, ideal)}\right) + \frac{1}{2}\left(1 - \frac{D(Lo, Le)}{MWL_{max}/2}\right) \tag{6}$$

This novel measure of instructional efficiency is aimed at solving the theoretical issues emerged in the discussion of Sect. 2.4. In fact, let us consider the illustrative learners, their performance and effort scores, presented in Table 1, and depicted in Figs. 2 and 4. The application of the parabolic model to these learners generates a new set of efficiency scores, as depicted in Fig. 5.

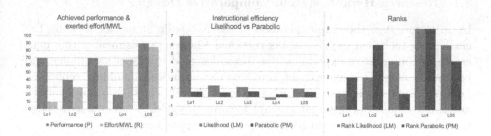

Fig. 5. A comparison between the likelihood model and the parabolic model of instructional efficiency, with five illustrative types of learner.

As it is possible to see, the efficiency score computed by the parabolic model (PM) for the first learner Lo^1 has been drastically reduced from the score computed by the likelihood model (LM). This is because of the bounded range within

0 and 1 of the parabolic model as well as its capacity to penalise learners whose intersection between performance and mental workload is not close to the *ideal* point on the parabola, and far from the expected exertable mental workload level given the achieved performance. However, the rank of Lo^1, out of five learners, is 1 (the best) for the likelihood model, and 2 for the parabolic model, thus not drastically different in the group. On the one hand, Lo^2 has instead earned a rank of 4 with the parabolic model, against 2 reached with the likelihood model, loosing position in the group. This is reasonable, given the fact that this learner has exerted very low effort, with a moderate performance, thus the underlying instructional design should not be considered as very efficient, because probably it did not engage the learner. On the other hand, Lo^3 has achieved rank 1 with the parabolic model, against rank 3 with the likelihood model. In this case, the efficiency of the underlying instructional design could be considered good, as it might have engaged the learner because of the good level of performance reached. Lo^4 was the worst both for the likelihood and the parabolic models, demonstrating a consistent outcome. This learner exerted a good amount of mental workload, but achieved very low performance, thus reasonably deriving that the underlying instructional design was not efficient. For this learner, it is also possible to see the effect of the parabolic model not to produce negative efficiencies, as instead possible with the likelihood model. Eventually, Lo^5 was a learner who exerted a very high mental workload, but still positively achieving a very high performance. Although this is good, because the performance scores actually points to a good learning experience, the exertable effort could have been reduced, thus the underlying instructional condition cannot be considered optimal in terms of efficiency.

3.1   Research Hypothesis and Comparative Design

In order to gauge the empirical value of the parabolic model for tackling the challenging technical problem of instructional efficiency assessment within education, a comparative experiment has been designed to assess its validity and informativeness. This experiment is replicable and indeed should be replicated multiple times across various studies in order to validate such a novel model, and this article is the very first attempt towards this goal. A research hypothesis is set below and the detailed research design is depicted in Fig. 6.

'H_1: IF the parabolic model (PM) is employed to compute the instructional efficiencies of a set of instructional designs,
THEN it is expected that it exhibits a good concurrent validity with the likelihood model (LM) but a superior discriminant validity and higher information gain'

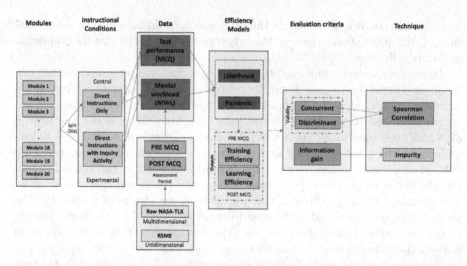

Fig. 6. The comparative experimental design diagram with details on instructional conditions, collected data, models of instructional efficiency employed, the evaluation criteria and methods employed to assess them.

Data for this experiment was collected in various taught modules at the Technological University Dublin, in the context of a larger research project in education [31,32,34]. All procedures performed involving human participants were in accordance with the ethical standards of the institutional research committee and with the 1964 Helsinki Declaration and its later amendments or comparable ethical standards. Ethical approval was obtained by the ethics committee of the above institution. Informed consent was obtained from all individual participants involved in the experiment, who were also provided with a study information sheet and could withdraw the study at any point in time. This experiment deals with two instructional design conditions. The first condition followed the traditional direct instruction approach to learning, while the second design extended it with a collaborative inquiry activity. In detail, the former approach involved a theoretical explanation of a chosen topic, whereby the instructor presented the information through direct instructions, projected to a white board, and verbally narrated. The latter approach extended the former approach with a guided inquiry activity amongst participants based on the use of cognitive trigger questions. Both groups received direct instructions, while only the experimental group subsequently participated in the collaborative inquiry activity. In the wider research project that originated such an experiment [31–34], the purpose of the second condition was to establish whether the additional inquiry activity could improve the efficiency of learners when compared to those learners who receive direct instructions only. Further details on the rationale behind the two conditions is not necessary here, since the goal is the comparison of two instructional efficiency models. For further detail, the reader is referred to our other published work [31,32,34]. In the experiment set here, any two different instructional conditions, assuming their difference, could have also been suitable. In fact, the more replications of this experiment, the better for its evaluation and thus validation.

In the first instructional condition, after the topic was presented to the class by an instructor, on the one hand the control group participants received questionnaires aimed at quantifying the effort and mental workload they experienced, using the Rating Scale Mental Effort (RSME) [51] and the raw version of NASA task load index (R-NASA) [9], models described in Sect. 2.3. Subsequently to these self-reporting questionnaires, a multiple-choice questionnaire (MCQ) associated to the taught topic was administered to the control group. On the other hand, the experimental group, the remaining half of the class, was split into teams of three or four participants for the inquiry activity. The participants discussed and exchanged information related to the topic leading to informed agreements collaboratively. The participants then wrote the shared answers individually to the cognitive trigger questions, part of the inquiry activity. Subsequently, the participants in the experimental group, similarly to those in the control group, received the same self-reporting questionnaires (RSME, R-NASA, and MCQ). Once the participants in both groups completed the MCQ, they were provided again with another RSME and Raw-NASA questionnaires. Filling the questionnaire on both occasions (pre and post MCQ) allows for the computation of both the training and the learning efficiencies, as they are related to different stages of the learning process [47]. Efficiency scores were then calculated using both the RSME and the R-NASA for each model of efficiency, namely the likelihood model (LM), used as baseline, and the parabolic model (PM), resulting in a total of eight different efficiency models, as shown in Table 2.

Table 2. Experimental configuration of the likelihood model (LM) and the parabolic model (PM) of instructional efficiency, with both the use of the Rating Scale Mental Effort (RSME) and the raw NASA Task Load index (RNASA) for the assessement of mental workload (MWL), and a multiple choice questionnaire (MCQ) for the assessment of test performance.

Model label	Efficiency type	Instructional model	MWL	Performance
LrEff-LM-RNasa	Learning	Likelihood (LM)	R-NASA	MCQ
LrEff-LM-Rsme	Learning	Likelihood (LM)	RSME	MCQ
LrEff-PM-RNasa	Learning	Parabolic (PM)	R-NASA	MCQ
LrEff-PM-Rsme	Learning	Parabolic (PM)	RSME	MCQ
TrEff-LM-RNasa	Training	Likelihood (LM)	R-NASA	MCQ
TrEff-LM-Rsme	Training	Likelihood (LM)	RSME	MCQ
TrEff-PM-RNasa	Training	Parabolic (PM)	R-NASA	MCQ
TrEff-PM-Rsme	Training	parabolic (PM)	RSME	MCQ

3.2   Evaluation Criteria

To assess the instructional efficiency models, namely the likelihood model (LM) and the parabolic model (PM), with their 8 variations, a set of evaluation criteria are selected, as described below, namely concurrent validity, discriminant validity and information gain.

Concurrent validity is the capacity of a measure to actually represent an underlying construct, in this case instructional efficiency, and it can be demonstrated by correlating the efficiency scores generated by a new model, here the parabolic model (PM), with those from another well-known model, in this case the likelihood model (LM). Concurrent validity is in practice measured with a correlation test.

Discriminant validity is aimed at measuring whether two constructs that theoretically should not be highly related to each other are, in fact, not related to each other. In this experiment the capability of the likelihood model, and the parabolic model is assessed, to better separate training and learning efficiencies, as two independent constructs and, in practice, this is achieved by performing a correlation test between the training and learning efficiency scores of each model.

Information gain is the level of impurity in a group of observations. It measures how much 'information' a variable provides about a target variable. In this research, it is used to understand which instructional efficiency model leads to efficiency scores that provide a higher amount of information about whether an observation belongs to a specific group (control or experimental). It is a measure of reduction in entropy (H) by transforming a set of data in some way. In practice, it is calculated by comparing the entropy of the data before and after a transformation. $H = \sum_i -p_i log_2 p_i$, with p the probability of class i that means the proportion of class i in a set. The higher the entropy the less the information content. The idea is to look at how much it is possible to reduce the entropy of the parent node (group) by segmenting on a given child (efficiency score). Formally, $IG = H_p - \sum_{i=1}^{n} p_{ci} H_{ci}$, where H_p is the entropy of the parent node, n is the number of child segments of the target variable, p_{ci} is the probability that an observation is in child i (the weighting), and H_{ci} is the entropy of child i. To compute the information gain the following steps are necessary:

1. split the efficiency score variable of each efficiency model into 5 bins;
2. calculate the entropy for each bin;
3. calculate the proportion of all records in each bin;
4. compute the entropy of the parent node (group);
5. subtract the sum of the entropy scores of the bin weighted by the proportion of data they represent from the root node entropy, obtaining information gain.
6. repeat the steps above for all 20 taught modules and for each instructional efficiency model and their variations.

The information gain associated to each version of an instructional efficiency model will be assigned a rank value from 1 to 8, 1 to the model with the most information gain units (I.G.), 8 to the model with the least I.G. units, per taught module, and the rank values will be aggregated across all the taught 20 modules.

This aggregated value is referred to as the sum of rank values. Subsequently, the efficiency models will be ranked again from 1 to 8 based on this sum of rank values, with 1 indicating the least sum of rank values achieved, 8 the highest. This will be referred to as the ranking position across models. In summary, the efficiency models that achieve lower ranking position will be deemed superior, in terms of average information gain across taught modules.

4   Results and Evaluation

The data collected contained 455 observations across 20 university modules in computer science as per Table 3. Most of the taught topics were different and data was collected over 3 years, each over two academic semesters, and participants in each class were different than those in all the other classes, thus independent to each other.

Table 3. Distribution of participants across taught modules in computer science and how they were split across control and experimental groups.

Module ID	Module name	Control	Experimental	Total learners
1	Research methods	14	15	29
2	Research hypothesis	20	16	36
3	Visualising geo spatial data	5	7	12
4	Operating systems	20	18	38
5	Problem solving	14	11	25
6	Data mining	10	9	19
7	Literature review	7	8	15
8	Research hypothesis	8	8	16
9	Strings	10	12	22
10	Program design	15	15	30
11	Machine learning	5	8	13
12	Image processing	7	9	16
13	Research methods	8	9	17
14	Statistics	6	7	13
15	IT forensics	19	14	33
16	Literature comprehension	7	9	16
17	Virtual memory	8	7	15
18	Research hypothesis	18	14	32
19	Literature review	16	15	31
20	Operating systems	14	13	27

The following scores were computed using collected data:

1. RSME (Rating Scale Mental Effort) scores (R) for each participant: pre and post a multiple choice questionnaire (training and learning);
2. a Raw NASA-TLX (Nasa Task Load Index) scores (R) for each participant: pre and post a multiple choice questionnaire (training and learning);
3. a performance score (P), in percentage, gathered from the application of a multiple choice questionnaire tailored to each taught module, and designed with the expert lecturer for that taught topic;
4. an efficiency score for each participant, by employing the two mental workload assessment techniques of 1 and 2, both for the two phases (training and learning), and for both the two models of instructional efficiency (likelihood and parabolic). In total 8 efficiency scores are produced for each participant, in line with the models defined in Table 2.

4.1 Concurrent Validity

All the efficiency scores were paired up with each other for each learner, and for each instructional efficiency model (LM and PM) and their 8 variations (Table 2), grouped by taught module (Table 3). The non-parametric Spearman correlation test was performed for each of these paired lists. The Pearson correlation instrument was not used since its assumptions were not met. Figure 7(a) illustrates the number of statistically significant correlations of the models, grouped by learning and training efficiency (LrEff, TrEff), and by the mental workload self-reporting assessment instrument employed (RSME, R-NASA). Figure 7(b) shows the average correlation coefficient r_s of these significant correlations.

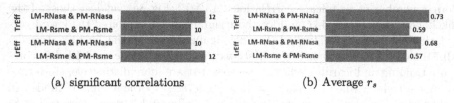

    (a) significant correlations   (b) Average r_s

Fig. 7. Concurrent validity of the parabolic model (PM) of instructional efficiency with the likelihood model (PM) with a) depicting the number of significant correlation tests across the 20 taught modules, and b) their average Spearman correlation coefficients.

Out of 20 possible modules, the parabolic model has shown, for more than half of them, a high concurrent validity with the likelihood model, with average correlation coefficients higher than 0.57, these being statistically significant ($\alpha <$ 0.05). The lack of a perfect correlation was expected, since the parabolic model measures instructional efficiency differently than the likelihood model. However, the fact that for more than half of the modules the two models of instructional efficiency produce scores moderately and highly correlated, it shows that the underlying construct they are actually measuring is similar, and not drastically different.

4.2 Discriminant Validity

The correlation between the training and learning efficiency scores of each model (PM and LM) were examined using Spearman's correlation test to determine their discriminant validity across the 8 models (Table 2) and the taught modules (Table 3). The Spearman test was used because the assumption of the Pearson test were not met. Figure 8a illustrates the number of statistically significant correlations between the efficiency score pairs, while Fig. 8b their average spearman's correlation (r_s).

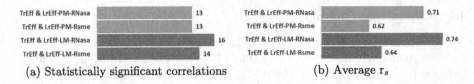

(a) Statistically significant correlations   (b) Average r_s

Fig. 8. Discriminant validity of the parabolic model (PM) of instructional efficiency with the likelihood model (PM) with a) depicting the number of significant correlation tests across the 20 taught modules, and b) their average Spearman correlation coefficients. (Color figure online)

Results demonstrate that the parabolic model (PM) has led to both the lowest number of significant correlations ($13 + 13$, Fig. 8a), against those of the likelihood model ($16 + 14$), and for those significant, it exhibited the lowest correlation coefficients (0.71, 0.62, Fig. 8b) against those of the likelihood model (0.74, 0.64). This is promising as it shows that the parabolic model led to compute training and learning efficiency scores that are more distinctive, since they do not correlate, when compared to those generated by the likelihood model. In other words, evidence suggests that the parabolic model (green bars of Fig. 8) has a superior discriminant validity than the likelihood model (blue bars).

4.3 Information Gain

Information gain was calculated for each of the efficiency models (Table 2) in order to explore which one provides the most information about whether or not an observation belongs to the control or experimental group, for each of the 20 modules (Table 3). In other words, through a measure of information gain, it is possible to determine which efficiency model provides the 'purest' segmentation with respect to these two groups. Figure 9 shows the distribution of the information gain values for these models.

Table 4 provides a summary of all the information gain units (I.G. units) calculated for all of these efficiency models across the 20 modules, and ranked by lower to higher, that means from the model that exhibits on average lower entropy to that of higher entropy.

Table 4. Ranking of efficiency score models based on the Information gain (I.G.) units, with Tr indicating the training phase, Lr the learning phase, Rsme the Rating Scale Mental Effort, RNasa the Raw Nasa Task load Index, PM the parabolic model, and LM the likelihood model of instructional efficiency.

Efficiency model	Rank Val. Sum	I.G. Avg	I.G. StDev.	Ranking Pos.
TrEff-PM-Rsme	74	0.218	0.141	1
TrEff-LM-RNasa	80	0.195	0.132	2
TrEff-PM-RNasa	83	0.176	0.084	3
LrEff-PM-Rsme	88	0.187	0.145	4
LrEff-LM-RNasa	90	0.171	0.109	5
LrEff-PM-RNasa	91	0.190	0.143	6
LrEff-LM-Rsme	97	0.167	0.144	7
TrEff-LM-Rsme	109	0.126	0.085	8

The parabolic model of instructional efficiency, as it is possible to observe from the ranks of Table 4 (highlighted rows), provided higher information gain (less entropy) across model variations when compared to the variations of the likelihood model, thus had lower rank values on average. In fact, for the training phase, the parabolic model had a sum of rank values lower than the likelihood model (74 vs 80). Similarly, for the learning phase, it has a lower rank values than the likelihood model (88 vs 90). The application of the unidimensional measure of effort, or that of the multi-dimensional measure of mental workload, did not provide clear evidence of the superiority of one measure over the other for producing lower ranks. Thus they seem equivalent, and as a consequence, the multidimensional measure might be preferable, as it can give more information on the learner's behaviour for post-hoc analysis. In summary, the parabolic model tends to generate efficiency scores with higher information gain than those produced by the likelihood model, as confirmed by the general lower rank values, and higher averages of information gain units.

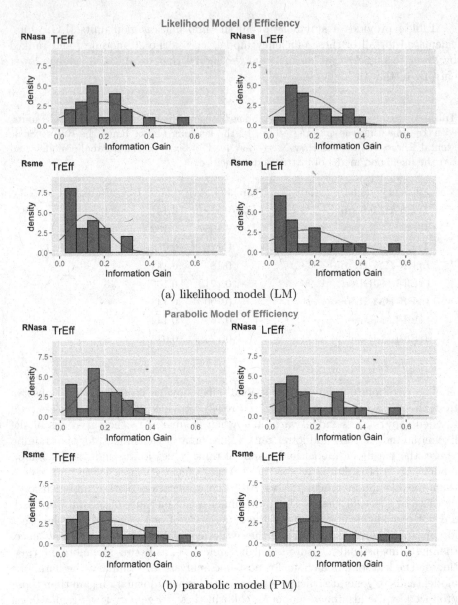

(a) likelihood model (LM)

(b) parabolic model (PM)

Fig. 9. Density plots of information gain values per efficiency model, with Tr indicating the training phase, Lr the learning phase, Rsme the Rating Scale Mental Effort, RNasa the raw Nasa Task load Index, PM the parabolic model, and LM the likelihood model of instructional efficiency.

5   Summary and Future Work

Instructional efficiency is a measurable concept within education and it has gained importance for the quantitative assessment of the efficiency of instructional designs. After a description of the deviational and the likelihood model of instructional efficiency, two well-known models employed within education, and after highlighting their advantages and disadvantages, the constructs of effort and mental workload have been briefly reviewed. This is because the above models of instructional efficiency are based upon a measure of effort or workload, which is combined with a measure of test performance. Additionally, on one hand, the main assumption behind these models is that efficiency is the capacity to achieve established goals, assessed with test performance measures, at the minimal expense of resources [12], assessed with perceived effort or mental workload. However, on the other hand, this article, through the proposal of a novel model of instructional efficiency, the *parabolic model*, challenged this assumption. Through illustrative examples, and by employing the various cognitive load types, fundamental components of the Cognitive Load Theory, it has been shown how this assumption is not always reasonable. This novel and one of its kind model is based upon the assumption that the relationship between mental workload and performance has an inverted-U shape, similarly to the well-known Yerkes-Dodson law of stress and performance [49]. Performance should peak with moderate mental workload, an *ideal* point, and be at the minimal level when experienced mental workload is either at a minimal or maximal level, that means underload or overload.

An empirical experiment has been designed, part of a larger study within education, aimed at investigating the inferences produced by this novel model when compared to the likelihood model of instructional efficiency. Empirical evidence is promising at it shows how the parabolic model has a good concurrent validity with the likelihood model, reasonably demonstrating its capacity to actually measure the construct of instructional efficiency. However, it has a better discriminant validity as demonstrated by a lower correlation between the efficiency scores of the training and the learning phases. Eventually, the parabolic model has led to efficiency scores with a higher information gain, as assessed by employing a measure of information entropy, highlighting its potential for the evaluation of instructional designs with practical implications for the disciplines of teaching and learning and generally for education. Future work are needed to further validate the parabolic model of instructional efficiency. This includes the replication of the experiment conducted in this study over additional instructional designs, and a further assessment of the efficiency scores generated by the parabolic model across a larger set of evaluation criteria [23,26], such as for example sensitivity, reliability, predicting validity.

References

1. Atkinson, R., Shiffrin, R.: Human memory: a proposed system and its control processes. In: Psychology of Learning and Motivation, vol. 2, pp. 89–195. Academic Press (1968)

2. Baddeley, A.: Is working memory still working? Am. Psychol. **56**, 851–864 (2001)
3. Bittner, A.C., Jr., Byers, J.C., Hill, S.G., Zaklad, A.L., Christ, R.E.: Generic work-load ratings of a mobile air defense system (LOS-F-H). Proc. Hum. Factors Soc. Annu. Meet. **33**(20), 1476–1480 (1989)
4. De Jong, T.: Cognitive load theory, educational research, and instructional design: some food for thought. Instr. Sci. **38**(2), 105–134 (2010)
5. Fischer, S., Lowe, R.K., Schwan, S.: Effects of presentation speed of a dynamic visualization on the understanding of a mechanical system. Appl. Cogn. Psychol. **22**(8), 1126–1141 (2008)
6. Gerjets, P., Scheiter, K., Catrambone, R.: Can learning from molar and modular worked examples be enhanced by providing instructional explanations and prompting self-explanations? Learn. Instr. **16**(2), 104–121 (2006)
7. Hancock, G., Longo, L., Hancock, P., Young, M.: Mental workload. In: Salvendy, G., Karwalski, W. (eds.) Handbook of Human Factors & Ergonomics, 5 edn., Chap. 7. Taylor & Francis (2021)
8. Hart, S.G.: NASA-task load index (NASA-TLX); 20 years later. Proc. Hum. Factors Ergon. Soc. Annu. Meet. **50**(9), 904–908 (2006)
9. Hart, S.G., Staveland, L.E.: Development of NASA-TLX (task load index): results of empirical and theoretical research. In: Hancock, P.A., Meshkati, N. (eds.) Human Mental Workload, Advances in Psychology, vol. 52, pp. 139–183. North-Holland, Oxford (1988)
10. Hendy, K.C., Hamilton, K.M., Landry, L.N.: Measuring subjective workload: when is one scale better than many? Hum. Factors **35**(4), 579–601 (1993)
11. Hoffman, B.: Cognitive efficiency: a conceptual and methodological comparison. Learn. Instr. **22**(2), 133–144 (2012)
12. Hoffman, B., Schraw, G.: Conceptions of efficiency: applications in learning and problem solving. Educ. Psychol. **45**(1), 1–14 (2010)
13. Junior, A.C., Debruyne, C., Longo, L., O'Sullivan, D.: On the mental workload assessment of uplift mapping representations in linked data. In: Longo, L., Leva, M.C. (eds.) H-WORKLOAD 2018. CCIS, vol. 1012, pp. 160–179. Springer, Cham (2019). https://doi.org/10.1007/978-3-030-14273-5_10
14. Kalyuga, S., Sweller, J.: Rapid dynamic assessment of expertise to improve the efficiency of adaptive e-learning. Education Tech. Research Dev. **53**, 83–93 (2005)
15. Kantowitz, B.H.: 3. mental workload. In: Advances in Psychology, vol. 47, pp. 81–121. Elsevier (1987)
16. Kantowitz, B.H.: Attention and mental workload. In: Proceedings of the Human Factors and Ergonomics Society Annual Meeting, vol. 44, pp. 3–456. SAGE Publications, Los Angeles (2000)
17. Kester, L., Lehnen, C., Van Gerven, P.W., Kirschner, P.A.: Just-in-time, schematic supportive information presentation during cognitive skill acquisition. Comput. Hum. Behav. **22**(1), 93–112 (2006)
18. Liu, Y., Wickens, C.D.: Mental workload and cognitive task automaticity: an evaluation of subjective and time estimation metrics. Ergonomics **37**(11), 1843–1854 (1994)
19. Longo, L.: Human-computer interaction and human mental workload: assessing cognitive engagement in the world wide web. In: Campos, P., Graham, N., Jorge, J., Nunes, N., Palanque, P., Winckler, M. (eds.) INTERACT 2011. LNCS, vol. 6949, pp. 402–405. Springer, Heidelberg (2011). https://doi.org/10.1007/978-3-642-23768-3_43

20. Longo, L.: Formalising human mental workload as non-monotonic concept for adaptive and personalised web-design. In: Masthoff, J., Mobasher, B., Desmarais, M.C., Nkambou, R. (eds.) UMAP 2012. LNCS, vol. 7379, pp. 369–373. Springer, Heidelberg (2012). https://doi.org/10.1007/978-3-642-31454-4_38
21. Longo, L.: Formalising human mental workload as a defeasible computational concept. Ph.D. thesis, Trinity College (2014)
22. Longo, L.: A defeasible reasoning framework for human mental workload representation and assessment. Behav. Inf. Technol. **34**, 758–786 (2015)
23. Longo, L.: On the reliability, validity and sensitivity of three mental workload assessment techniques for the evaluation of instructional designs: a case study in a third-level course. In: Proceedings of the 10th International Conference on Computer Supported Education, CSEDU 2018, Funchal, Madeira, Portugal, 15–17 March 2018, vol. 2, pp. 166–178 (2018)
24. Longo, L., Barrett, S.: Cognitive effort for multi-agent systems. In: Yao, Y., Sun, R., Poggio, T., Liu, J., Zhong, N., Huang, J. (eds.) BI 2010. LNCS (LNAI), vol. 6334, pp. 55–66. Springer, Heidelberg (2010). https://doi.org/10.1007/978-3-642-15314-3_6
25. Longo, L., Leva, M.C. (eds.): H-WORKLOAD 2017. CCIS, vol. 726. Springer, Cham (2017). https://doi.org/10.1007/978-3-319-61061-0
26. Longo, L., Orrú, G.: An evaluation of the reliability, validity and sensitivity of three human mental workload measures under different instructional conditions in third-level education. In: McLaren, B.M., Reilly, R., Zvacek, S., Uhomoibhi, J. (eds.) CSEDU 2018. CCIS, vol. 1022, pp. 384–413. Springer, Cham (2019). https://doi.org/10.1007/978-3-030-21151-6_19
27. Longo, L., Orrú, G.: Evaluating instructional designs with mental workload assessments in university classrooms. Behav. Inf. Technol. **0**(0), 1–31 (2020)
28. Miller, G.A.: The magical number seven plus or minus two: some limits on our capacity for processing information. Psychol. Rev. **63**(2), 81–97 (1956)
29. Moray, N.: Mental Workload: Its Theory and Measurement, vol. 8. Springer, Boston (2013). https://doi.org/10.1007/978-1-4757-0884-4
30. Moustafa, K., Longo, L.: Analysing the impact of machine learning to model subjective mental workload: a case study in third-level education. In: Longo, L., Leva, M.C. (eds.) H-WORKLOAD 2018. CCIS, vol. 1012, pp. 92–111. Springer, Cham (2019). https://doi.org/10.1007/978-3-030-14273-5_6
31. Orrú, G., Gobbo, F., O'Sullivan, D., Longo, L.: An investigation of the impact of a social constructivist teaching approach, based on trigger questions, through measures of mental workload and efficiency. In: Proceedings of the 10th International Conference on Computer Supported Education (CSEDU 2018) vol. 2, pp. 292–302 (2018)
32. Orrú, G., Longo, L.: Direct instruction and its extension with a community of inquiry: a comparison of mental workload, performance and efficiency. In: Proceedings of the 11th International Conference on Computer Supported Education, CSEDU 2019, Heraklion, Crete, Greece, 2–4 May 2019, vol. 1, pp. 436–444 (2019). https://doi.org/10.5220/0007757204360444
33. Orrú, G., Longo, L.: The evolution of cognitive load theory and the measurement of its intrinsic, extraneous and germane loads: a review. In: Longo, L., Leva, M.C. (eds.) H-WORKLOAD 2018. CCIS, vol. 1012, pp. 23–48. Springer, Cham (2019). https://doi.org/10.1007/978-3-030-14273-5_3

34. Orru, G., Longo, L.: Direct and constructivist instructional design: a comparison of efficiency using mental workload and task performance. In: Longo, L., Leva, M.C. (eds.) H-WORKLOAD 2020. CCIS, vol. 1318, pp. 99–123. Springer, Cham (2020). https://doi.org/10.1007/978-3-030-62302-9_7

35. Paas, F., Van Merrienboer, J.J.G., Adam, J.: Measurement of cognitive load in instructional research. Percept. Mot. Skills **79**, 419–430 (1994)

36. Paas, F., Van Merrienboer, J.J.: The efficiency of instructional conditions: an approach to combine mental effort and performance measures. Hum. Fact. J. Hum. Fact. Ergon. Soc. **35**(4), 737–743 (1993)

37. Plass, J.L., Moreno, R., Brünken, R.: Evaluating Instructional Designs Cognitive Load Theory, 1st edn. Cambridge University Press, New York (2010)

38. Reed, S.K.: Human Cognitive Architecture, pp. 1452–1455. Springer, Boston (2012). https://doi.org/10.1007/978-1-4419-1428-6

39. Rizzo, L., Dondio, P., Delany, S.J., Longo, L.: Modeling mental workload via rule-based expert system: a comparison with NASA-TLX and workload profile. In: Iliadis, L., Maglogiannis, I. (eds.) AIAI 2016. IAICT, vol. 475, pp. 215–229. Springer, Cham (2016). https://doi.org/10.1007/978-3-319-44944-9_19

40. Rizzo, L., Longo, L.: Inferential models of mental workload with defeasible argumentation and non-monotonic fuzzy reasoning: a comparative study. In: Proceedings of the 2nd Workshop on Advances in Argumentation in Artificial Intelligence, co-located with XVII International Conference of the Italian Association for Artificial Intelligence, AI^3@AI*IA 2018, Trento, Italy, 23 November 2018, pp. 11–26 (2018)

41. Rizzo, L.M., Longo, L.: Representing and inferring mental workload via defeasible reasoning: a comparison with the NASA task load index and the workload profile. In: Proceedings of the 1st Workshop on Advances in Argumentation in Artificial Intelligence AI3AI-IA. CEURS (2017)

42. Rubio Valdehita, S., Ramiro, E., García, J., Puente, J.: Evaluation of subjective mental workload: a comparison of SWAT, NASA-TLX, and workload profile methods. Appl. Psychol. **53**, 61–86 (2004)

43. Smith, P.C., Street, A.: Measuring the efficiency of public services: the limits of analysis. J. Roy. Stat. Soc. Ser. A (Stat. Soc.) **168**(2), 401–417 (2005)

44. Sweller, J.: Evolution of human cognitive architecture. Psychol. Learn. Motiv. **43**(2003), 216–266 (2003)

45. Sweller, J.: Element interactivity and intrinsic, extraneous, and Germane cognitive load. Educ. Psychol. Rev. **22**, 123–138 (2010)

46. Tuovinen, J.E., Paas, F.: Exploring multidimensional approaches to the efficiency of instructional conditions. Instr. Sci. **32**, 133–152 (2004)

47. Van Gog, T., Paas, F.: Instructional efficiency: revisiting the original construct in educational research. Educ. Psychol. **43**(1), 16–26 (2008)

48. Wickens, C.D.: Multiple resources and mental workload. Hum. Factors **50**(3), 449–455 (2008)

49. Yerkes, R.M., Dodson, J.D., et al.: The Relation of Strength of Stimulus to Rapidity of Habit-Formation. Punishment: Issues and Experiments, pp. 27–41 (1908)

50. Young, M.S., Brookhuis, K.A., Wickens, C.D., Hancock, P.A.: State of science: mental workload in ergonomics. Ergonomics **58**(1), 1–17 (2014)

51. Zijlstra, F., Doorn, L.: The construction of a scale to measure perceived effort. Department of Philosophy and Social Sciences, p. 53, January 1985

Radical Connectionism – Implications for Mental Workload Research

Aidan Byrne[✉]

Medical School, Swansea University, Swansea, UK

Abstract. While Mental Workload has been widely described in terms of the limited power of a digital computer, this analogy is becoming increasingly untenable. More recently the philosophical concept of Connectionism and the computational model of Parallel Distributed Processing (PDP) have provided an alternative paradigm for Mental Workload which explains some of the unexpected findings in recent research. It also suggests both that cognitive overload is a common, everyday problem and one which is heavily dependent on the whole environment in which it is measured.

Keywords: Mental workload · Connectionism · Parallel Distributed Processing · Cognitive psychology

1 Introduction

Mental Workload is now an established paradigm in both cognitive research and workplace based improvement methodology [1, 2] but lacks a widely accepted neuroanatomical/physiological explanation [3, 4].

Many researchers have characterized the human brain analogous to a digital computer with components such as a central processor, working memory, long term memory, with each device having a limited capacity to process information [5, 6]. The consequence being that if demand exceeds capacity, performance will deteriorate. This paradigm has been reinforced by functional MRI (fMRI) imaging which has allowed researchers to isolate specific areas of the brain associated with specific tasks [7].

However, the digital paradigm is becoming increasingly untenable. Firstly, while fMRI studies have located areas of the brain which 'light up' in response to specific task demands, it has proved impossible to provide single anatomical locations for many required components [8]. For example, the brain stores large amounts of information, but there are no neuroanatomical locations that can be categorized as 'memory' and correspondingly, localized damage to the brain does not cause loss of specific memories. Further, generalized brain disease such as Alzheimer's dementia does not cause piecemeal loss of memory as if individual files were damaged, but rather a 'graceful deterioration' [9] with memories gradually fading and becoming more difficult to recall.

Secondly, the digital paradigm has been supported by the concept of neurons which depolarize or 'fire' in an 'all or nothing' manner which allows direct comparison to a digital computer whose logic circuits are either 'on' or 'off'. However, more recent

L. Longo and M. C. Leva (Eds.): H-WORKLOAD 2021, CCIS 1493, pp. 37–44, 2021.
https://doi.org/10.1007/978-3-030-91408-0_3

neurophysiological research has suggested that the interaction of neurons is actually at the level of the dendrite, with information encoded as analogue changes in voltage and conductance [10]. These changes then lead to neuron action potentials which vary in both strength and duration, so that neural activity is not seen as on/off in a digital manner, but varies continuously in an analogue manner.

Lastly, if the brain functioned as a digital processor, it would be expected that it would function accurately and effectively under low workload and as task demands increased, it would have a stable demand threshold above which performance deteriorated. Studies in anesthetists working in real or simulated operating theatres however, do not show this pattern of measured mental workload/performance. Instead, studies have shown evidence of excess workload in almost all clinical situations, [11–14] with a gradual decrease in mental workload over seven years of training [15]. In addition, it is not explicable that the subjects under study were working normally and not committing regular errors, which suggests that the digital paradigm is not adequate. This also suggests that the cognitive workload associated with even simple tasks may be much higher than previously recognized with that complexity masked by our brain's natural ability to cope with our existence in rapidly changing environments. In particular, the finding that the Mental Workload of fully trained and experienced anaesthetists was higher than that of trainees in the later stages of their training was not explained by current theory [15].

2   Analogue Computation

Although much less well known than digital computers, analogue computers have been constructed using a wide variety of components, but share the property that each component influences the activation of other components in a continuously varying manner, massively increasing the potential computational power when compared with digital computation [16]. Although past designs have used physical gears/rotors or even fluids, more recent electronic designs are composed of a large number of electronic components or nodes, linked by connections which can be inhibitory or facilitatory. A series of input nodes are linked to a series of output nodes through a complex series of 'hidden' nodes which, together form an effective computer described as Parallel Distributed Processing (PDP). The computer is exposed to a large number of training inputs which reinforce 'correct' outputs and suppress 'incorrect' outputs. These designs, with only a few hidden nodes, have been shown to be capable of being trained, for example, to recognize faces in a manner which appears similar to human cognition [17]. The philosophical concept of this type of computation has been described as 'connectionism' [18].

Digital computers, are started, run through a computational process, and deliver an exact result in a predictably fixed time, after which they cease operation. Electronic analogue computers by comparison, are effectively always on, with components set in a specific 'activation state'. Any change in input results in the network 'relaxing' into a new activation state. Each activation state may produce a single output, an oscillation between two or more outputs or a continued pattern of instability. Further, the final result is not determined by the input, but is more likely to be a range of results with different probabilities [19].

Analogue computers do not have separate components such as 'processor' or 'memory'. All the components contribute to the processing power and the systems memory is encoded by the way components are connected together and the form of their inter-actions. Importantly, there is no 'programme', 'variables' or 'rules', with the results emerging through the interaction of the inputs and the starting activation state of the network. So, for example, in a digital computer programmed to recognize faces, there would be different variables for components such as eye color, skin color, and nose shape. In contrast, an analogue computer would have specific activation states for individual people, with multiple nodes involved in each [20].

The above shows that digital and analogue computers have very different responses to incorrect inputs and/or damage to their components. Digital computers are very sus-ceptible to damage in that any failure at any point in the process will result in either an incorrect result, or more likely an 'error' message. Analogue computers, because of their distributed nature are much more resilient and in many cases, substantial damage can be inflected on their circuitry with little or no change in their function.

3 The Brain as an Analogue Computer

The human brain can therefore considered to be a massive array of interconnected nodes, with each node anatomically located to a single dendrite. The connections between each node are encoded as changes in voltage, changes to intracellular ions and proteins as well as the release of neurotransmitters at synapses. Some interactions will also be influenced by wider physiological processes such as the release of hormones such as adrenaline and melatonin in response to external influences such as hunger or threat.

The suggestion is also that the distinction between peripheral senses, input systems, processor, activation pathways and effectors is also blurred in that it would be expected that the total computation power of the system is effected by all these components and, for example, visual processing would be expected to start at retinal level through interactions between neighboring rods/cones and continue as signals ascend thought the pathway to the cerebral cortex. The consequence is that while localized neuronal dam-age, for example, brain trauma, affecting an input/output system could cause blindness or localized paralysis, it would not be expected to produce specific deficits to higher pro-cesses such as personality or specific memories. This is compatible with current research on brain function with, for example, functional Magnetic Resonance Imaging (fMRI) in that it would be expected that some areas of the brain would be more involved with, for example, visual processing, abstract reasoning or fear, but to identify specific loci in the brain to specific functions would ignore the reality of distributed processing [7].

The sensory system is therefore seen as a 'bottom up' process by which incoming sensory information is processed through an ascending system of interactions which results in activation states which represent meaning. For example, the pattern of light which activates retinal cells results in a pattern of neuronal activation which may pro-gressively encode individual photons, to areas of light/dark and color, to edges, shapes, patterns, faces and then the concepts of 'Jane', 'pleased', 'Hello' and the initiation of conversation.

At the same time there is a 'top down' process by which active activation states prioritize specific sensory pathways and effectively impose existing concepts onto the incoming sensory information, so that our overall interpretation of the world around us is both a construct of what we expect as well as what we experience. The available evidence suggests that the majority of our experience is constructed internally with sensory input supplying only a minority of the information used [21].

In the same way, our actions are initiated by activation states representing higher concepts which initiate descending pathways relating to, for example, thirst, walking to tap, leg movements/balance correction and finally individual muscle group activation. Correspondingly, our actions are shaped by ascending feedback systems which allow most of us to walk, but few of us to play guitar or dance beautifully.

This also suggests that there is an activation state which represents 'OK', which gradually changes to an activation state of 'Problem' in response to pain/threat/hunger. The 'Problem' activation state would be expected to result in increased cognitive activity in an attempt to solve the problem. It would also be expected that the 'OK' state would be associated with all the sensory input agreeing with the current internal model, so that 'things are happening as expected'. In contrast, if sensory input did not conform to the internal model, it would be expected to result in the activation of the 'Problem' activation state and an increase in cognitive activity in an attempt to solve the problem. The 'Problem' state could be considered as an explanation of the 'Fight or Flight' state.

In this paradigm, working memory has no physical representation but is rather a function of new activation states tending to 'overwrite' existing activation states, so that only a small number of activation states can be active at any one time. While similar activation states would be expected to overwrite each other, it is likely that dissimilar activation states would not tend to do so. This would support research which suggests that there is more than one component to working memory [22]. Mental workload would also increase if two different tasks require the simultaneous use of the same sensory pathway in that each task will tend to generate its own activation state within that pathway. So, either one activation state will predominate, the pathway will oscillate between the two states or no stable state will emerge, producing results consistent with Wicken's multiple resource theory [23]. These two examples, follow the principle, stated above, that while analogue computers do not contain rules, their emergent behavior appears 'rule like'.

In addition, it suggests that the confidence/significance of the task would also be important. For example, if a subject felt very confident and that the task was of low significance they would tolerate minor differences between their own internal model and reality, producing an activation state of 'OK', resulting in an acceptance of their internal model, 'relaxation' into a state where few resources were used and an association with low measures of mental workload. In contrast, a different subject who felt themselves to be incompetent and the task to be vital, would be expected to focus on even trivial differences between their own internal model and reality, generating an internal state of 'Problem' leading to active sensory activity and the activation of multiple activation states which would be associated with high levels of measured mental workload [24].

The implication is therefore that overall, our brain structure is the result of a long term and massively complex interaction between our DNA, our environment and the physical properties of our physical components. While this determines the overall shape and composition of our brains, its function is determined by an interaction between us and our environment with abilities gradually developed through years of experience, response and feedback. Short term memory would therefore be encoded in rapidly changing aspects of neurons, such as ion/protein concentrations and longer term memory encoded as structural changes in synaptic connections and dendrite morphology [19].

Such a paradigm has attracted criticism for an apparent return to behaviorist theory, with the brain reduced to the status of a 'black box' conditioned to produce specific responses through cycles of trial, response and reward/punishment [25]. Although an analogue brain would be expected to exhibit such behavior, it ignores the much greater complexity suggested here. For example, it would be expected that a child growing up in a society would learn internal activation states representing 'true', 'wrong', 'pleasant' and 'beautiful'. Therefore, in an individual presented with a cake and told not to eat it, we might expect the production of multiple activation states representing 'nice', 'wrong', 'punishment', 'respect' and 'consequences', but whether the presentation of the cake resulted in the output of 'eat' or 'don't eat' would depend on the individual's genetic makeup, their entire life experience and the activation state of their brain just prior to the choice being presented.

4 Consequences for Mental Workload Theory

The above paradigm is based on the understanding that the world around us presents us with a complexity which no existing computer or brain can deal with in real time. Our brains therefore rely heavily on existing internal models to which highly selected sensory input is added to produce an interpretation of our surroundings [18, 26].

Mental workload is therefore correctly defined as a function of the demands of a task relative to the abilities of the individual. Increasing workload will eventually exceed the capacity of the brain to generate adequately accurate activation states and overload would be expected to result in poor performance. However, rather than overload being conceptualized as excess processing demands on a central processor, it is seen as a failure to extract the appropriate information from the environment or due to a failure to generate an effective internal model. Existing measures of mental workload in the form of subjective, physiological and secondary task measures therefore, would be expected to be valid [1].

This paradigm also aligns closely with the four stages of learning first outlined by Broadwell in 1969 [27], but widely used elsewhere.

So, in the study of anesthetists during their training noted earlier, [15] novices lacked the necessary sensory filters to extract meaning from the complex theatre environment and knew that a supervisor would deal with any problems, so showed confidence, low mental workload and would be described as 'unconsciously incompetent'. Over a period of weeks, the trainees became aware of the complexity of the task, but were unable to rapidly develop the required sensory filters, internal models and motor skills, so entered a period of high workload and 'conscious incompetence'. This can be seen as them consciously constructing an internal model by actively extracting meaning from their environment. Over the next seven years, the trainees developed the sensory filters, internal models and motor skills to more rapidly construct internal models and so deal effectively with the majority of tasks. They therefore became 'consciously competent' and showed low mental workload.

The explanation of the finding of increased mental in fully qualified/permanent staff was unexpected, but can be seen as the experienced staff only using sensory information to confirm that their internal model is correct, rather than using sensory information to construct a new reality. This would be expected to be associated with high levels of confidence/low levels of reported mental workload and, to external observers, a high level of performance [28]. However, the reduction in the use of external sensory input would be expected to result in decreased responsiveness to a secondary task, as used in this study, [15] with an apparent increase in mental workload. In addition, it would be expected that the experienced staff would be less aware of both their surroundings and their own actions, as described as a state of 'unconscious competence'.

This would also suggest that while the main problem for trainees would be cognitive overload, permanent staff would be more susceptible to confirmation bias by relying on their own internal models rather than gaining vital information from around them.

5 Conclusions

This paradigm leads us to several conclusions on human cognition that lead to testable predictions.

Firstly it characterizes our environment as overwhelmingly complex so that cognitive overload would be expected to be a common rather than a rare mental state. Measurement of the mental workload of individuals using objective methods undergoing normal day to day tasks would be expected to identify signs of cognitive overload.

Secondly, our ability to function on a daily basis is therefore dependent on internal schemata and expectations rather than an accurate analysis of the world around us. This predicts that experience/familiarity are key determinants of workload, with mental workload rapidly decreasing as an individual gains experience of the task and the environment.

Thirdly, workload would also be highly sensitive to changes in both the task and its environment. This predicts that especially for those with highly developed skills situated in highly standardized environments, minor changes may influence mental workload, even if the changes do not directly relate directly to the primary task.

Fourthly, individual confidence will be a key determinant of mental workload. This predicts that if an individual loses confidence in their interpretation of the environment or their ability to complete the task, their mental workload will increase. Extreme levels of uncertainty on their own may lead to cognitive collapse.

Lastly, tasks which may be identified as subjectively high workload, for example, academic examinations or mental mathematic would be expected to use very limited resources and show low levels of workload measured objectively. In contrast, everyday tasks which may be identified as low workload, such as shopping, driving a car or walking in a city involve the extraction of meaning from a complex environment and may therefore show high levels of workload measured objectively.

This new paradigm of mental workload supports much of the existing research and explains some experimental findings which previously seemed inexplicable. However, further research to explore the above predictions will be required before it can be accepted as a valid interpretation of human cognition.

References

1. Young, M.S., Brookhuis, K.A., Wickens, C.D., Hancock, P.A.: State of science: mental workload in ergonomics. Ergonomics **58**(1), 1–17 (2015)
2. Wickens, C.D.: Mental Workload: Assessment, Prediction and Consequences, pp. 18–29. Springer, Cham (2017)
3. Hancock, P.A.: Whither Workload? Mapping a Path for Its Future Development, pp. 3–17. Springer, Cham (2017)
4. Babiloni, F.: Mental workload monitoring: new perspectives from neuroscience. In: Longo, L., Leva, M.C. (eds.) H-WORKLOAD 2019. CCIS, vol. 1107, pp. 3–19. Springer, Cham (2019). https://doi.org/10.1007/978-3-030-32423-0_1
5. Orru, G., Longo, L.: The evolution of cognitive load theory and the measurement of its intrinsic, extraneous and Germane loads: a review. Commun. Comput. Inf. Sci. **1012**, 23–48 (2018)
6. Tricot, A., et al.: Working memory resource depletion effect in academic learning: steps to an integrated approach. In: Longo, L., Leva, M.C. (eds.) H-WORKLOAD 2020. CCIS, vol. 1318, pp. 13–26. Springer, Cham (2020). https://doi.org/10.1007/978-3-030-62302-9_2
7. Prat, C.S., Mason, R.A., Just, M.A.: An fMRI investigation of analogical mapping in metaphor comprehension: the influence of context and individual cognitive capacities on processing demands. J. Exp. Psychol. Learn. Mem. Cogn. **38**(2), 282–294 (2012)
8. Olsen, R.K., Robin, J.: Zooming in and zooming out: the importance of precise anatomical characterization and broader network understanding of MRI data in human memory experiments. Curr. Opin. Behav. Sci. **32**, 57–64 (2020)
9. Tasnimi, M.: Connectionism: the pros and cons author name. Int. J. Res. English Lang. Lit. Humanit. **22** (2015)
10. Daniel, R., Rubens, J.R., Sarpeshkar, R., Lu, T.K.: Synthetic analog computation in living cells. Nature **497**(7451), 619–623 (2013)
11. Byrne, A.J., Sellen, A.J., Jones, J.G.: Errors on anaesthetic record charts as a measure of anaesthetic performance during simulated critical incidents. Br. J. Anaesth. **80**(1), 58–62 (1998)
12. Woods, B., Byrne, A., Bodger, O.: The effect of multitasking on the communication skill and clinical skills of medical students. BMC Med. Educ. **18**(1), 76 (2018)
13. Davis, D.H.J., Oliver, M., Byrne, A.J.: A novel method of measuring the mental workload of anaesthetists during simulated practice. Br. J. Anaesth. **103**(5), 665–669 (2009)
14. Byrne, A., Tweed, N., Halligan, C.: A pilot study of the mental workload of objective structured clinical examination examiners. Med. Educ. **48**(3), 262–267 (2014)
15. Byrne, A.J., Murphy, A., McIntyre, O., Tweed, N.: The relationship between experience and mental workload in anaesthetic practice: an observational study. Anaesthesia **68**(12), 1266–1272 (2013)
16. Small, J.S.: The Analogue Alternative: The Electronic Analogue Computer in Britain and the USA, 1930–1975. Routledge, London (2001)
17. Grossman, S., et al.: Convergent evolution of face spaces across human face-selective neuronal groups and deep convolutional networks. Nat. Commun. **10**(1), 1–13 (2019)
18. O'Brien, G., Opie, J.: How do connectionist networks compute? Cogn. Process. **7**(1), 30–41 (2006)
19. O'Brien, G.: Connectionism, analogicity and mental content. Acta Anal. **22**, 111–131 (1998)
20. Alvarado Barrios, G., Retamal, J.C., Solano, E., Sanz, M.: Analog simulator of integro-differential equations with classical memristors arXiv (2018)
21. Mitchell, M.: Complex systems: network thinking. Artif. Intell. **170**(18), 1194–1212 (2006)
22. Funahashi, S.: Working memory in the prefrontal cortex. Brain Sci. **7**(12), 49 (2017)

23. Wickens, C.D.: Multiple resources and mental workload. Hum. Factors J. Hum. Factors Ergon. Soc. **50**(3), 449–455 (2008)

24. Omosehin, O., Smith, A.P.: Do cultural differences play a role in the relationship between time pressure, workload and student well-being? In: Longo, L., Leva, M.C. (eds.) H-WORKLOAD 2019. CCIS, vol. 1107, pp. 186–204. Springer, Cham (2019). https://doi.org/10.1007/978-3-030-32423-0_12

25. Huang, J.: Imitating the brain with neurocomputer a 'new' way towards artificial general intelligence. Int. J. Autom. Comput. **14**(5), 520–531 (2017)

26. Kostenko, A., Rauffet, P., Moga, S., Coppin, G.: Operator functional state: measure it with attention intensity and selectivity, explain it with cognitive control. In: Longo, L., Leva, M.C. (eds.) H-WORKLOAD 2019. CCIS, vol. 1107, pp. 156–169. Springer, Cham (2019). https://doi.org/10.1007/978-3-030-32423-0_10

27. Broadwell, M.M.: Teaching for learning (XVI.). Gospel Guard. **41**, 1–3 (1961)

28. Pediconi, M.G., Bigi, S., Brunori, M., Genga, G.M., Venzi, S.: In the sky between expertise and unexpected feelings and resources of pilots' resilient ego: a psychoanalytic point of view. In: Longo, L., Leva, M.C. (eds.) H-WORKLOAD 2020. CCIS, vol. 1318, pp. 27–57. Springer, Cham (2020). https://doi.org/10.1007/978-3-030-62302-9_3

Fundamental Frequency as an Alternative Method for Assessing Mental Fatigue of Distance Learning Teachers

José Juan Cañas(✉), Enrique Muñoz-de-Escalona, and Jessica F. Morales-Guaman

Mind, Brain and Behaviour Research Centre, University of Granada, Granada, Spain
{delagado,enriquemef}@ugr.es, jessicamorales@correo.ugr.es

Abstract. Online education is gaining ground in our society due to the introduction of new educational technologies and the pandemic situation we are experiencing. The experience is showing that online teaching makes an extra demand on mental resources as compared to face-to-face teaching. For this reason, we are in need of methodologies to measure this demand for resources in order to propose how to mitigate it. In this paper we propose a methodology based on acoustic voice analysis to measure the mental resource demand of teachers. This methodology is similar to that being used successfully in other fields. The advantages of this methodology are that it does not require any costly and intensive instrumentation to record and analyse data. The only two instruments that the methodology requires are a tape recorder and a software for analysing the acoustic parameters of the voice that can be installed on the teachers' own computer.

Keywords: Online teaching · Mental fatigue · Voice fundamental frequency

1 Introduction: Mental Workload and Mental Fatigue of Teachers

Human being requires energy to perform mental and physical activities. We could say that this energy, which is obtained through nutrition and stored in the body, is limited and it can be depleted [1–4]. Human performance is directly linked to the quantity and quality of available resources (energy) which are available to cope with the execution of tasks [2–5]. Hence, we can say that performance is directly linked to human mental workload [5, 6] and mental fatigue [7, 8]. We can define mental workload as the result of establishing a division between demanded resources (mediated by task complexity) and available resources (mediated by intrinsic factors, such as individual differences, mental activation, sleep deprivation etc.) [5, 9]. The division of both factors can result into three different possible scenarios: mental overload (if demanded resources are much higher than available resources), balanced situation (if demanded and available resources are balanced) and mental underload (if available resources are much higher than demanded resources). The former and the latter are unbalanced situations, which would ultimately affect operators' wellbeing and performance and would increase risks, particularly in the employment context [1, 10–12]. Mental overload can be caused by excess in demanded

© Springer Nature Switzerland AG 2021
L. Longo and M. C. Leva (Eds.): H-WORKLOAD 2021, CCIS 1493, pp. 45–59, 2021.
https://doi.org/10.1007/978-3-030-91408-0_4

resources, but in can also be due to a lack of available resources induced by the emergence of mental fatigue. Thus, we can see that mental workload construct is closely linked with mental fatigue, which can be defined as a condition of cognitive impairment and low alertness that affects performance and is caused by resource depletion through time performing certain cognitive/s task/s [13]. Mental workload [14–16] and mental fatigue [17–20] have been considered responsible for weakened human performance as well as the main causes of work-related accidents. For this reason, the measurement of both constructs continues to be one of the greatest challenges to be faced nowadays by Ergonomists and Human Factors researchers [21–29], but it also extends to other spheres such as the educational field.

For the past few decades, due to the technological changes that have been introduced in education, we are witnessing a progressive shift from face-to-face teaching to online teaching. Moreover, this change is accelerating due to the pandemic situation we have been experiencing since the beginning of 2020 when many colleges and universities have been forced to adopt online teaching. This change is having consequences at all levels of the educational system, but mainly in the practices, behaviours and psychological processes of its two main members, teachers and students. Teachers and students are reporting negative psychological effects of online teaching. It is therefore important that research is carried out to find out what these negative effects are, what their causes are and what measures we can propose to mitigate them.

One of the negative effects of online teaching is related to the mental resources of teachers and students. This negative psychological effect is also being observed in other areas where computer-mediated communication is taking precedence over face-to-face communication. Many of these areas have witnessed the emergence of a phenomenon known as Zoom fatigue, which is common to all situations where people have replaced face-to-face communication with communication through audio-visual media. Zoom fatigue is a term that refers to the symptoms a person feels when communicating with other people through audio-visual technology, usually a computer. Although the term has become very popular nowadays, it has the disadvantage that it refers to a particular technology, the Zoom platform. Some authors therefore prefer to replace Zoom with other terms such as Computer Mediated Communication so that the phenomenon includes communication experiences through all audio-visual technologies. Therefore, we would be talking about mental fatigue and mental workload due to computer mediated communication irrespective of the platform used for this communication [30]. No matter what we call it, all researchers agree that the phenomenon is due to an excessive demand on mental resources because communication is done through audio-visual means rather than face-to-face.

This extra demand on mental resources due to computer-mediated communication is currently being intensively researched, and some explanations have already been suggested. For example, [31] has suggested that in face-to-face interaction we rarely consciously attend to our own gestures and other non-verbal cues. As research on nonverbal synchrony has shown, nonverbal behaviour is simultaneously effortless and incredibly complex [32]. However, in computer-mediated communication, non-verbal behaviour is still complex, but users have to put more effort into sending and receiving signals.

While this explanation may be valid, it is clear that there may be other possible explanations as well and we need to do more research on mental fatigue and mental workload in computer-mediated communication, especially in online teaching and in order to do so we need tools to do that research. Fortunately, we currently have extensive research on mental workload and mental fatigue in many laboratory and applied contexts [33–36] that can be used to investigate this phenomenon of computer-mediated communication and to propose methods to mitigate the effects of online teaching on teachers' and students' mental workload and mental fatigue.

2 Tools for Measuring Mental Workload and Mental Fatigue in E-learning

In order to investigate the mental workload and mental fatigue of teachers during online teaching, it is necessary to have a methodology to measure their mental resources. In many disciplines, over the last decades, researchers have devised several methods to measure the mental resources a person has while performing a task [37, 38].

All these methods can be classified in various ways according to several criteria. The first criterion is the time at which the amount of resources is recorded. According to this criterion we can distinguish between "offline methods" and "online methods". Offline methods basically consist of estimating the amount of mental resources after the task has been completed, whereas online methods measure the amount of resources during the performance of the task. In online teaching, we could measure the amount of resources of teachers at the end of their lesson (offline procedure), but if we want to know how these resources change during task performance, we would need to use an online procedure.

However, regardless of whether the assessment is offline or online, we have to select a method from the categories that have been proposed. The first of these categories includes all methods that are based on measuring task performance. These methods are based on the assumption that task performance reflects the amount of mental resources a person has. If those resources are few, performance will be poor, while if they are many, performance will be good. A subcategory of these methods is what we call "concurrent task performance-based methods", which consist of asking the person to perform a task that is called a secondary task while he/she is performing his/her main task, which is the one he/she has to perform on the job. Basically, these methods measure the performance of the secondary task and apply the following logic: since both the primary and the secondary task have to share the same resources, the performance of the secondary task is a reflection of how many resources are "left over" after the primary task has been performed. If we observe that the secondary task performs very well, we can interpret that the primary task requires few resources. Conversely, if the secondary task performs poorly, it means that the primary task is consuming most of the resources. These performance-based methods are difficult, if not impossible, to use during an online teaching because it would mean asking the teacher to perform a secondary task while explaining his or her subject to the students. This secondary task would interfere in an unacceptable way with the teachers' explanation.

There is a second category of methods that we call "subjective methods" which consist of asking the person to give a subjective estimate of his/her currently available mental resources, usually using a scale of numerical intervals on which the available mental resources can be expressed from least to most during the performance of the task. Although, these methods would allow the teacher to give an estimate of his/her mental resources, they would also have the disadvantage of interfering with his/her task of explaining the course contents to the students.

Finally, the third category of methods, known as psychophysiological methods, are based on our knowledge of the relationship between mental resources and certain psychophysiological parameters. There are currently several psychophysiological methods, all of which have advantages and disadvantages. Most of these currently proposed methods of psychophysiological recording (recordings of eye parameters such as blink rate, pupil diameter, recordings of the electrical activity of the cerebral cortex, etc.) require a great deal of technical expertise and the use of some particular recording equipment, which is expensive and would require the teacher to be equipped with it in order to adequately record the physiological parameters. These drawbacks would rule out these physiological methods if we want to use them widely in research on mental workload and mental fatigue of teachers teaching online.

Recently some researchers have explored performance-based evaluation methods on online teaching. For example, [39] have explored the possibility of measuring mouse movements and keyboard presses of students. The researchers installed an especial software on students' computers in a MATLAB programming course. This software collected data on mouse movement and keystrokes as students performed practical tasks assigned to them by teachers during their classes. At the same time, the students answered the NASA-TLX questionnaire, a questionnaire that measures subjective mental workload. The data obtained were subjected to a classification procedure based on the K-Nearest Neighbour (KNN) algorithm. With this ranking procedure the authors were able to predict students' subjective estimates of mental workload from the patterns of keyboard presses and mouse movements. The authors concluded that it is possible to use these performance measures during online teaching to estimate mental workload and mental fatigue. However, this procedure has a serious drawback: in most online classes, students and teachers do not have to be typing or moving the mouse. In most online classes, teachers explain content verbally and students ask questions verbally. Only in some classes, in particular in practical classes and in topics related to computer input, teachers and students have to press the keyboard and move the mouse. For this reason, if online classes are dominated by verbal behaviour, it would be necessary to develop procedures for assessing mental workload and mental fatigue based on voice analysis.

In the field of air traffic control, [40] have proposed that a measure of a persons' mental resources can be obtained by analysing some acoustic parameters of the human voice, namely the fundamental frequency of the voice (F0). This proposal is based on our knowledge that in communication between two people, it is of crucial importance that both are able to perceive the emotional state of the other. Thus, in order to be able to perceive the emotional state of the person with whom we are communicating, human beings use various signals, the most relevant of which are facial gestures. Human beings are very good at expressing our inner psychological states through facial gestures. However, although less effective, another feature of human communication that also shows the inner psychological state is the voice, more specifically, certain acoustic parameters of the voice. It would therefore be possible to analyse the acoustic characteristics of the voice to infer the psychological states of the speakers. In the case of air traffic controllers, who have to communicate constantly with pilots and collateral controllers, the acoustic characteristics of their voice can show the state of their mental resources. The results obtained by these researchers in the laboratory had confirmed this hypothesis, and had been replicated in analyses of recordings of actual air traffic controllers communicating with pilots and collaterals during their working day [41]. Therefore, they could be used as a basis for the development of a similar methodological approach to infer the state of teachers' mental resources during online teaching.

The scientific justification for the proposal of this alternative can be found in empirical studies in which a more or less large set of parameters have been measured and the effects that some factors have on them have been analysed [42]. Many of these experimental studies have manipulated independent variables that hypothetically may have an effect on some of these acoustic parameters [43]. The results of these studies have gradually outlined what of these parameters are the most sensitives to changes in mental states. In this way, most of the studies carried out coincide in identifying F0 as the parameter that best reflects states of stress, load and mental fatigue. F0 is the lowest frequency of a periodic waveform. In the case of the human voice, when producing a sound, the vocal cords vibrate at a certain speed by rapidly opening and closing with small puffs of air. The sound produced is composed of a spectrum of frequencies that we can decompose to obtain the lowest frequency of the spectrum. That lower frequency of the sound produced is what we call F0. It should be noted that, although they are related, we should not confuse F0 with the pitch of a sound, in this case the voice. While pitch is a unit of measurement of "perception", we could say that F0 defines the "physical" measurement of sound, and this can be obtained by making a recording of the voice by placing a wide-range microphone directly in the throat, above the vocal folds, but below the resonant structures of the vocal tract. Pitch, on the other hand, is a "psychological" measure of how frequencies are perceived by the human nervous system through the ear and is measured by the "Mel Scale". The name Mel comes from the word melody, to indicate that it is based on the human perception of tones. Thus, the relationship between F0 and pitch would be similar to the relationship between the physical intensity of sound and the decibel scale, the latter being a perceptual psychological measure of sound intensity. In any case, since the relationship between frequency and pitch is a complex relationship that takes us into the field of psychophysics and takes the perspective of the listener and not the speaker, which is what interests us in this research; researchers have preferred to measure F0 directly in their research on the relationship between mental states and the physical parameters of the voice instead of pitch.

The first empirical data on the relationship between F0 and mental states related to mental resources was obtained in a now classic study by [44] in which a group of participants were asked to perform a series of tasks in which the researchers manipulated the levels of mental load, thus inducing different levels of stress. The results indicated that under experimentally induced stress conditions there was an increase in F0 relative to baseline, an increase in jitter (a measure of disturbance in frequency) and shimmer (a measure of disturbance in the amplitude of the acoustic wave), an increase in high-frequency harmonic energy, and a decrease in spectral noise.

Human speech is divided into three sub-processes, namely breathing, phonation and resonance and it can be measured using many physical parameters. Traditionally, these parameters have been analysed and studied by speech therapists in relation to the diagnosis and treatment of speech pathologies [45], although for several decades, they have also been studied with the aim of designing automatic speech recognition and production tools [46]. However, the results of these neuropsychological studies also allow us to hypothesise about the parameters that may be of most interest for detecting mental states. In this sense, of the three speech processes, it is phonation that has been identified by researchers as being responsible for the variation in acoustic parameters that reflect the mental states we are studying. The parameters of phonation depend on the functioning of the larynx and, more specifically, the vocal folds. However, some authors have pointed out that F0 also depends on the breathing process and, since breathing is related to the stress response, they propose that we should also consider them when explaining the relationship between these parameters and mental states.

[47] have reviewed the experimental literature on the psychophysiological mechanisms responsible for speech control and have identified two major mechanisms that act simultaneously and have to be kept in balance. First, we have a mechanism, which in neuroscientific terminology would belong to the category of "bottom-up" mechanisms because they are activated by environmental stimuli. These bottom-up mechanisms are responsible for activating the system and determine the effort a person needs to make in the face of external demands. It is this mechanism that would affect F0. Secondly, there would be an "up-down" mechanism (activated by the brains' response) that primarily controls the variability of these parameters.

There is a brain structure known as the Anterior Cingulate Cortex (ACC) that is responsible for maintaining the balance between these two mechanisms. This structure is part of an executive attentional network and its main role is to regulate the processing of information from other networks, both sensory and emotional [48]. There is a connection between the ACC and the vagus nerve (VN) which is involved in the regulation of breathing which is the initial process of speech production. But this nerve also plays an important role in the response, especially in stress, to environmental demands. The vocal apparatus is connected to the two bifurcated pathways of the NV and the ACC. On the one hand, the superior laryngeal nerve, which originates from the VN, is known to innervate the cricothyroid muscle involved in vocal fold stretching and pitch regulation [49]. On the other hand, the ACC's executive pathways to brainstem nuclei involved in "fight or flight mode" [50] and its "up-down" regulation (e.g., [51, 52]) are also part of particular pathways that execute psychomotor and vocal behaviour (e.g., [53, 54]). Possibly, the connection between the ACC and the autonomic circuitry of the NB and other connections to the laryngeal nerves may serve as a major pathway for voice stress output during cognitive and emotional load. Therefore, based on neuropsychological research we can infer that fatigue might affect different phases of speech production [55].

In summary, after this brief review of empirical studies to date, we can say that there is empirical evidence to assume that it might exist a relationship between F0 and mental states, in particular mental fatigue. Moreover, current knowledge about the neuropsychological basis of human speech allows us to explain these effects. Therefore, in this study we have explored the possibility of extending these results to find out whether a methodology could be designed to measure the mental resources of teachers who teach online. In this research, we asked a group of five female university professors and one male secondary school teacher to record what they said during their lectures using an app on their mobile phones. These recordings were then analysed to investigate whether the F0 of the teachers' voices changed during their lectures. Our hypothesis, according to the previous results, was that the F0 of the teachers' voices would increase throughout the lesson, showing their mental fatigue.

3 Methodology

3.1 Materials and Instruments

To obtain the recordings of the lessons, teachers were asked to use their mobile phone standard recording application and to send us the recording file in.wav format for analysis. The F0 analysis was carried out with a specific software named "Praat". Praat is a scientific license free tool for analyzing spectrograms of audio records. It was developed at the University of Amsterdam by Paul Boersma and David Weenink in 1992 and it is constantly being updated with improvements implemented by authors, some of them suggested by users [56]. Once the audio file is loaded you can obtain multiple audio parameters such as fundamental frequency, intensity, volume, formants, etc. In this study we used Praat software for obtaining the fundamental frequency intervals average.

3.2 Participants

Since this was our first study on the effect of mental fatigue on F0 during online teaching, we decided to simplify the objectives and hold constant several variables that we hypothesized might interact with this effect. For this reason, to investigate the between subjects differences we selected only female teachers to avoid gender interaction effects. We know that F0 is different for women and men, but the interaction between mental fatigue and gender could be explored in future studies. Thus, five female teachers from the University of Granada participated in the research. The ages ranged from 29 to 40 years and the average age was 33. We asked them to select and record a lesson that represented a standard lesson that they would teach to their students. Because each teacher had different teaching styles, the lessons of the five teachers were of different lengths.

To investigate the within-subject differences, we asked a 63 years old secondary school teacher to participate in the study. He recorded his lessons of different lengths over seven days.

3.3 Procedure

The teachers participating in the research were asked to record their voice during their lesson with their mobile phone. For obtaining the recording they could use any standard application they already had installed on their mobile phones.

This study was carried out in accordance with the recommendations of the local ethical guidelines of the committee of the University of Granada institution called Comité de Ética de Investigación Humana. The protocol was approved by the Comité de Ética de Investigación Humana. All subjects gave written informed consent in accordance with the Declaration of Helsinki.

4 Results

To analyse the evolution of F0 during the online lessons of participants in both experimental groups, we divided the entire time period of the lessons into 2 min intervals and obtained the average F0 for each of these intervals.

4.1 First Experimental Group: University Lecturers

The recordings of the five university lecturers were of approximately the same length, but to average them all we took only the first 25 intervals, covering the first 50 min of the recording.

We can see in the Fig. 1 that F0 increased linearly through intervals, as trend analysis revealed, $F(1, 23) = 6.79$, $p < .05$. The estimated linear function was F0 = 166,92 + ,173 Intervals. The R Square was, 228.

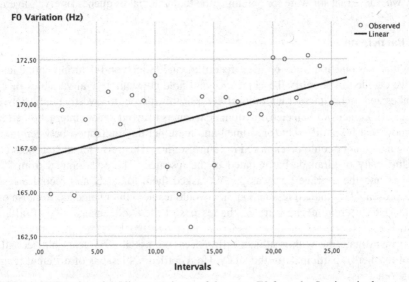

Fig. 1. Estimation of the linear tendency of the mean F0 from the 5 university lectures

4.2   Second Experimental Group: Secondary School Teacher

The Secondary School teachers' recordings were of approximately the same length, but to average them all we only took the first 23 intervals, covering the first 46 min of each lesson. Figure 2 shows that F0 increased linearly through intervals, as trend analysis revealed, $F(1, 21) = 2,82$ p $< .10$. The estimated linear function was F0 $= 223,63 +$,175 Intervals. The R Square was, 118.

Therefore, the results showed that, according to our hypothesis, F0 increased over the course of the lesson taught by the teachers.

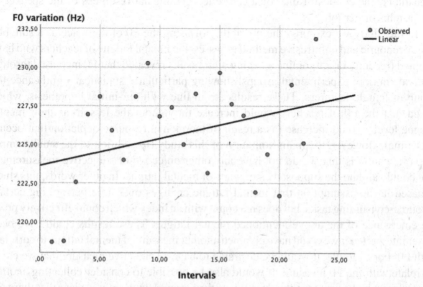

Fig. 2. Estimation of the linear tendency of the mean F0 from the 7 days of online teaching of the Secondary School Teacher

Although in the case of the secondary school teacher the linear upward trend did not become statistically significant, in the case of the 5 female university teachers this trend did reach significance.

5   Discussion

Online teaching is not new in our society, however, the pandemic we are experiencing has accelerated its implementation at all levels of education. Universities and schools have asked their teachers to adopt the online methodology within a few months and these teachers have started to experience problems they were unaware of before. One of these problems is the emergence of mental fatigue, which is a consequence of the excessive demand on mental resources involved in communicating via a computer.

The knowledge we have about this mental fatigue experienced by teachers in online teaching, which some call "Zoom Fatigue", is very scarce and we need to set up research projects to find out what are its characteristics and what are the factors that determine it. These research projects need a suitable methodology to be able to measure mental fatigue and mental workload within the context of online teaching. For this reason, it would be worthwhile to invest efforts in developing such methodologies. The main characteristic of the online teaching condition is that the teacher mainly uses his or her voice (at the expense of non-verbal behaviour) to explain the contents of his or her lessons to the students. Therefore, a viable proposal would be to develop methodologies for assessing mental fatigue based on the analysis of the acoustic characteristics of the voice. As is already being demonstrated in other areas of Human Factors (e.g. air traffic control), the acoustic characteristics of the voice can reflect the mental resources of the speaker to perform his or her job.

In this study we explored the possibility of using the F0 of the voice as a suitable, easy, economic and unintrusive method for assessing mental fatigue of teachers who have adopted (recently or not) online teaching. Our results revealed that F0 increased through intervals in both experimental groups, showing particularly statistical significance the group of female lecturers. These results are in line with our initial hypothesis, which stated that the F0 of teachers would increase throughout the lesson, as their mental fatigue levels would increase (as a result of the mental resource depletion that occurs over time). However, the main limitation of this study (in addition to the small sample of participants) is that we do not have any other objective or subjective measurement that could validate the supposed emergence of mental fatigue. In other words, this study is based in the assumption that mental fatigue emerges over time performing certain resource-consuming tasks, but does not count with an index which could effectively proof the emergence of the above-mentioned mental fatigue. These results could have been better interpreted if we could have obtained another measure of mental fatigue to correlate with F0. For example, it would be desirable to have a subjective measure that we could correlate with the F0 measure. It would also be possible to consider collecting another physiological measure over the duration of the lesson. However, it is clear that there are problems in being able to introduce other measures, whether subjective or physiological, during the delivery of the lesson. It is precisely these problems that made us exploring the possibility of using F0 to predict mental fatigue. It would be methodologically difficult to request the level of mental fatigue that a teacher is experiencing every two minutes. It would also be complicated and very intrusive to use eye tracking equipments in order to collect their pupil diameter or blink rate. Although this last procedure is not ruled out in future research, because some applications that measure eye movements through computer webcams are emerging and we will have to explore them to determine if they could be used for our purposes in this research.

For this reason, it will be necessary to carry out further laboratory research under controlled conditions, in which F0 is measured and analysed simultaneously with subjective and psychophysiological variables, in order to check whether they correlate and detect mental fatigue in a similar way. An example of this research has been carried out by [57] who conducted a laboratory experiment involving 17 participants aged between 24 and 40 years. Each participant completed three sessions with the Multi-Attribute Task Battery II (MATB-II) of one hour each and distributed over a week every two days. The task configuration set allowed an increase in cognitive demands as the experimental session progressed. During the MATB-II sessions, certain ocular parameters (pupil size and blink rate) were recorded and their voice as well, so that their fundamental frequency could be analysed. Participants also reported their experienced mental fatigue level every two minutes during task performance. All this data was combined with data obtained from smart wristbands (Xiaomi Smart Band 4) worn by the participants continuously during the week-long experiment, which allowed them to monitor the hours and quality of their sleep. The results showed an increase in mental fatigue as the experimental tasks progressed: 1) task performance was impaired over time, 2) subjective mental fatigue reports increased over time, 3) blink rate and F0 increased over time, which is consistent with the increase in subjective mental fatigue and performance impairment and 4) a decrease in pupil size over time was also observed, which is consistent with the hypothesis that the smaller the pupil size the greater the experienced mental fatigue. Therefore, these results suggested that F0 is a variable that can be used to assess mental fatigue as other psychophysiological (pupil diameter and blink rate), subjective and performance measures.

6 Conclusions and Further Research

Our results are in line with the evidence about the relationship between F0 and mental fatigue. These results, in the field of online teaching, are a continuation of those found in the research, that continues showing evidence about the increase in F0 that occurs as mental fatigue arises, in different domains [44, 47, 55, 57]. However, what is needed now, aside from continuing clarifying the link between these two elements, is to know which factors impact on this relationship between mental fatigue and F0. It is clear that human speech is also affected by individual characteristics of people and by the external conditions in which communication takes place. For example, we know that voice frequency depends on the gender of the speaker. Women have a higher-pitched voice, i.e. with higher frequencies, than men, who have lower-pitched voices (lower frequencies). In addition, voice pitch becomes deeper with age. In the same way, certain factors such as background noise, message content, message receiver, etc., can also affect F0. Therefore, since our ultimate goal will be to develop automatic voice analysis software to detect mental fatigue, we need to be aware of all these demographic and contextual factors so that we can take them into account in the development of such software. In other words, we cannot expect to develop universal software that does not take into account individual factors and characteristics of the particular teacher whose voice we are analysing. Therefore, we can say that to date it has only been empirically demonstrated that mental fatigue has an effect on F0 [44, 47, 55, 57], but more research work is needed to know when and in what form this effect is found, in order to develop a reliable and valid F0 analysis algorithm for developing an application that can be incorporated for assessing mental fatigue in real time.

It will also be necessary to compare the effect of mental fatigue on teachers depending on whether they teach online or face-to-face. Due to the pandemic situation in which this research has been conducted, we have not been able to make this comparison, as we could not obtain face-to-face teaching recordings. However, when face-to-face teaching resumes, this comparison should be a priority. Finally, further research, with extended sample size, will need to consider measuring other psychophysiological and subjective parameters that could be used to validate F0 as a valuable mental fatigue measure that can overcome the traditional limitations of psychophysiological measures.

References

1. Kahneman, D.: Attention and Effort, vol. 1063. Prentice-Hall, Englewood Cliffs (1973)
2. Wickens, C.D.: Multiple resources and mental workload. Hum. Fact. **50**(3), 449–455 (2008). https://doi.org/10.1518%2F001872008X288394
3. Hockey, R.: The Psychology of Fatigue: Work, Effort and Control. Cambridge University Press, Cambridge (2013)
4. Hockey, G.R.J.: Compensatory control in the regulation of human performance under stress and high workload: a cognitive-energetical framework. Biol. Psychol. **45**(1), 73–93 (1997)
5. Wickens, C.D.: Multiple resources and performance prediction. Theor. Issues Ergon. Sci. **3**(2), 159–177 (2002). https://doi.org/10.1518/001872008X288394. 2008 50: 449
6. Raufi, B.: Hybrid models of performance using mental workload and usability features via supervised machine learning. In: Longo, L., Leva, M.C. (eds.) H-WORKLOAD 2019. CCIS, vol. 1107, pp. 136–155. Springer, Cham (2019). https://doi.org/10.1007/978-3-030-32423-0_9
7. Evans, M., Harborne, D., Smith, A.: Developing an objective indicator of fatigue: an alternative mobile version of the Psychomotor Vigilance Task (m-PVT). In: Longo, L., Leva, M.C. (eds.) H-WORKLOAD 2018. CCIS, vol. 1012, pp. 49–71. Springer, Cham (2019). https://doi.org/10.1007/978-3-030-14273-5_4
8. Fan, J., Smith, A.: Mental workload and other causes of different types of fatigue in rail staff. In: Longo, L., Leva, M.C. (eds.) H-WORKLOAD 2018. CCIS, vol. 1012, pp. 147–159. Springer, Cham (2019). https://doi.org/10.1007/978-3-030-14273-5_9
9. Muñoz-de-Escalona, E., Canas, J.: Online measuring of available resources. In: H-Workload 2017: The First International Symposium on Human Mental Workload, Dublin Institute of Technology, Dublin, Ireland, 28–30 June (2017). https://doi.org/10.21427/D7DK96
10. Young, M.S., Stanton, N.A.: Malleable attentional resources theory: a new explanation for the effects of mental underload on performance. Human Factors **44**(3), 365–375 (2002). 10.1518%2F0018720024497709
11. Fan, J., Smith, A.P.: The impact of workload and fatigue on performance. In: Longo, L., Leva, M.C. (eds.) H-WORKLOAD 2017. CCIS, vol. 726, pp. 90–105. Springer, Cham (2017). https://doi.org/10.1007/978-3-319-61061-0_6
12. Sawaragi, T., Horiguchi, Y., Hina, A.: Safety analysis of systemic accidents triggered by performance deviation. 제어로봇시스템학회 국제학술대회 논문집, 1778–1781 (2006). https://doi.org/10.1109/SICE.2006.315635
13. Lorist, M.M., Boksem, M.A., Ridderinkhof, K.R.: Impaired cognitive control and reduced cingulate activity during mental fatigue. Cogn. Brain Res. **24**(2), 199–205 (2005)
14. Edwards, T., Martin, L., Bienert, N., Mercer, J.: The relationship between workload and performance in air traffic control: exploring the influence of levels of automation and variation in task demand. In: Longo, L., Leva, M.C. (eds.) H-WORKLOAD 2017. CCIS, vol. 726, pp. 120–139. Springer, Cham (2017). https://doi.org/10.1007/978-3-319-61061-0_8
15. Brookhuis, K.A., de Waard, D.: Monitoring drivers' mental workload in driving simulators using physiological measures. Accid. Anal. Prev. **42**(3), 898–903 (2010). https://doi.org/10.1016/j.aap.2009.06.001
16. Paxion, J., Galy, E., Berthelon, C.: Mental workload and driving. Front. Psychol. **5**, 1344 (2014). https://doi.org/10.3389/fpsyg.2014.01344

17. Taylor, A.H., Dorn, L.: Stress, fatigue, health, and risk of road traffic accidents among professional drivers: the contribution of physical inactivity. Annu. Rev. Public Health **27**, 371–391 (2006). https://doi.org/10.1146/annurev.publhealth.27.021405.102117

18. Grandjean, E.: Fitting the Task to the Man: A Textbook of Occupational Ergonomics. Taylor & Francis, London (1989)

19. Dawson, D., Ian Noy, Y., Härmä, M., Åkerstedt, T., Belenky, G.: Modelling fatigue and the use of fatigue models in work settings. Accid. Anal. Prev. **43**(2), 549–564 (2011)

20. Hopstaken, J.F., van der Linden, D., Bakker, A.B., Kompier, M.A., Leung, Y.K.: Shifts in attention during mental fatigue: evidence from subjective, behavioral, physiological, and eye-tracking data. J. Exp. Psychol. Hum. Percept. Perform. (2016). 2016-01220-001 [pii]

21. MuñozdeEscalona, E., Cañas, J.: Latency differences between mental workload measures in detecting workload changes. In: Longo, L., Leva, M.C. (eds.) H-WORKLOAD 2018. CCIS, vol. 1012, pp. 131–146. Springer, Cham (2019). https://doi.org/10.1007/978-3-030-14273-5_8

22. Muñoz-de-Escalona, E., Cañas, J.J., van Nes, J.: Task demand transition rates of change effects on mental workload measures divergence. In: Longo, L., Leva, M.C. (eds.) H-WORKLOAD 2019. CCIS, vol. 1107, pp. 48–65. Springer, Cham (2019). https://doi.org/10.1007/978-3-030-32423-0_4

23. Muñoz-de-Escalona, E., Cañas, J.J., Leva, C., Longo, L.: Task demand transition peak point effects on mental workload measures divergence. In: Longo, L., Leva, M.C. (eds.) H-WORKLOAD 2020. CCIS, vol. 1318, pp. 207–226. Springer, Cham (2020). https://doi.org/10.1007/978-3-030-62302-9_13

24. Novstrup, A., Goan, T., Heaton, J.: Workload assessment using speech-related neck surface electromyography. In: Longo, L., Leva, M.C. (eds.) H-WORKLOAD 2018. CCIS, vol. 1012, pp. 72–91. Springer, Cham (2019). https://doi.org/10.1007/978-3-030-14273-5_5

25. Comberti, L., Leva, M., Demichela, M., Desideri, S., Baldissone, G., Modaffari, F.: An empirical approach to workload and human capability assessment in a manufacturing plant. In: Longo, L., Leva, M.C. (eds.) H-WORKLOAD 2018. CCIS, vol. 1012, pp. 180–201. Springer, Cham (2019). https://doi.org/10.1007/978-3-030-14273-5_11

26. Kartali, A., Janković, M., Gligorijević, I., Mijović, P., Mijović, B., Leva, M.: Real-time mental workload estimation using EEG. In: Longo, L., Leva, M.C. (eds.) H-WORKLOAD 2019. CCIS, vol. 1107, pp. 20–34. Springer, Cham (2019). https://doi.org/10.1007/978-3-030-324 23-0_2

27. de Frutos, P., Rodríguez, R., Zhang, D., Zheng, S., Cañas, J., MuñozdeEscalona, E.: COMETA: an air traffic controller's mental workload model for calculating and predicting demand and capacity balancing. In: Longo, L., Leva, M.C. (eds.) H-WORKLOAD 2019. CCIS, vol. 1107, pp. 85–104. Springer, Cham (2019). https://doi.org/10.1007/978-3-030-32423-0_6

28. Maggi, P., Ricciardi, O., Di Nocera, F.: Ocular indicators of mental workload: a comparison of scanpath entropy and fixations clustering. In: Longo, L., Leva, M.C. (eds.) H-WORKLOAD 2019. CCIS, vol. 1107, pp. 205–212. Springer, Cham (2019). https://doi.org/10.1007/978-3-030-32423-0_13

29. Faulhaber, A., Friedrich, M.: Eye-tracking metrics as an indicator of workload in commercial single-pilot operations. In: Longo, L., Leva, M.C. (eds.) H-WORKLOAD 2019. CCIS, vol. 1107, pp. 213–225. Springer, Cham (2019). https://doi.org/10.1007/978-3-030-32423-0_14

30. Nadler, R.: Understanding "Zoom fatigue": theorizing spatial dynamics as third skins in computer-mediated communication. Comput. Comp. **58**, 102613 (2020)

31. Bailenson, J.N.: Nonverbal overload: atheoretical argument for the causes of Zoom fatigue. Technol. Mind Behav. **2**(1), 1–6 (2021)

32. Kendon, A.: Movement coordination in social interaction: some examples described. Acta Physiol. (Oxf) **32**, 101–125 (1970)

33. Longo, L., Leva, M.C. (eds.): Human Mental Workload: Models and Applications: First International Symposium, H-WORKLOAD 2017, Dublin, Ireland, 28–30 June 2017. Springer, Cham (2017). https://doi.org/10.1007/978-3-319-61061-0

34. Longo, L., Leva, M.C. (eds.): Human Mental Workload: Models and Applications: Second International Symposium, H-WORKLOAD 2018, Amsterdam, the Netherlands, 20–21 September 2018. Springer, Cham (2019). https://doi.org/10.1007/978-3-030-14273-5

35. Longo, L., Leva, M.C. (eds.): Human Mental Workload: Models and Applications: Third International Symposium, H-WORKLOAD 2019, Rome, Italy, 14–15 November. Springer, Cham (2020). https://doi.org/10.1007/978-3-030-32423-0

36. Longo, L., Leva, M.C. (eds.): Human Mental Workload: Models and Applications: Fourth International Symposium, H-WORKLOAD 2020, Granada, Spain, 3–5 December 2020. Springer, Cham (2020). https://doi.org/10.1007/978-3-030-62302-9

37. Wickens, C.: Mental workload: assessment, prediction and consequences. In: Longo, L., Leva, M.C. (eds.) H-WORKLOAD 2017. CCIS, vol. 726, pp. 18–29. Springer, Cham (2017). https://doi.org/10.1007/978-3-319-61061-0_2

38. Charles, R.L., Nixon, J.: Measuring mental workload using physiological measures: a systematic review. Appl. Ergon. **74**, 221–232 (2019)

39. Pimenta, A., Gonçalves, S., Carneiro, D., Fde-Riverola, F., Neves, J., Novais, P.: Mental workload management as a tool in e-learning scenarios. In: International Conference on Pervasive and Embedded Computing and Communication Systems (PECCS), pp. 25–32 (2015)

40. MuñozdeEscalona, E., Cañas, J.J., MoralesGuaman, J.F.: Fundamental frequency as an alternative method for assessing mental fatigue. In: Longo, L., Leva, M.C. (eds.) H-WORKLOAD 2020. CCIS, vol. 1318, pp. 58–75. Springer, Cham (2020). https://doi.org/10.1007/978-3-030-62302-9_4

41. Cañas, J.J., Muñoz-de-Escalona, E., Lopez de Frutos, P., Rodríguez, R., Celorrio, F.: Estimation of Air Traffic Controller's fatigue based on the analysis of the human Voice's Fundamental Frequency. Paper submitted for publication (2021)

42. Cho, S., Yin, C.S., Park, Y., Park, Y.: Differences in self-rated, perceived, and acoustic voice qualities between high- and low-fatigue groups. J. Voice **25**(5), 544–552 (2011). https://doi.org/10.1016/j.jvoice.2010.07.006

43. Whitmore, J., Fisher, S.: Speech during sustained operations. Speech Commun. **20**(1–2), 55–70 (1996)

44. Mendoza, E., Carballo, G.: Acoustic analysis of induced vocal stress by means of cognitive workload tasks. J. Voice **12**(3), 263–273 (1998)

45. Jackson, M.C.: La voz normal y patológica [The normal and pathological voice]. Buenos Aires. Médica Panamerica (2019)

46. Jurafsky, D., Martin, J.H.: Speech and Language Processing: An Introduction to Speech Recognition, Computational Linguistics and Natural Language Processing. Prentice Hall, Upper Saddle River (2008)

47. Van Puyvelde, M., Neyt, X., McGlone, F., Pattyn, N.: Voice stress analysis: a new framework for voice and effort in human performance. Front. Psychol. **9**, 1994 (2018)

48. Posner, M.I., Rothbart, M.K.: Research on attention networks as a model for the integration of psychological science. Annu. Rev. Psychol. **58**, 1–23 (2007)

49. Kreiman, J., Sidtis, D.: Foundations of Voice Studies: An InterdisciplinaryApproach to Voice Production and Perception. Wiley, Hoboken (2011)

50. Cacioppo, J.T., Tassinary, L.G., Berntson, G.G.: Handbook of Psychophysiology, 3rd Edn. Cambridge University Press, Cambridge (2007)

51. Thayer, J.F., Lane, R.D.: A model of neurovisceral integration in emotion regulation and dysregulation. J. Aect. Disord. **61**, 201–216 (2000)

52. Lane, R.D.: Neural substrates of implicit and explicit emotional processes: aunifying framework for psychosomatic medicine. Psychosom. Med. **70**, 214–231 (2008)

53. Vogt, B.A., Gabriel, M.: Neurobiology of Cingulate Cortex and Limbic Thalamus. Birkhauser, Boston (1993)

54. Paus, T.: Primate anterior cingulate cortex: where motor control drive and cognition interface. Nat. Rev. Neurosci. **2**, 417–424 (2001)

55. Krajewski, J., Batliner, A., Golz, M.: Acoustic sleepiness detection: framework and validation of a speech-adapted pattern recognition approach. Behav. Res. Methods **41**(3), 795–804 (2009)

56. Boersma, P., Van Heuven, V.: Speak and unSpeak with PRAAT. Glot Int. **5**(9/10), 341–347 (2001)

57. Vallecillo, I.: Evaluation of the impact of fatigue on air traffic control through a laboratory tested methodology. Master's thesis on Occupational Risk Prevention. University of Granada (2020)

A Systematic Review of Older Drivers in a Level 3 Autonomous Vehicle: A Cognitive Load Perspective

Bilal Alam Khan[1]([✉]), Maria Chiara Leva[2], and Sam Cromie[1]

[1] Centre for Innovative Human Systems, School of Psychology,
Trinity College Dublin, Dublin, Ireland
{khanbi,sdcromie}@tcd.ie
[2] Technological University Dublin, Dublin, Ireland
mariachiara.leva@tudublin.ie

Abstract. With current advancement in technology, it is expected and hoped that even a conditional or level 3 (L3) autonomous vehicle could alleviate older adults' mobility issues. These conditional or level 3 autonomous vehicles allow the driver to engage in non-driving task (NDRT), but, it can request the driver to assume control of the vehicle via 'Takeover request' when it has reached its operational limits. Considering this could be a challenging for older drivers with their declined cognitive, perceptual, and motor capacities. A systematic review has been conducted to produce literature on their issues in a L3 autonomous vehicle. This review mainly focuses on older drivers' challenges, perception of workload in AVs and takeover performance. This review is hoped to provide relevant literature on the subject and may help researchers improve and pursue research gaps identified in this paper.

Keywords: Older drivers · Level 3 autonomous vehicles · Takeover request · Workload

1 Introduction

According to WHO's report on Global health and ageing, the world population is becoming older. Older adults are a loosely defined population group belonging to the age group of 65 and above. Currently, the older adults population is at around 730 million and is estimated to reach around 1.5 billion by 2050. This trend is more pronounced in the developed countries such as the USA, UK, Japan, etc.; the primary reason attributed to this growing trend is better medical health facilities in the developed countries [38].

Older drivers are frequently cited as a vulnerable road user group. With age-related declines, they often have to either limit their driving exposure or cease the driving completely. This causes mobility issues in older drivers. Mobility for older adults is part of their daily life, with studies linking continued mobility

© Springer Nature Switzerland AG 2021
L. Longo and M. C. Leva (Eds.): H-WORKLOAD 2021, CCIS 1493, pp. 60–77, 2021.
https://doi.org/10.1007/978-3-030-91408-0_5

accessibility to healthy ageing and quality of life [6]. Retirement limits the mobility for older drivers as the number of work-related trips gets reduced. Therefore, the only travelling exposure they get is when they go shopping, medical visits, family get-together, recreational purposes, etc. For older adults, car driving is often the most preferred choice of transportation not only because of safety and perceived comfort as it enables them to go to the actual destination itself which may not be the case with public transportation. Moreover, older adults are more exposed to fatalities when using public transportation and as passengers [11,27].

1.1 Challenges of Older Drivers

Driving is a dynamic task requiring interaction between different functionalities such as cognition, perception, and motor movement. Drivers with age over 65 experience age-related declines in all of these functionalities. Because of age-related declines in these functionalities – older adults have been found to have slower reaction time, limited or reduced useful field of view (UFOV), and experience increased frailty [14,27]. Some studies have reported that older drivers have the highest rate of crashes per kilometres, have higher traffic convictions, and are overinvolved in right-of-way crashes [16,28]. Based on these studies and media hype, it is natural to assume that older drivers are an unsafe vehicle user group on the road. However, most of these studies have estimated risk in terms of the number of accidents over the miles driven and used it as a basis to compare different age groups. This type of metrics to compare risk across different age groups, however theoretically not inaccurate, have some logical issues. For example, older drivers are known to adopt some habits to counteract their age-related declines. These compensatory behaviour include avoiding rush hours, driving alone and for short distances, avoiding driving at night or in bad weather conditions, which reduce their overall exposure in terms of distance [9,33]. Also, most of the accidents only get included in the official databases they result in some serious injury or when an insurance claim is being made. Older drivers experience age-related frailty and are also more likely to get a serious injury from an accident which may not cause much harm to a teenager, this leads to a sampling bias, called, 'Frailty bias'. Therefore, to do a fair risk factor analysis comparison across age, it should be based on yearly mileage exposure or on similar metrics that can encapsulate the older driver compensatory behaviour. Conversely, older drivers are underrepresented in single-vehicle crashes, crashes related to loss of speed or risky manoeuvring. Their involvement in crashes as non-responsible parties is very few as well, which suggest they drive slowly and more cautiously which reduces their chances of getting hit. The 'over-representation of older drivers crashes at the intersection' has got disproportionate attention and focus, while it is also an important direction to look at, more often their under-representation in single-vehicle crashes or as non-responsible parties has been ignored [10]. This study also concluded that older drivers are cautious, conservative, and defensive drivers. Another study by Hakamies-Blomqvist in 2002, compared older drivers against drivers of other age groups based on the yearly mileage exposure and concluded that older drivers is indeed a safer driving cohort [12]. Older drivers usual driving strategy is to drive slowly, cautiously, and at a pace, they can manage, however, at intersections, this strategy fails because of the high density of vehicles at intersections, the pace of the individual vehicle is usually decided by the speed of traffic that put pressure on older drivers to drive faster than their conservative limits which could overwhelm their capacities. Moreover, driving at intersection requires the driver to gain situational awareness by taking secondary looks, follow right-of-way, and keep track of different traffic signs. All of these procedures put excessive demand on cognitive functioning of the driver, which in the case of older drivers is affected by age. Hence, their over-representation in the crashes at intersection [32]. Also, they are more risk to themselves than to others on road, so there is a need to develop and redesign traffic infrastructure to cater to the needs of this growing population age group. Semi-autonomous vehicles, in theory, have the potential to solve these mobility issues of older drivers by acting as a co-pilot that will work with the driver and support them in difficult driving situations and manoeuvre. These vehicles could aid the older drivers in high congestion scenarios such as intersections where they are already over-represented in crashes. This study in the following sections will discuss the issues of older drivers and autonomous vehicles in detail.

1.2   Autonomous Vehicles

Autonomous vehicles (AVs) are evolving at a very rapid pace, however, it will still take a couple of years before we can expect a complete self-driving vehicle [37]. AVs are defined as vehicles that will be able to move safely on roads by sensing the road environment with little to no human involvement at all. According to SAE (2014), AVs are categorized into six-level, ranging from level 0 to level 5; the details about each level has been explained in Table 1 [34]. It is expected that in the near future, highly and conditional autonomous vehicles are going to dominate the AV market [37]. These vehicles provide the driver with the option to engage in non-driving related tasks (NDRTs) such as texting, watching a video, eating, talking with a passenger, etc. The idea that older drivers mobility issues can be alleviated by semi-autonomous vehicles is frequently touted in articles, seminars, and research papers; however, not much research has been done that actually involves older drivers in autonomous vehicles to support these claims [4,43]. These vehicles could, at least in theory, help older drivers to continue to drive longer and safer. Most of the research that involves older drivers and autonomous vehicles is in the form surveys or review articles [4,5,30]. However, thorough research needs to be done to substantiate these claims and to understand their outreach, benefits, and shortcomings as well.

1.3   Takeover Request

Level 3 or conditional automation - even with their limited automation - enables the driver to engage in the non-driving related task (NDRT). They have limited automation in the sense that under very specific situations such as construction zone, school zone or broken vehicle ahead, etc., the driver may have to take back control of the vehicle. The system will notify the driver of these situations by initiating a 'Takeover request (TOR)' to the driver to take control of the vehicle – which could be a visual, aural, or tactile or a combination of these . The system will also provide a lead takeover time (LTOT) to the driver within which they have to take back controls of the vehicle. After the notification of the takeover request, the driver has to shift their attention to driving, gain sufficient situational awareness so that they may make a smooth and safe transition [7]. The time it takes the driver to assume control in response to a TOR is called Response takeover time (RTOT). This paradigm of TOR has been a focus of much interest in the research community with studies looking into the modality of the takeover request (verbal, visual, or tactile), takeover time, the cognitive load, the psychological state of the driver during automation, Situational awareness, engagement of the driver in NDRT during a takeover, etc. [3,8,31,35] The majority of these researches aim at supporting the driver, engaged in NDRT to regain control of the vehicle. Takeover time is highly dependent on the driver's cognitive capabilities, the driver's mental state, the workload at the time of notification, and the driver's engagement in a non-driving task [22,41].

Table 1. Shows the taxonomy and definition of different levels of automation as described by SAE in SAE 2014.

Level	Name	SAE definition
0	*No automation*	It can only provide some driver assistance in terms of night vision, navigation system, or lane departure warnings
1	*Driver assistance*	It provides lateral and longitudinal control of the vehicle but not both simultaneously
2	*Partial automation*	This level can perform both the lateral as well as the longitudinal control simultaneously, which enables the driver to disengage from driving physically; however, the driver still has to monitor the driving activity at all times and is responsible for the safety of the vehicle
3	*Conditional driving automation*	It provides all the functionalities of level 2 automation with the addition that the driver does not need to monitor the driving activity at all. However, they may still be needed behind the wheels to take over the vehicle if or when the system reaches its limits
4	*High driving automation*	This level of automation can drive completely without human intervention within certain areas, however, it may require human presence to operate the vehicle outside those areas
5	*Full driving automation*	This level is fully automated in the truest sense as it does not require human presence at all and can drive under all conditions

1.4   Workload of a Takeover Request

The transition from autonomous driving to manual driving, commonly referred in the literature as Takeover of vehicle, has been studied extensively. The factors that may affect this transition include driving environment (traffic density, weather), NDRTs (watching a video, eating, reading, etc.), vehicle configurations (lead takeover time, modality of TOR), driver state and age. Among these factors, engagement in the NDRTs has a significant effect on the takeover performance in terms of the workload it induces on the driver. Studies have manipulated this workload either in a naturalistic environment by engaging in NDRTs such as reading, writing an email, or watching a video or using standardised tasks such as n-back task or SuRT task [2, 29].

Most researchers reported engagement in NDRTs have negatively influenced the takeover performance while others found a certain level of engagement to be beneficial, particularly in the cases of underload conditions which may cause drowsiness in the drivers. Studies have reported that even 15 min of automation induces drowsiness [8, 36]. This idea that engagement in NDRTs could alleviate the signs of drowsiness since it was induced as a result of underload conditions was explored by researchers. Miller et al. (2015) conducted a study in a driving simulator found that participants who engaged in reading a text or watching a video showed fewer signs of drowsiness than those who did not engage in NDRT [24]. Conversely, other studies found that drivers who engaged in non-driving related activities showed poorer takeover performance [42]. It should be mentioned here that most of these studies did not directly manipulate the workload of NDRTs, with the exception of Zeeb et al. (2016) where the difficulty of NDRTs (reading vs proof-reading) was manipulated as a proxy to workload [42]. These results suggest that a moderate workload would produce optimum results [21].

As mentioned earlier, one of the factors that influence takeover performance is the age which has not been studied much. Considering the importance of workload in takeover performance, it would be intriguing to look into the influence of these two factors together on the takeover performance. Based on these results, older drivers - with their age-related cognitive declines - could find the engagement in a Non-driving task more challenging than normal driving itself and their performance could be affected as a result of it.

To date, there does not exist a systematic review available – to the best of the authors' knowledge – on the perception of workload in a level 3 autonomous vehicle by older drivers. The motivation behind this systematic review is to take the first step and collate all the studies that have been done on the performance, perception, and attitudes of older drivers in autonomous vehicles and their HMI system during a takeover request scenario. It is the authors' hope that collecting all the relevant researches in a single review article would help understand the current research direction and also provide future pathways. The paper is structured as follows: the first section details the introduction and background, followed by the methodology including search strategy, inclusion/exclusion criteria and review methodology used in this paper. Finally, this paper reports the findings of all the selected publications and discusses them briefly.

2 Materials and Methods

This systematic review is based on the PRISMA method – Preferred Reporting Items for Systematic Reviews and Meta-Analyses [25]. Per the stated method, the problem statement was defined, followed by the scope of this study, and inclusion/exclusion criteria were described. After outlining these fundamental terms of this systematic review, the relevant literature was screened and identified by scanning their titles and abstract, the screened literature then was either included or excluded depending on the inclusion/exclusion criteria. Finally, the included papers were studied thoroughly and taken forward for further review to ascertain if they are relevant to the problem statement defined below.

2.1 Problem Statement

"What is the influence of age or age-related declines on the performance and perception of workload by the older driver in a level 3 autonomous vehicle?" This research question was developed based on the statement of the PRISMA and the guidelines of PICOS – Population, Intervention, Comparator, Outcomes and Study design [25]. The purpose of this study is to collate and report studies conducted on older drivers in automated vehicles and identify possible future directions based on their reported results.

2.2 Search Strategy

A comprehensive phrase search was conducted using the following keywords: 'older drivers 'OR' older adults 'OR' elderly 'AND' takeover request 'OR' takeover 'OR' take over 'OR' transition of control 'AND' level 3 automation 'OR' conditional automation 'OR' conditional autonomous vehicles 'OR' autonomous vehicles 'OR' automated vehicles'. The search was done on April 2021.

These search keywords were used to look for relevant studies in these databases: PubMed, Scopus, Web of Science, ACM digital library, APA PsycInfo, IEEE Xplore, Google Scholar, Science Direct, and EMBASE.

A total of 274 articles were selected initially using the above-mentioned search phrase. After title and abstract screening, further removal of duplicates articles from various search engines and removing non-peer-reviewed conference articles, and book chapters; further exclusion of the papers was done if their full texts were not available, see Fig. 1. Finally, 38 papers were considered for full review and after carefully reviewing the articles based on their relevance to the above-mentioned problem statement, 9 papers were included and their findings were reported in this review.

2.3   Scope of the Review and Inclusion/Exclusion Criteria

Eligibility Criteria. The studies that were included in this review must fulfil all of the below-mentioned criteria:

I The study must be about the transition from automation to manual control of the vehicle; the transition could either be as a result of system failure or a planned takeover.

II The study must have words like takeover request, takeover time or transition of control in the text.

III The study must have included older drivers as the participants or have used age as an independent variable or have studied age as a factor influencing driving performance.

IV The study must be about conditional automation (SAE level 3 automated vehicles).

V The study has to be written in English.

The studies which did not have full text available or were review articles or published as book chapters or non-experimental papers such as survey articles, review papers, interview papers or were published in a non-peer review journal or conference were excluded. There were no criteria set on publication date – relevant papers published from any date were accepted.

3   Results

In this section, different findings related to the older drivers' workload and performance issues have been reported in Table 2. This table include summary and findings of the reviewed literature from a workload perspective.

3.1   Takeover Measures

A range of takeover measures have been adopted by different studies to quantify takeover performance and takeover quality. Takeover performance is commonly defined as the performance of a driver during a takeover scenario, which means how quickly the driver responded to the takeover request and how safely they drove after assuming the controls. Usually takeover performance is quantified using time based measures such as Lead takeover time (or Time budget), Takeover time or Reaction takeover time, Indicator time, lane deviation, brake inputs, etc. and quality based measures in terms of safe and conservative aspect of takeover. The measures commonly used to quantify the qualitative aspect of takeover performance are steering wheel angle, steering wheel reversal rate, minimum time to collision, lateral and longitudinal acceleration, collisions and critical encounters, etc.

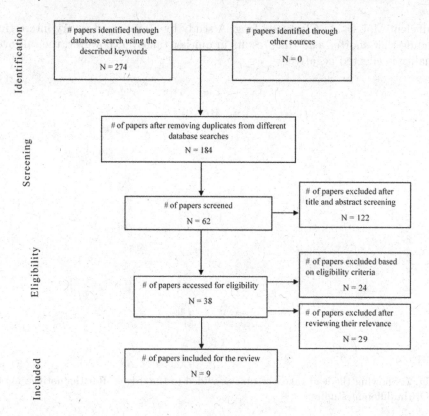

Fig. 1. Showing procedure followed in this survey to select studies based on the PRISMA, 2009 [25].

Lead Takeover Time. Lead takeover time or Time budget is defined as the time provided by the vehicle system at the initiation of a TOR within which the driver has to assume controls of the vehicle [7]. The lead takeover time (LTOT) should be sufficient for the driver so that they may disengage from the NDRT, gain sufficient situational awareness, and assume vehicle control. The Fig. 2 showed lead takeover time opted by different studies selected in this review. Majority of the studies have opted for a lead takeover time below 10 s with lead time below 5 s to be categorized as urgent or critical takeover Fabian Doubek, 2020. The same can be observed from the Fig. 2 as well - most of the studies opted for a LOT of below 10 s with the exception of Shuo Li et al. which used a much longer LTOT of 20 s. They provided the reason behind adopting a longer LTOT to be the cognitive declines associated with age and avoiding the risk of developing stress in older drivers from critical takeover (below 5 s).

The issue of the influence of lead takeover time on takeover performance has yet to be understood clearly. Studies have reported contradictory findings on this issue. A few reporting lead takeover time below 5 s to be not sufficient for a safe takeover Van den Beukel, 2013. While others reported this lead time to be sufficient Mok et al.; Clark and feng. A study by [7] reported a very interesting finding that shorter lead time results in quicker takeover, however, the takeover quality is affected negatively.

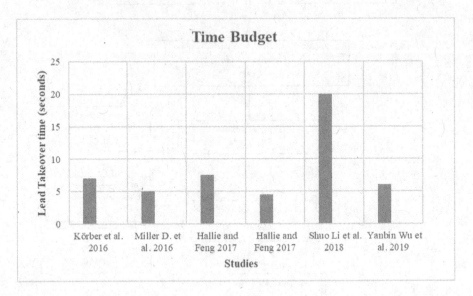

Fig. 2. Showing the lead takeover time provided to the driver after the notification of TOR in different studies.

Response Takeover Time. Response takeover time or simply Takeover time is defined as the time it takes the driver to make the conscious input in response to the takeover request. The conscious input has been defined as the manoeuvre of the steering wheel angle of 2° and/or 10% movement of accelerator or brake pedal positions [26]. Figure 3 shows a comparison of response takeover times between older and younger drivers as reported in the studies selected for this review. An interesting observation from the same figure is that for both older and younger drivers the response takeover time lies below 5 s. This is a very important result from the point of view of vehicle manufacturers as they would be well informed about optimum lead takeover time should be so as to not overwhelm the driver but be achievable in the practical terms as well. Also, it can be observed that in most of the studies conducted on older drivers' performance in a l3 automation, the performance (in terms of takeover time) is almost comparable to younger drivers, if not better in some studies. The only exception reported is by [18], where there is observable difference in performance between the two groups. The reason reported by the authors for this apparent difference in performance is that they have adopted a longer lead takeover time of 20 s. The older drivers being cautious and slow drivers used this time budget to assume vehicle control as their own pace. This led to increasing their response takeover time, but their takeover quality improved significantly.

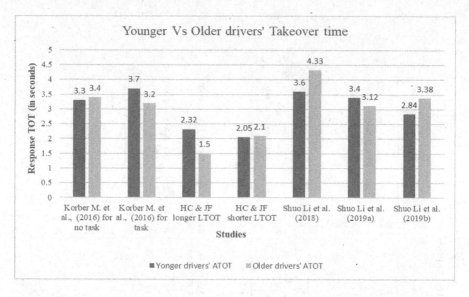

Fig. 3. Showing comparison between younger and older drivers' actual time it took them to respond to the TOR notification.

Some other frequently used measures of takeover performance has been defined below for better clarity and understanding.

- **Reaction Time (RT):** It is defined as the time it takes the driver after the initiation of TOR and to the manual driving position. The manual driving position is the position when the subjects' eyes on the road, hands on the steering wheel and feet on the pedals. It is a measure of how quickly participants respond to the TOR.
- **Takeover Time (TOT):** It is the time it takes the driver after the initiation of TOR to their conscious input to the vehicle, which in defined in literature as a manoeuvre of the steering wheel angle of 2° and/or 10% movement of accelerator or brake pedal positions [26]. It is also used as independently as Time-steer-1 and Time-Brake-0.1 in a study by Wu et al. (2019).
- **sdSteer:** It refers to the standard deviation of the steering wheel angle. It is a measure of the smoothness of the manoeuvre.
- **Indicator Time:** It refers to the time taken by the driver after the TOR to the driver's input of indicator signal for a lane change. It measures how quickly the participants started changing the lane.
- **Minimum Time-to-Collision (TTC):** It is an effective measure in assessing the severity of potential collisions. It refers to the time required for the test vehicle to collide with the stationary vehicle obstructing the driving lane if it continues at its speed at the time it changes to the next lane completely.
- **Steering Wheel Angle:** It angle represents the standard deviation in degree from the centre position of the steering wheel.

Table 2. Showing the review of the selected papers

S. No	Study	Participants	NDRT	Workload observed	Workload estimated	Lead takeover time (LTOT)	Response takeover time (RTOT)
1	[15]	YD: 36 (age 19 to 28) and OD: 36 (age 60 to 79)	20 Questions task (cognitive distraction)	Yes, by manipulating situational complexity (NDRT and traffic density)	No	7 s	YD: 3.3 (No task) and 3.7 (task); OD: 3.4 (No task) and 3.2 (task)
2	[23]	YD: 12 (age 15 to 19), MD: 12 (age 17 to 69), and OD: 12 (age 70 to 81)	Watching a movie, reading a story on a tablet, and supervising the car's driving	Yes, engagement in NDRTs	No	5 s	X
3	[2]	YD: 17 (age) and OD: 18 (age)	Voluntary on the choice of participant	Yes, engagement in NDRTs	No	7.5 s and 4.5 s	YD: 2.18 and OD: 1.71
4	[18]	YD: 37 (age 20 to 35) and OD: 39 (age 60 to 81)	Read aloud a text from a mounted device	Yes, engagement in NDRTs	No	20 s	OD: 4.32 s and YD: 3.60 (mean of all weather conditions)
5	[39]	115 participants (age 18 to 75) divided into 5 groups of 23 participants in each age group	No NDRT	Yes, by scheduled manual transition	No	6 s	X
6	[19]	YD: 37 (age 20 to 35) and OD: 39 (age 60 to 81)	Read aloud a text from a mounted device	Yes, engagement in NDRT	Yes NASA RTLX score	20 s	OD: 3.12 s and YD: 3.4 s
7	[17]	YD: 37 (age 20 to 35) and OD: 39 (age 60 to 81)	Read aloud a text from a mounted device	Yes, engagement in NDRT	No	20 s	OD: 3.38 s and YD: 2.84 s
8	[40]	YD: 12 (age 19 to 32), MD: 12 (age 37–50), and OD: 12 (age 56 to 74)	Two types of NDRT: 1. watching a video for 30 min; 2. watching video for 10 min, playing game for 10 min and then watching video for 10 min	Yes, engagement in NDRT	No	6 s	X
9	[13]	YD: 24 (age 20 to 24) and OD: 24 (age 66 to 76)	Watching a video	No	No	X	X

*For acronyms (YD, OD, MD, etc.) see Table 3 in appendix section.

4   Discussion

With age-related declines, older drivers are more prone to fatal crashes and thus have been suggested to be the key population group to get benefited from automation, since, automation has been frequently claimed to reduce traffic accidents [43]. However, only a few studies have investigated the challenges of older drivers in automation. In this review, these studies - on older driver's performance and perception of workload - have been collated to facilitate further research in this direction. This review has looked into these studies from the point of view of the workload, because an optimum level of workload is conducive for good takeover performance. Takeover paradigm is a distinctive element of level 3 autonomous vehicle, which allows the driver to disengage from driving and involve in other activities (reading, watching, etc.) within the operational limits of the system, beyond which the driver would have to assume controls.

Older drivers are a vulnerable road user cohort because of their age-related declines in cognitive, sensory, and motor functionalities – all of which are critical to the takeover scenarios in driving conditional AVs. The takeover request represents a safety-critical paradigm in which the driver has to assume control of the vehicle when the vehicle system reaches its limit. This puts additional workload demand on the older drivers' already declined cognitive capabilities. Moreover, this capability to switch attention quickly is called attention switching which degrades significantly with ageing [1, 20]. Therefore, it is reasonable to assume that older drivers would find the takeover request scenario particularly challenging and this may further translate into the deterioration of their driving performance during the takeover. However, studies have reported the opposite of this assumption, as can be observed from the Table 2 and Fig. 3. The performance of the older drivers during a takeover situation has not been affected by age and is comparable to younger and middle-aged drivers. A study investigated and compared the takeover performance of older and younger driver's engagement in the secondary task and reported no difference in takeover performance across the age [23]. However, it was noted that older drivers drove slower as compensation to the age-related declines. Similar results were reported by Körber et al. (2016), along with the observation that older drivers were more cautious during the takeover of the vehicle [15]. Clark and Feng (2017) studied the effect of age, level of engagement, and influence of takeover notification (4.5 or 7.5 s) on driver takeover performance [2]. They reported that older drivers' performance was similar to younger drivers for both lead takeover times. Although their performance was similar to younger drivers, the authors reported that the older drivers would prefer a longer lead takeover time. They also found that those older drivers who got more engaged in the secondary task and would brake harder during the takeover. This suggests that older drivers do indeed adopt additional driving strategies to counter the effects of age-related declines even during the takeover scenario. This could explain the similar driving performance of older drivers to younger drivers during a takeover scenario. However, this needs to be researched further to ascertain the validity of the older drivers' self-management strategies in explaining these results. Also, it should be noted here that although most of these studies mentioned here, have indeed manipulated workload using NDRT or other situational complexity such as Traffic density. However, none of them has estimated the perceived workload by older drivers in a takeover scenario.

In contrast, the study by Li S. et al. (2018), showed that age-related declines negatively affects the takeover performance and takeover quality of older drivers [18]. They investigated the effect of age and weather conditions on takeover performance using a driving simulator. The results concluded that older drivers took a longer time to react, and showed compensatory behaviour such as harder braking and acceleration in line with previous research done on older drivers' performance [12]. The takeover performance of younger drivers was affected much more negatively by bad weather conditions than that of older drivers. The researcher Li S. has conducted a series of studies on older drivers to investigate the issue of older driver mobility in autonomous vehicles. In a subsequent study in 2019, Li S. et al., tried to investigate the effect of age and level of disengagement on takeover performance. The authors reported that older drivers required longer takeover time, longer reaction time as well as indicator time [17]. The explanation mentioned by the authors is that the older drivers are more cautious in reassuming the vehicle control, thus taking a long time to gain sufficient situational awareness or it could be because of age-related cognitive and functional declines, which have slowed their information processing capabilities and reaction time. They also reported that age doesn't have any effect on takeover quality. One of the possible reasons for this result could be that the takeover time provided in this study was 20 s, much higher than what other researchers have used, see Fig. 2. It was suggested that by taking a longer time during the takeover, the older drivers have compensated for their age-related declines. In that way improving takeover quality. These results were in line with the research by Gold et al. (2013), which suggested that providing a shorter takeover time to the driver will result in a quicker takeover transition, however, the takeover quality will be compromised [7]. In another study done in 2019, Li S. et al. researched the development of an age-friendly HMI for AVs. They designed three age-friendly HMIs and conducted experiments to evaluate the effect of these HMIs on workload, performance, and attitudes [19]. The three HMIs reported in the study were R-HMI, V-HMI, and R+V HMI. R-HMI is one that provides the reason of the takeover to the driver, V-HMI updates the vehicular status and its surrounding to the driver when they are disengaged from dirving, and R+V HMI does both. The choice of these HMIs was based on the survey and interview study the author conducted before with the older drivers about their preferences and expectations. This is the only study - that we found - that had estimated the older drivers perception of workload using NASA RTLX score. They also reported that older drivers would prefer and had performed better than younger drivers for an HMI system that updates the driver of the vehicle status and provides them with the reason for the takeover request, see Fig. 3. This study was very relevant from the vehicle manufacturers' perspective to develop an age-friendly vehicle and also important to the researchers working in this field.

Recently, a few studies have tried to investigate the older driver states and attitudes in autonomous vehicles. Wu et al. conducted two studies on older driver drowsiness in AVs. In the paper published in 2019, the authors investigated the effects of scheduled transitions to manual driving on driver drowsiness and performance and the age differences therein [39]. They found the transition to manual driving may alleviate the issue of drowsiness in autonomous vehicles. However, these positive effects do not last very long – just a 10 min autonomous driving environment would be sufficient to counter these effects. It was also reported that older drivers' performance was negatively influenced by the scheduled manual transition – they responded more slowly in both steering and braking at the critical event. The authors concluded that scheduled manual driving does not have any significant positive impact on drivers' drowsiness – it can only maintain the drivers' arousal level for 10 min afterwards. In the case of older drivers, authors recommended not using such a system as it would create an unnecessary task- switching demand on them. In 2020, Wu et al. investigated the effect of age on engagement in NDRT to counter drowsiness in an automated vehicle [40]. Karolinska sleepiness scale along with eye blink duration was used as measures to determine the level of drowsiness and the effect of NDRT on it. They found that younger drivers were prone to drowsiness and involvement with NDRT has improved their performance in comparison to that without engaging in NDRT. While for older drivers, it was reported that NDRT did not affect the drowsiness but had a negative influence on the performance of the driver. Another dimension into older drivers' attitudes was pursued by Huang and Pitts in 2020, where they investigated the age differences in perception of alerts for takeover and their modalities [13]. They reported that both age group drivers favoured alert modality which included all three types of sensory signal (aural, visual, and tactile). They also found differences in attention patterns where older drivers focused more on the road than younger drivers. However, none of these two studies reported the effect of different alerts (of takeover notification) on the perception of workload by older drivers, as it has been reported above that an optimum level of workload is conducive for a good takeover performance. Therefore, while employing different modalities of takeover notification, their effect on drivers' workload should also be estimated.

5   Future Work

The results reviewed in this paper suggest that older drivers can indeed assume control of the vehicle within the reasonable stipulated time, with their takeover performance being comparable or in some cases better than the younger drivers. However, more research is still needed to understand the full scope of these results, as most of these studies are done on a very simplistic environments such as a broken vehicle ahead, or presence of a construction zone, etc. Also, it should be noted that the issues of older drivers' perception towards takeover request, their cognitive state, and their perception of workload during the takeover scenario are yet to be addressed fully. These are still open research questions.

It will be an interesting dimension to observe older drivers' behaviour and estimate their mental workload using physiological measures such as eye tracking, EEG, or camera during a takeover scenario. Another path could be to observe their behaviour with the vehicle HMI system under different loading conditions and assess the effect of workload on trust in automation. One possible research course could be an adaptive notification delivery system for takeover request, which senses the cognitive load of the older drivers and provide concise information based on their state, so that additional information would not overwhelm them, thereby degrading their performance. These are some of the future research courses that could be pursued so that an age-friendly vehicle HMI system that actually supports the older drivers' mobility issues can be realised.

One of the shortcomings of this review is that this has been too narrowly focused on older drivers and level 3 automation. A more generalised approach dealing with age differences in autonomous vehicles can be taken for the future studies where instead of looking into level 3 automation and takeover request, the challenges of older drivers will be reviewed in all levels of automation. Also, a more thorough review will be required as the research in this direction progresses and then a clear trend in the literature could be possible to establish. As of now, with only 9 papers, it is difficult to observe a consistent trend. Thus, a future review could compare older drivers' workload perception as well as other psychological states (fatigue, stress, situational awareness, etc.), behaviour, attitude, preferences, etc. in different levels of automation. This will ensure that vehicle manufacturers and other relevant actors in the traffic industry have sufficient information to work on - so that the older drivers and other vulnerable road user groups in general, could be facilitated using the semi-autonomous vehicle technology.

Acknowledgement. This work was conducted with the financial support of the Science Foundation Ireland Centre for Research Training in Digitally-Enhanced Reality (d-real) under Grant No. 18/CRT/6224.

A   Appendix

Table 3. Table of different acronyms used in this paper

S. No	Acronym	Full form
1	NDRT	Non Driving Related Task
2	SAE	Society of Automotive Engineers
3	L3	Level 3 autonomous vehicles as per SAE classification of AVs
4	AV	Autonomous Vehicles
5	TOR	Takeover Request
6	LTOT	Lead Takeover Time
7	RTOT	Reaction Takeover Time
8	HMI	Human-Machine Interface
9	RT	Reaction Time
10	TOT	Takeover Time
11	TTC	Time to Collision
12	YD	Younger Driver
13	MD	Middle aged Drivers
14	OD	Older Drivers
15	R-HMI	HMI that provides the 'reason' of a takeover request to the driver
16	V-HMI	HMI that gives the driver status of the vehicle and of its surroundings
17	R+V HMI	HMI that provides both functinalities of R-HMI and V-HMI

References

1. Arnau, S., Möckel, T., Rinkenauer, G., Wascher, E.: The interconnection of mental fatigue and aging: an eeg study. Int. J. Psychophysiol. **117**, 17–25 (2017). https://www.sciencedirect.com/science/article/pii/S0167876016308790
2. Clark, H., Feng, J.: Age differences in the takeover of vehicle control and engagement in non-driving-related activities in simulated driving with conditional automation. Accid. Anal. Prev. **106**, 468–479 (2017). https://www.sciencedirect.com/science/article/pii/S000145751630313X
3. Desmond, P.A., Hancock, P.A., Monette, J.L.: Fatigue and automation-induced impairments in simulated driving performance. Transp. Res. Rec. **1628**(1), 8–14 (1998). https://doi.org/10.3141/1628-02
4. Eby, J., Kouvaris, C., Nielsen, N., Wijewardhana, L.: J. High Energy Phys. **28**, 1 (2016)
5. Faber, K., van Lierop, D.: How will older adults use automated vehicles? assessing the role of avs in overcoming perceived mobility barriers. Transp. Res. Part A: Policy Prac. **133**, 353–363 (2020), https://www.sciencedirect.com/science/article/pii/S0965856419312091
6. Gabriel, Z., Bowling, A.: Quality of life from the perspectives of older people. Ageing Soc. **24**(5), 675–691 (2004). https://doi.org/10.1017/S0144686X03001582
7. Gold, C., Damböck, D., Lorenz, L., Bengler, K.: Take over! how long does it take to get the driver back into the loop? Proc. Hum. Factors Ergon. Soc. Ann. Meeting **57**, 1938–1942 (2013)

8. Gonçalves, J., Happee, R., Bengler, K.: Drowsiness in conditional automation: proneness, diagnosis and driving performance effects. In: 2016 IEEE 19th International Conference on Intelligent Transportation Systems (ITSC), pp. 1–4 (2016)

9. Hakamies-Blomqvist, L.: Aging and fatal accidents in male and female drivers. J. Gerontol. **49**(6), 286–290 (1994)

10. Hakamies-Blomqvist, L.: Why do older drivers give up driving. Accid. Anal. Prev. **30**(3), 3015–3312 (1998)

11. Hakamies-Blomqvist, L.: The 5th european transport safety lecture: Ageing europe: The challenges and opportunities for transport safety (2003)

12. Hakamies-Blomqvist, L., Raitanen, T., O'Neill, D.: Driver ageing does not cause higher accident rates per km. Transp. Res. Part F: Traffic Psychol. Behav. **5**(4), 271–274 (2002). https://doi.org/10.1016/s1369-8478(03)00005-6

13. Huang, G., Pitts, B.: Age-related differences in takeover request modality preferences and attention allocation during semi-autonomous driving. In: HCI (2020)

14. Klein, R.: Age-related eye disease, visual impairment, and driving in the elderly. Hum. Factors **33**(5), 521–525 (1991). https://doi.org/10.1177/001872089103300504, pMID: 1769672

15. Körber, M., Gold, C., Lechner, D., Bengler, K.: The influence of age on the takeover of vehicle control in highly automated driving. Transp. Res. Part F: Traffic Psychol. Behav. **39**, 19–32 (2016)

16. Langford, J., Koppel, S.: Epidemiology of older driver crashes - identifying older driver risk factors and exposure patterns. Transp. Res. Part F: Traffic Psychol. Behav. **9**(5), 309–321 (2006). https://www.sciencedirect.com/science/article/pii/S1369847806000234, older drivers' safety and mobility: Current and future issues

17. Li, S., Blythe, P., Guo, W., Namdeo, A.: Investigating the effects of age and disengagement in driving on driver's takeover control performance in highly automated vehicles. Transp. Plan. Technol. **42**, 470–497 (2019)

18. Li, S., Blythe, P., Guo, W., Namdeo, A.: Investigation of older driver's take-over control performance in highly automated vehicles in adverse weather conditions. IET Intell. Transp. Syst. **12**, 1157–1165 (2018)

19. Li, S., et al.: Evaluation of the effects of age-friendly human-machine interfaces on the driver's takeover performance in highly automated vehicles. Transp. Res. Part F-traffic Psychol. Behav. **67**, 78–100 (2019)

20. Lorist, M., Klein, M., Nieuwenhuis, S., De Jong, R., Mulder, G., Meijman, T.: Mental fatigue and task control: planning and preparation. Psychophysiology **37**, 614–625 (2000)

21. Ma, S., et al.: Promote or inhibit: An inverted u-shaped effect of workload on driver takeover performance. Traffic Injury Prev. **21**(7), 482–487 (2020). https://doi.org/10.1080/15389588.2020.1804060, pMID: 32822218

22. Merat, N., Jamson, A., Lai, F., Carsten, O.: Highly automated driving, secondary task performance, and driver state. Hum. Factors **54**(5), 762–771 (2012). https://doi.org/10.1177/0018720812442087

23. Miller, D., et al.: Exploring Transitional Automation with New and Old Drivers. SAE Technical Paper (2016)

24. Miller, D., et al.: Distraction becomes engagement in automated driving. In: Proceedings of the 59thAnnual Meeting of the Human Factors and Ergonomics Society, pp. 1676–1680 (2015)

25. Moher, D., Liberati, A., Tetzlaff, J., Altman, D.G.: Preferred reporting items for systematic reviews and meta-analyses: the prisma statement. BMJ 339 (2009). https://www.bmj.com/content/339/bmj.b2535

26. Mok, B., Johns, M., Lee, K.: Timing of unstructured transitions of control in automated driving. pp. 1167–1172, South Korea (2015)
27. O.E.C.D.: Ageing and transport: mobility needs and safety issues (2001). https://doi.org/10.1787/9789264195851-en
28. Pollatsek, A., Romoser, M.R.E., Fisher, D.L.: Identifying and remediating failures of selective attention in older drivers. Current Dir. Psychol. Sci. **21**(1), 3–7 (2012). https://doi.org/10.1177/0963721411429459, pMID: 23082045
29. Radlmayr, J., Gold, C., Lorenz, L., Farid, M., Bengler, K.: How traffic situations and nondriving related tasks affect the take-over quality in highly automated driving. In: Proceedings of the Human Factors and Ergonomics Society Annual Meeting, vol. 58, pp. 2063–2067 (2014)
30. Rahman, M.M., Deb, S., Strawderman, L., Smith, B., Burch, R.: Evaluation of transportation alternatives for aging population in the era of self-driving vehicles. IATSS Res. **44**(1), 30–35 (2020). https://www.sciencedirect.com/science/article/pii/S0386111218301353
31. Rauch, N., Kaussner, A., Krüger, H., Boverie, S., Flemisch, F.: The importance of driver state assessment within highly automated vehicles (2009)
32. Romoser, M., Fisher, D.: Effects of cognitive and physical decline on older drivers' side-to-side scanning for hazards while executing turns (2017)
33. Rothe, J.: The Safety of Elderly Drivers. Transactions Publishers, London (1990)
34. S.A.E.: Taxonomy and definitions for terms related to on-road motor vehicle automated driving systems (2014). https://saemobilus.sae.org/content/j3016_201609
35. Stanton, N., Young, M.: Driver behavior with adaptive cruise control. Ergonomics **48**, 1294–1313 (2005)
36. Takeda, Y., Sato, T., Kimura, K., Komine, H., Akamatsu, M., Sato, J.: Electrophysiological evaluation of attention in drivers and passengers: toward an understanding of drivers' attentional state in autonomous vehicles. Transp. Res. Part F: Traffic Psychol. Behav. **42**, 140–150 (2016). https://doi.org/doi.org/10.1016/j.trf.2016.07.008
37. UKAutodrive: lords get latest on UK trials (2016). http://www.ukautodrive.com
38. W.H.O.: Ageing and health (2018).https://www.who.int/news-room/fact-sheets/detail/ageing-and-health
39. Wu, Y., Kihara, K., Takeda, Y., Sato, T., Akamatsu, M., Kitazaki, S.: Effects of scheduled manual driving on drowsiness and response to take over request: a simulator study towards understanding drivers in automated driving. Accid. Anal. Prev. **124**, 202–209 (2019)
40. Wu, Y., et al.: Age-related differences in effects of non-driving related tasks on takeover performance in automated driving. J. Saf. Res. **72**, 231–238 (2020)
41. Young, M., Stanton, N.: Malleable attentional resources theory: a new explanation for the effect of mental underload on performance. Hum. Factors **44**, 365–375 (2002)
42. Zeeb, K., Buchner, A., Schrauf, M.: Is take-over time all that matters?: the impact of visual-cognitive load on driver take-over quality after conditionally automated driving. Accid. Anal. Prev **92**, 230–239 (2016)
43. Zmud, J., Ecola, L., Phleps, P., Feige, I.: The future of mobility: Scenarios for the united states in 2030 (2013). http://www.jstor.org/stable/10.7249/j.ctt5hhw3n Accessed 25 May 2021

Applications

On EEG Preprocessing Role in Deep Learning Effectiveness for Mental Workload Classification

Kunjira Kingphai[✉] and Yashar Moshfeghi

NeuraSearch Laboratory, Department of Computer and Information Sciences,
University of Strathclyde, Glasgow, Scotland
{kunjira.kingphai,yashar.moshfeghi}@strath.ac.uk

Abstract. A high mental workload level could significantly contribute to mental fatigue, decreased performance, or long-term health problems [14]. Recently, deep learning models have been trained on Electroencephalogram (EEG) signals to detect users' mental workload. While such approaches show promising results, they either ignore the noise element inherent in the EEG signals or apply a random set of preprocessing techniques to reduce the noise. Such a lack of uniform preprocessing techniques in cleaning the EEG signals would not allow the comparison of the effectiveness of deep learning models across different studies even when they use the data collected from the same experiment. Therefore, in this study, we aim to investigate the effect of preprocessing techniques defined by neuroscientists in the effectiveness of deep learning models. To do so, we focused on the preprocessing techniques that can be automated and do not need any human intervention, namely a high-pass filter, the ADJUST algorithm, and a re-referencing. Using a publicly available mental workload dataset, STEW, we investigate the effect of these preprocessing techniques in three state-of-the-art deep learning models named Stacked LSTM, BLSTM, and BLSTM-LSTM. Our results show that ADJUST has the most significant effect on the performance of our models compare to other steps. Our findings also show that EEG signals that were prepossessed using the high-pass filter, ADJUST algorithm and re-referencing provided the highest classification performance across the investigated deep learning models. We believe this paper provides an important step towards defining a uniform methodological framework for using deep learning models on EEG signals.

Keywords: EEG · Preprocessing · Mental workload · Classification · Deep learning

1 Introduction

Measuring mental workload (MWL) is an important task, and the main aim of the psychological community to understand human performance, which can be affected if MWL is too high or too low. Researchers have shown that MWL

© Springer Nature Switzerland AG 2021
L. Longo and M. C. Leva (Eds.): H-WORKLOAD 2021, CCIS 1493, pp. 81–98, 2021.
https://doi.org/10.1007/978-3-030-91408-0_6

can be measured using administering questionnaires, performance measures, or neurophysiological like brain activity [31]. In particular, studies have shown that Electroencephalography (EEG) signals are highly correlated with real-time mental workload status [10]. This is because EEG signals are capable of capturing brain activities with high temporal resolutions [2]. Thus, advanced deep learning models have been developed to capture variance characteristics in the EEG signals to classify MWL status accurately. Examples of such models are the works using Convolutional Neural Network (CNN) [19], Recurrent Neural Network (RNN) [18], and Bidirectional Long Short-Term Memory-Long Short Term Memory (BLSTM-LSTM) [8] as their models.

However, the neuroscience community have shown that EEG signals are subject to noise. As a result, many efforts have been dedicated in the past to advance data preprocessing techniques to reduce noise and standardised procedures of cleaning EEG data have been formed [1,4,9].

However, the deep learning works using EEG signals do not follow a standard data cleaning procedure. Due to such inconsistencies in their data preprocessing framework, first, the real effect of the deep learning models cannot be measured. Second, the results obtained from different studies cannot be compared against each other even when they are using the data collected from the same experiment. Thus, the research on the standardised artefact removal step in deep learning continues to be an open problem.

Therefore, in this paper, we aim to investigate the following research question: "What are the effects of different preprocessing techniques in the effectiveness of deep learning models using EEG signals to predict MWL levels?". Since our aim to investigate the effect of preprocessing techniques in deep learning models and ultimately to incorporate them in such models, in this paper, we focus on those preprocessing techniques that can be executed automatically (without any human intervention), namely a high-pass filter, the ADJUST algorithm, and a re-referencing. We investigate the effect of these preprocessing techniques in three state-of-the-art deep learning models used for MWL prediction named Stacked LSTM, BLSTM, and BLSTM-LSTM [8]. For our analysis, we employed an available mental workload Scenario called STEW [21].

The paper is structured as follow. Section 2 provide a background of MWL and research works related to its prediction. Then, in Sect. 3, the methodology will be described. Results and discussion can be found in Sect. 4. Finally, the conclusion are given in Sect. 5.

2   Background

The MWL has been realised as an important factor in subject performance within a complicated working system. Either overload or underload could reduce performance and directly impact the effectiveness and quality of the working system. Therefore, MWL monitoring and prediction has become a crucial task to guarantee a functional and effective human-system collaboration [22]. Conventionally, MWL has been assessed through self-report mechanisms such as questionnaire or by measuring the performance of a secondary task [42]. However, to perform post-task self-report feedback or performance measurement, subjects must be trained to understand the tool used for expressing their MWL [39]. So, such techniques could themselves increase subject's workload. Thus, recent studies have investigated the possibility of predicting MWL via brain activity captured using EEG. The main advantage of such a technique is that it is unobtrusive allowing the MWL to be captured in real-time [3].

However, neuroscientists have found that EEG signals can be easily contaminated by noise (artefacts). The source of EEG artefacts can be internal and external. The internal or physiological artefacts include ocular activity (EOG), muscle activity (EMG), or cardiac activity (ECG or EKG) [16]. The external ones might be from instruments or subject's body movement [16]. The noises in the EEG signal could affect data quality and decrease model performance in further analysis. Therefore, the artefacts removal is a necessary prerequisite step before any exploitation of the obtained EEG signals [35].

2.1 Mental Workload Prediction

A subject's mental workload levels could be effectively predicted from EEG signals. Recently, deep learning has successfully been used in EEG analysis due to its capacity to capture good feature representation from data [32]. While, some researchers have used noise reduction techniques as part of their EEG preprocessing stage, the effectiveness of each of these techniques on deep learning models for MWL classification has not yet been investigated. This has resulted in lack of uniform framework to be followed, and in turn makes the comparisons of such models impossible.

For example, Kurnar et al. [18] have applied a band-pass filter in the raw EEG to remove unwanted signals and employed a deep recurrent neural network (RNN) to classify four levels of the cognitive workload. As a result, they have gained average accuracy of 92.5% in their classification. The band-pass filter has also been adopted into Maneesh Bilalpur et al. [5] study. However, the range of frequencies has been set at a different value; in this study, it has been set between 0.1 45 Hz. Moreover, the authors have also further rejected noisy epochs by visual inspection. Finally, noisy ICA components corresponding to eye-blinks and movements have been manually removed. The artefact removed data has been used to classify two levels of mental workload induced by acoustic parameters by using a deep convolutional neural network (CNN) classifier. The F1-score of 0.64 has been obtained. The other type of filter which has been applied is a notch filter. In [43], Zhang et al. have applied 50 Hz notch filter in their study and a Butterworth band-pass filter between 0.5 Hz 50 Hz. Then, the EEG signals from all channels have been re-referenced to the average of two ear electrodes. However, the authors have left ocular artefacts in their data. A three-class mental workload induced by n-back tasks with easy, medium, and hard difficulty levels has been categorized by the proposed two-stream neural networks (TSNN). The proposed model has achieved an average accuracy of 91.9%. Same as the previous work, the Butterworth filter has been employed in [41] as well; however, it has been used with a low-pass cutoff frequency 40 Hz. To correct the artefacts from eye movements, the authors have employed ICA in their preprocessing procedure. Then, the cleaned data has put into an ensemble deep learning model (EL-SDAE) for the binary MW classification problem. The model has achieved 92% accuracy of mental workload recognition. As observed from the literature, deep learning researchers working with the EEG have attempted to remove noise from their data using the exited preprocessing techniques proposed by the neurobiologist. However, there is no single procedure of preprocessing that everybody is following. In particular, the band-pass filter technique, which seems to be the most commonly used tool, has been defined at a diverse range.

Another aspect is that event people perform classification using the same dataset; they apply the different preprocessing techniques in their experiment. For example, Lim et al. [21] have performed MWL classification by using their own dataset named STEW. In the artefact removal stage, the authors have used high-pass filter 1 Hz, notch filter and Artifact Subspace Reconstruction (ASR). Then, they have re-referenced data to average for removing artefacts from muscle movement and clean the noise. Authors have obtained 69% MWL classification accuracy from a Support Vector Regression (SVR) model. The STEW dataset has also been adopted into Chakladar et al. [8] study for MWL level classification as well. However, in this study, the authors have removed the artefacts from EEG signals using only a band-pass filter technique. The filter has allowed signal between 4 32 Hz to pass. Then, the preprocessed data has been feed into various model for estimating human workload levels. They have performed an analysis in two Tasks: 1) "No task" and 2) "SIMKAP-based multitasking activity". The proposed Bidirectional Long Short-Term Memory- Long Short-Term Memory (BLSTM-LSTM) model has outperformed other models in their study. The model has reached 86.33% and 82.57% classification accuracy for study 1) and 2), respectively. Moreover, from the literature, it can also be observed that the effect of the preprocessing procedure has not been a considered factor in the analysis.

Although there are several EEG preprocessing guidelines provided by the neuroscientists [4,11,13], there are quite broad and no universally adopted. Researchers, therefore, have to decide themselves which technique to use for effectively removing noise. Also some existing pipelines have certain visual inspection and manual labelling as part of their process [6]. While these methods can be very useful to reduce the noise in signals, they suffer from three issues. First these methods are time-consuming, particularly when we are dealing with a large dataset. Second, then can introduce bias in the analysis [36]. Finally, they limit the use of such pipelines in automated processes.

Also, since the effect of preprocessing steps in deep learning paper for EEG analysis has not been examined, the comparability of results from different studies is impractical. Therefore, to find the effect of automatically preprocessing techniques in deep learning models clearly, we replicated Chakladar et al. paper [8]. The reasons we choose this paper because the authors have evaluated models by using a publicly MWL Scenario, and their proposed model has become state-of-the-art of this Scenario. As we tried to investigate the effect of preprocessing techniques, our artefact removal procedure is different from the original paper. Details of the used Scenario and a framework for EEG artefact removal that can be executed automatically for deep learning analysis is described in the next section.

3 Methodology

3.1 Data Acquisition

In this study, the STEW Scenario taken from [21] was used. The Scenario contains 48 subject's EEG signals collected from 14 electrodes (AF3, F7, F3, FC5, T7, P7, O1, O2, P8, T8, FC6, F4, F8, AF4), sampled 128 Hz. The participants are all males from the university's graduate population whose recruited via open email. They do not have any neurological, psychiatric or brain-related diseases and never participated in any prior EEG experiment. The signals have been recorded in two states; the resting state and the testing state. In the resting state, subjects were asked to sit on the chair and did not perform any task for 3 min; their EEG was recorded and used as the resting state. In the testing state, subjects performed the Simultaneous Capacity (SIMKAP) multitasking activity with EEG being recorded, and the final 3 min of the recording is used as the workload Task. The first and last 15 s of data from each recording were excluded to reduce effects from any between task activity, resulting in recordings of 2.5 min (150 s). Finally, the sample size of signals in each state is 19200 samples. After each segment of the experiment, subjects were also asked to rate their MWL using a rating scale of 1 to 9. In the analysis steps, the 9-point rating scale has been categorised into three mental workload level: low (1–3), moderate (4–6) and high (6–9).

3.2 EEG Preprocessing

EEG preprocessing consist of several techniques. Some can automatically eliminate noise from data, and others have to be performed manually. In this paper, we aim to investigate the effect of preprocessing techniques that can only performed automatically, i.e. without any human intervention. The advantage of an automatic processing analysis is that it avoids the problem of bias from manually marking artefact by visual inspection [36]. Therefore, we investigate the effect of three main preprocessing techniques namely a high-pass filter, the ADJUST algorithm, and a re-referencing.[1] As a result of this we have four experimental scenarios, as follows:

– **Scenario 1 - Raw Data:** No preprocessing has been conducted on the data.

---

[1] All preprocessing techniques were performed using EEGLAB v12, running under the cross-platform MATLAB environment.

Table 1. Experimental scenarios

Scenario	Preprocessing process
1	None (Raw data)
2	High-pass filtering
3	High-pass filtering and ADJUST
4	High-pass filtering, ADJUST and Re-reference

– **Scenario 2 - High-pass filter:** In this scenario, the EEG signal was filtered using 1 Hz high-pass filter to remove slow linear trends. Signal with frequencies greater than a certain value was kept. A default of zero-phase FIR filter was used.
– **Scenario 3 - ADJUST:** In this scenario, to separate the artefact components from the EEG signals, Independent Component Analysis (ICA) was applied on the filtered signals from the previous step (i.e. Scenario 2) using the Runica function [23]. The artefact component from ICA analysis was automated inspect by ADJUST [27]. Then, the identified artefacts components were removed without manual correction.
There is a general guideline proposed by Mognon et al. [27] for Running ADJUST; however, we omitted those steps that required manual intervention such as visual inspection.
– **Scenario 4 - Re-referencing:** In this scenario, we were re-referencing the EEG signal by averaging electrical activity measured across all scalp channels. Generally, user can do re-reference using either averaging with all channels or reference channel(s). The reference channel(s) usually attache at the earlobe or around the eye as the EOG channel. In this step, we desired to average the electrical activity with all channels because our adopted dataset does not contain any reference channel.

Our four experimental scenarios are summarised in Table 1.

Figure 1 and 2 show sample data before and after preprocessing techniques applied in Scenario 4. We observed that the artefacts were removed effectively by a high-pass filter, the ADJUST algorithm, and a re-referencing techniques.

3.3 EEG Feature Extraction and Selection

The purpose of feature extraction is to capture EEG signal characteristics. In literature, there are various features have been used in EEG classification. Power spectral density (PSD) [24] seem to be the most wildly used feature. They can be divided into sub-band of delta (0.5–4 Hz), theta (4–8 Hz), alpha (8–12 Hz), beta (12–30 Hz) and gamma (30–100 Hz). Each band appear in a different state of the human brain. The delta shows deeply asleep and not dreaming, theta happens when people drowsy and drifting down into sleep and dream, alpha shows a very relaxed and deepening into a meditation of people, and appear

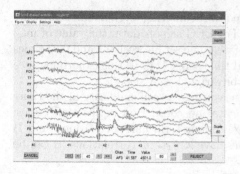 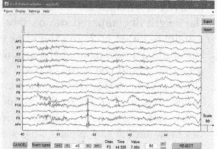

Fig. 1. Sample continuous time EEG channel data before preprocessing

Fig. 2. Sample continuous time EEG channel data after preprocessing

when people busily engaged in activities and conversation, and gamma reveals a hyper brain active and great for learning [16]. The time domain, linear domain and non-linear domain are other features that have also been used.

As for our features, we used the PSD alpha, PSD theta, skewness, kurtosis, approximate entropy and Hurst exponent which extracted from 14-channels, since they were reported to be the best feature set for this collection, tasks, and models [8].

Skewness and kurtosis are time-domain features. Approximate entropy and Hurst exponent are non-linear domain features. All features were extracted from each EEG channel, and the entire length of data was used for calculation. Since EEG data was collected with a sampling frequency 128 Hz, the signal was sampled 128 times per second. We calculated the features with a sliding window of size 512, and shifted 128 was used [21]. The details of each feature are elaborated below:

1. PSD alpha and PSD theta were extracted by a Fast Fourier transformation (FFT) [29].
2. Skewness [12], which is the degree of asymmetry in the distribution, was evaluated by (1)

$$Skewness = \frac{1}{N} \sum_{i=1}^{N} \frac{(X_i - X)^3}{\sigma^3} \tag{1}$$

If all the samples in a channel are uniformly distributed around the mean, they have a Gaussian distribution.
3. Kurtosis [12] showing the degree of peakedness in the distribution can be represented using (2). Channel value with highly-tailed or high kurtosis refers to the present of noise in the data.

$$Kurtosis = \frac{1}{N} \sum_{i=1}^{N} \frac{(X_i - X)^4}{\sigma^4} \tag{2}$$

4. Approximate entropy (ApEn) [30] is used to quantify the regularity and the unpredictability of fluctuations over time series. It can be represented in (3).

$$ApEn(m, r, N) = \phi^m(r) - \phi^{(m+1)}(r) \tag{3}$$

Where r is a parameter usually referred to the filtering level, and m represents the length of compared run of data. For EEG signals data, the value of m is usually to be set at 2, and the value of r is to be set between 0.1 and 0.25 times the standard deviation of the original time series [44]. In this experiment, we set m at 2, and the value of r was arbitrarily chosen at 0.2.

5. Hurst exponent (H) [15] is used for measuring the self-similarity of the time-series. When H equal to 0.5, it indicates no correlation in the time series; H lies between 0 to 0.5 means there are long-term anti-correlations, and H lies between 0.5 to 1 means time-series have long-term correlations. H can be evaluated by (4).

$$H = \frac{log(R/S)}{log(T)} \qquad (4)$$

where R denotes the range and standard deviation of the first n samples of time series data, respectively. T represent the span of time series data.

Finally, the total number of extracted features of a 14-channel data is 84 (14×6). All features were standardised before further analysis. The standardised method is going to be explained in the following section.

3.4   Models

To investigate the effect of preprocessing techniques, we verified our scenarios in three state-of-the-art deep learning models named Stacked LSTM, BLSTM, and BLSTM-LSTM adopted from [8]. These models have been used widely used in the EEG signal for MWL classification [17,28,37], and they are particularly useful for learning sequential data with long term dependencies [45].

Table 2. Deep learning model architectures

Model	Layers/Nodes
Stacked LSTM	L128-L64-L40-D32-D1 (D3)
BLSTM	BL128-D32-D1 (D3)
BLSTM-LSTM	BL256-L128-L64-D32-D1 (D3)

The deep learning models architectures are shown in Table 2. L, D, and BL refer to LSTM, Dense and BLSTM layer, respectively. For example, L128-L64-L40-L32 means LSTM layer with 128 units followed by the second LSTM with 64 units, the third LSTM with 40, and the Dense layer with 32 unites. While D1 in the last layer is a Dense layer with 1 unit used in Task 1, D3 is a Dense layer with 3 unit used in Task 2. In this study, a dropout rate was set at 0.2, and the Adam optimiser with an initial learning rate of 1e−04 was used for training all the deep learning models. Early stopping was also utilised to avoid overfitting problem. Moreover, we stopped training once the model performance stopped improving for 30 epochs.

3.5   Tasks

In this study, we performed classification in two tasks; the first task was a binary classification. The models were used to categorise EEG signal between resting state or no task and working state or during subject perform SIMKAP task. In the second task, we classified three MWL levels from subjective ratings, which compose of low, moderate and high, by using objective EEG spectral data. It was a multiclass classification. For Task 1, we used all 48 subjects' data, but for Task 2, we ignored data from S05, S24 and S42 as rating data was not available for these subjects.

3.6   Feature Standardisation

Both the intra- and inter-individual variability character can be found in the EEG signal. Consequently, the extracted features would have a poor generalizability property; moreover, unavoidable artefacts might still exist in the data. It is difficult to build a model for recognising the level of mental workload across subject [20]. Herein, the problem was eased by a personalised feature standardisation method [7,38], the extracted features were converted into the same scale across subjects by F_{scaled}. Assume the raw feature value is F_{raw}. L_w and U_w are the upper and lower whisker (limits), respectively, they are the measure's value distribution for generating box plot [40]. L_w = max (minimum feature value, lower quartile $-1.5 *$ interquartile range) and U_w = min (maximum value, supper quartile $+1.5 *$ interquartile range. The scaled feature value F_{scaled} is acquired from

$$F_{scaled} = \frac{F_{raw} - L_w}{U_w - L_w} \tag{5}$$

3.7   Metrics

We use six metrics to evaluate the effectiveness of the preprocessing techniques on deep learning model performance, as follows:

Sensitivity, also known as the true positive rate, is the proportion of the number of correct positive examples to the number classified as positive and is defined by

$$Sensitivity = \frac{TP}{(TP + FN)} \tag{6}$$

where true positives (TP) is a number of case that predicted positive, and it is true, and false negative (FN) is a number of case that predicted negative, and it is false.

Specificity, which is the same ratio for negative examples, can be defined by

$$Specificity = \frac{TN}{(TN + FP)} \tag{7}$$

where True Negatives (TN) is a number of case that predicted negative, and it is true and False Positive (FP) is a number of case that predicted positive, and it is false.

Precision refer to the ratio of correct positive examples to the number of actual positive examples and is defined by

$$Precision = \frac{TP}{(TP + FP)} \tag{8}$$

Accuracy which is the sum of the number of true positives and true negatives divided by the total number of examples.

$$Accuracy = \frac{TP + TN}{(TP + TN + FP + FN)} \tag{9}$$

The other two criteria used in this analysis are **False Accepted Rate** (FAR) and **False rejected rate** (FRR). Those criteria are usually applied for measuring the performance of a biometric system [34]. FAR occur when we accept an unauthorised case which should actually be rejected. This measurement is also known as Type II errors. FRR is the issue of the valid case which should be accepted are rejected. This refers to Type I errors. The FAR and FRR are represented in (10) and (11), respectively.

$$FAR = \frac{FP}{(TN + FP)} \tag{10}$$

$$FRR = \frac{FN}{(TP + FN)} \tag{11}$$

3.8   Experimental Procedure

As we have shown in Sect. 3.2, EEG preprocessing, we have four scenarios from the preprocessing techniques. In each scenario, EEG features were extracted, and then a set of 84 optimised features based on the original paper [8] was used in this experiment. In the model evaluation step, a cross-validation technique was applied. To do so, we firstly split 80% of the dataset to conduct model training and kept 20% of the data aside as an unseen test dataset. Then, the training dataset was further split into five folds of approximately equal size. That is 5-fold cross-validation. Within each loop of classification model training, one fold was treated as a validation set, and the model was trained on the remaining $5 - 1$ folds. Inside the loop, the selected features were standardised by using (5). Once the model was trained using 5-folds, we evaluated classification model performance by comparing a predicted level with the true labels of the unseen dataset.

4   Results and Discussion

This section discusses different experimental results along with the performance analysis of the proposed framework.

Table 3. The numbers in the parenthesis are the changed percentage of model performance in each scenario comparing with Scenario 1. * shows a statistical significant difference (p-value < 0.05) in model performance under three comparison condition (Scenario 1 versus 2, Scenario 1 versus 3, and Scenario 1 versus 4)

Model	Senario	Sensitivity	Specificity	Precision	Accuracy	FAR	FRR
Stacked LSTM	1	79.63	76.07	76.90	77.85	29.23	20.37
	2	81.78* (2.70%)	77.11* (1.37%)	78.13* (1.60%)	79.44* (2.04%)	22.89* (-21.69%)	18.22* (-10.5%)
	3	85.78* (7.72%)	85.26* (12.08%)	85.34* (10.98%)	85.52* (9.85%)	14.74* (-49.57%)	14.22* (-30.19%)
	4	**87.26*** **(9.58%)**	**87.78*** **(15.39%)**	**87.71*** **(14.06%)**	**87.52*** **(12.42%)**	**12.22*** **(-58.19%)**	**12.74*** **(-37.46%)**
BLSTM	1	78.81	76.96	77.38	77.89	23.04	21.19
	2	82.89* (5.18%)	76.97 (0.01%)	78.25* (1.12%)	79.93* (2.62%)	23.03 (-0.04%)	17.11* (-19.25%)
	3	87.19* (10.63%)	85.78* (11.46%)	85.98* (11.11%)	86.48* (11.03%)	14.22* (-38.28%)	12.81* (-39.55%)
	4	**88.30*** **(12.04%)**	**86.74*** **(12.71%)**	**86.94*** **(12.35%)**	**87.52*** **(12.36%)**	**13.26*** **(-42.45%)**	**11.70*** **(-44.79%)**
BLSTM-LSTM	1	83.85	79.56	80.40	81.70	20.04	16.15
	2	82.89* (-1.14%)	79.78 (0.28%)	80.39 (-0.01%)	81.33 (-0.45%)	20.22 (0.90%)	17.11* (5.94%)
	3	86.89* (3.63%)	88.44* (11.16%)	88.26* (9.78%)	87.67* (7.31%)	11.56* (-42.32%)	13.11* (-18.82%)
	4	**87.93*** **(4.87%)**	**90.96*** **(14.33%)**	**90.68*** **(12.79%)**	**89.44*** **(9.47%)**	**9.04*** **(-54.89%)**	**12.07*** **(-25.26%)**

(a) The effect of our four preprocessing scenarios in the mental workload classification in Task 1: resting state vs working state.

Model	Senario	Sensitivity	Specificity	Precision	Accuracy	FAR	FRR
Stacked LSTM	1	66.52	84.59	68.34	78.57	15.41	33.48
	2	70.96* (6.67%)	82.11* (-2.93%)	66.48* (-2.72%)	78.40 (-0.22%)	17.89* (16.09%)	29.04* (-13.26%)
	3	81.81* (22.99%)	90.44* (6.92%)	81.06* (18.61%)	87.57* (11.45%)	9.56* (-37.96%)	18.19* (-45.67%)
	4	**83.56*** **(25.62%)**	**91.83*** **(8.56%)**	**83.65*** **(22.40%)**	**89.07*** **(13.36%)**	**8.17*** **(-46.98%)**	**16.44*** **(-50.90%)**
BLSTM	1	22.52	95.94	73.52	71.41	4.06	77.48
	2	17.11* (-24.02%)	96.63 (0.72%)	71.74* (-2.42%)	70.12* (-1.81%)	3.37* (-17.00%)	82.89* (6.98%)
	3	24.11* (7.06%)	97.33* (1.45%)	81.89* (11.38%)	72.93* (2.13%)	2.67* (-34.24%)	75.89* (-2.05%)
	4	**29.04*** **(28.95%)**	**97.44*** **(1.56%)**	**85.03*** **(15.66%)**	**74.64*** **(4.52%)**	**2.56*** **(-36.95%)**	**70.96*** **(-8.42%)**
BLSTM-LSTM	1	68.22	85.74	70.52	79.90	14.26	31.78
	2	71.74* (5.16%)	87.17* (1.67%)	73.65* (4.44%)	82.02* (2.65%)	12.83* (-10.03%)	28.26* (-11.08%)
	3	85.56* (25.42%)	92.09* (7.41%)	84.40* (19.68%)	89.91* (12.53%)	7.91* (-44.53%)	14.44* (-54.56%)
	4	**86.59*** **(26.93%)**	**93.43*** **(8.97%)**	**86.82*** **(23.11%)**	**91.15*** **(14.08%)**	**6.57*** **(-53.93%)**	**13.41*** **(-57.80%)**

(b) The effect of our four preprocessing scenarios in the mental workload classification in Task 2: low vs moderate vs high MWL.

Scenario 1. For the Scenario 1, which we only used the raw data without any preprocessing, we observe from Table 3 that all adopted deep learning model is capable of capturing relevant information and classify with good model performance score. Specifically, the least sophisticated model like the Stacked LSTM provided a good starting point compared to chance.

Task 1. It can be seen from the data in Table 3a that the highest accuracy scores are from the BLSTM-LSTM model, followed by the BLSTM and Stacked LSTM model, which are 81.70%, 77.89% and 77.85%, respectively. It could be implied that the more sophisticated model provided the higher model accuracy. However, when looking at the sensitivity score, we observed a different pattern; that was, the sensitivity of the BLSTM model was slightly lower than the most unsophisticated model architecture like the Stacked LSTM. That means the BLSTM model marked subjects who were in resting state as in working state than other models did. On the other hand, we observed that the BLSTM model obtained the highest specificity score of 76.96% in Task 1. That means if subjects were not in a resting state, the BLSTM model was good at identifying non-resting state correctly than other models.

Task 2. When looking at model accuracy in Table 3b, we observe that the best model is still the BLSTM-LSTM, the second-best turn to be the Stacked LSTM, and the less effective one is the BLSTM. Model accuracy of the BLSTM-LSTM, LSTM, and BLSTM are 79.90%, 78.57%, and 71.41%, respectively. In this task, we observed that the lower sensitivity score in a more sophisticated model of the BLSTM compare with the Stacked LSTM was becoming more serious. While the Stacked LSTM achieved 66.52% sensitivity, the BLSTM obtained 22.52% sensitivity. That means the BLSTM could not classify the true level of the subject' MWL correctly. For example, when a subject was in the low level of MWL, the model seemed to mark low MWL level as medium or high. Furthermore, we observed that the BLSTM obtained a very high specificity score of 95.94%, then the BLSTM was good at identifying the non-considering MWL level correctly. For example, when subjects were not in the low level of MWL, the BLSTM model seemed to mark medium or high correctly than other models did.

Scenario 2. In Scenario 2, we removed the artefact components from our dataset for the first time using a high-pass filter technique. We observe the same pattern of the result from Table 3 as shown in the previous scenario, with some few exceptions. The exception is in Task 1.

Task 1. As can be seen from Table 3a, the highest model accuracy is from the BLSTM-LSTM, followed by the BLSTM, and Stacked LSTM. The accuracy of the BLSTM and Stacked LSTM increased by 2.62% and 2.04%, respectively, compared with them in Scenario 1. However, the accuracy of the BLSTM-LSTM model dropped by 0.45% comparing with its in Scenario 1. We observed that there was no decrease in the sensitivity score of the BLSTM, compared with the Stacked LSTM in this scenario.

Task 2. As shown in Table 3b, the best model is the same one, the BLSTM-LSTM; however, the second-best model become the Stacked LSTM and the less effective model to classify three levels of MWL is the BLSTM. The accuracy of the BLSTM-LSTM increased by 2.65%. However, for the Stacked LSTM and BLSTM, the accuracy decreased by 0.22% and 1.81%, respectively, compared with them in Scenario 1. In this task of Scenario 2, we still observed a sharp decrease in the sensitivity score of the BLSTM model comparing with Stacked LSTM. While the Stacked LSTM enhanced 70.96% sensitivity, the BLSTM acquired 17.11% sensitivity. Nevertheless, we observed that the BLSTM obtained the highest specificity score of 96.63% in this task.

From this data, we observed that we have some improvement in model performance, but there was also some decrease. It seems that a high-pass filter technique does not much contribute to model performance. Moreover, it might distort the EEG signal somehow and cause us to lose some information from the EEG data. Furthermore, the problem of the BLSTM model still appears in this scenario.

Scenario 3. In Scenario 3, we further removed the artefact components from our dataset by using the ADJUST algorithm. We observe the same pattern of the result from Table 3 as we have seen in Scenario 2 with a few exceptions. The exception is in Task 1.

Task 1. We observe from the data in Table 3a that the highest accuracy scores is from the BLSTM-LSTM, followed by the BLSTM and Stacked LSTM; their accuracy increase by 7.31%, 11.03% and 9.85%, respectively, compared with them in Scenario 1. We observed that the BLSTM obtain the highest sensitivity score in this task and follow by the BLSTM-LSTM and Stacked LSTM.

Task 2. For Task 2, considering the accuracy score in Table 3b, the best model is the BLSTM-LSTM, followed by the Stacked LSTM and the BLSTM. Model accuracy of the BLSTM-LSTM, Stacked LSTM and BLSTM rose by 12.53%, 11.45%, and 2.13%, respectively, compared with them in Scenario 1. In this scenario, we still observed a significant decreased of sensitivity score in the BLSTM, compared with the Stacked LSTM. While the Stacked LSTM enhanced 81.81% sensitivity, the BLSTM acquired 24.11% sensitivity. Furthermore, we observed that the BLSTM model obtained the highest specificity score of 97.33% in this task.

Generally, we see much progress in model performance in this scenario after we applied the ADJUST algorithm for further artefact removal from EEG signals. It seems that the ADJUST has much contributed to model performance. It can ease irrelevant information from data. However, we still observe the problem of low sensitivity in the BLSTM model in this scenario.

Scenario 4. In Scenario 4, we added more preprocessing technique in our pipeline, which is a re-referencing.

Task 1. Considering the accuracy score in Table 3a, the best model is the same one, the BLSTM-LSTM, which has a 9.47% improvement, compared with its in Scenario 1. In this scenario, the BLSTM and Stacked LSTM achieve the same accuracy. However, they have a different improvement rate. While the accuracy score of the BLSTM increased by 12.36%, the Stacked LSTM model improved by 12.42%, compared with them in Scenario 1. The sensitivity pattern of this scenario was the same as Scenario 3; the numbers were slightly increased.

Task 2. In Task 2, we observe the exact performance behaviour as found in Scenario 3 from Table 3b. Model accuracy of the BLSTM-LSTM, Stacked LSTM, and BLSTM increased by 14.08%, 13.36%, and 4.52%, respectively, compared with them in Scenario 1. A significant decreased of sensitivity score in the BLSTM model compared with Stacked LSTM was still be found. While the Stacked LSTM model enhanced 83.56% sensitivity, the BLSTM acquired 29.04% sensitivity. The BLSTM model still obtained the highest specificity score of 97.44%, but the numbers did not differ much from Scenario 3.

In summary, these results show that there is progress in model performance as we added more preprocessing techniques in the pipeline across different tasks. Furthermore, this behaviour consistent across all the metrics we are looking at, and we also see the exactly linear decrease of error, i.e. FAR and FRR, with some exceptions. The exception was in Scenario 2, when a high-pass filter was used. In this scenario, we observed an increase of error numbers in Task 1 of the BLSTM-LSTM model and Task 2 of the Stacked LSTM and BLSTM. As can be seen from Table 3a, FAR receiving from Task 1 of the BLSTM-LSTM model starts at 20.04%; however, after high-pass filtering, the number climbs to 20.22%. FRR, which starts at 16.15%, change to 20.22% after filtering. Considering Task 2 of the Stacked LSTM, as results shown in Table 3b, the increasing of error number found in FAR, which starts at 15.41% and climbs to 17.89% and FRR from the BLSTM rises by 6.98% after filtering. The smaller FAR and FRR values indicate that the model performs better. Conversely, the model could capture the data structure more effectively when they have larger sensitivity, sensitivity, precision, and accuracy value. Therefore, filtering the EEG signals to remove artefacts might be a common preprocessing step, but it could introduce temporal distortions in the signals. The other important observation is that after EEG signals were preprocessed using the ADJUST algorithm, the performances notably increased across the state-of-the-art deep learning models. Finally, we gain the highest classification performance across the deep learning models when using all preprocessing techniques. Hence, there are opportunities for deep learning models for getting a higher performance if we enhance the artefact removal techniques in the preprocessing state.

Moreover, the result also reveal that the unsophisticated model, i.e. Stacked LSTM, already provided a good starting point compared to chance using raw data. That means event simple deep learning model architecture can capture relevant information and do a few things. However, BLSTM had very low sensitivity, especially in Task 2: low vs medium vs high MWL. So, the bidirectional that go backwards did not seem to be contributing much. The cause of this problem could be from the training strategy of the bidirectional model. The idea of the bidirectional model is to concatenate two independent neural networks together; one input has been fed sequentially by time order, another in reverse time order [33]. For more generally, the model needs input from both the past and future. Practically, we do not have a future value of time series for the present time of prediction. Consequently, that would be the reason that why the model cannot categorise the MWL level effectively. Therefore, this study has raised an important questions of "How a bidirectional neural network can be applied on the time series?". Lastly, the BLSTM-LSTM which had the highest starting point and also end with the best performing. Especially, the result from Table 3a, BLSTM-LSTM, Task 1, show that the model accuracy increases from 81.70% to 89.44%. Then, the difference from the raw data, Scenario 1 compared with Scenario 4, become less different. Where in Task 2, the accuracy of BLSTM-LSTM climbs from 79.90% to 91.15% as shown in Table 3b.

In this analysis, we also performed the analysis of variance on ranks using the Kruskal-Wallis H test [25] for testing whether there were statistically significant differences between four scenarios of EEG preprocessing on models performance. We found that there was a statistically significant difference among four scenarios across three models ($p < 0.05$). Consequently, we performed a pair-wise comparison using the Mann-Whitney U test [26] for finding a difference between model performance trained by raw data and preprocessed data. The Mann-Whitney U test showed that there were statistically significant differences on the performance of models at Scenario 2, 3, and 4 compared to Scenario 1, which is our baseline for every model, with few exceptions. The asterisk in Table 3 shows the statistically significant results where the p-value < 0.05. This shows that the preprocessing techniques applied have a significant effect in improving the effectiveness of the deep learning model on EEG signals. Overall, even though the model is sophisticated, a suitable preprocessing pipeline still provided the advantage. Hence, there are opportunities for deep learning models for getting a higher performance if we enhance the artefact removal techniques in the preprocessing stage.

5 Conclusion

In this paper, we explored the effect of preprocessing techniques defined by neuroscientist in the effectiveness of deep learning models. To investigate the effect of preprocessing techniques, we focused only on the automated techniques named a high-pass filter, the ADJUST algorithm, and a re-referencing. Then, we verified the effect of these preprocessing techniques in three state-of-the-art deep learning models named Stacked LSTM, BLSTM, and BLSTM-LSTM by using a publicly available mental workload Scenario, STEW [21]. Our finding shows that ADJUST has the most effect on the performance across the investigated deep learning models compared to other techniques. Moreover, our results also show that EEG signals that were preprocessed using a high-pass filter, the ADJUST algorithm, and a re-referencing all together provided the highest classification performance across the models. However, we also observed that raw signals still suffice for classification as seen from each model, especially in BLSTM-LSTM. The model starts from a very good starting point in both Tasks. The more the model becomes sophisticated, the more potential they find relevant information from raw data. Therefore, it means that the need for preprocessing become less important. Hence, in future work, we should consider building the deep learning model sophisticated enough to encompass the preprocessing inside it automatically.

In this paper, we investigated the effect of three artefact removal techniques, i.e. a high-pass filter, the ADJUST algorithm, and a re-referencing. Our positive findings encourage further research to study the effect of other artefact removal techniques. Furthermore, we would also like to evaluate the effect of these techniques on a boarder range of deep learning models, e.g. CNN. Finally, we will investigate how we can incorporate the EEG preprocessing techniques into the deep learning model.

References

1. Makoto's preprocessing pipeline. https://sccn.ucsd.edu/wiki/Makoto's_preprocessing_pipeline
2. Arico, P., et al.: Reliability over time of EEG-based mental workload evaluation during air traffic management (ATM) tasks. In: 2015 37th Annual International Conference of the IEEE Engineering in Medicine and Biology Society (EMBC), pp. 7242–7245. IEEE (2015)
3. Berka, C., et al.: EEG correlates of task engagement and mental workload in vigilance, learning, and memory tasks. Aviation Space Environ. Med. **78**(5), B223–B244 (2007)
4. Bigdely-Shamlo, N., Mullen, T., Kothe, C., Su, K.M., Robbins, K.A.: The prep pipeline: standardized preprocessing for large-scale EEG analysis. Front. Neuroinformatics **9**, 16 (2015). https://www.frontiersin.org/article/10.3389/fninf.2015.00016
5. Bilalpur, M., Kankanhalli, M., Winkler, S., Subramanian, R.: EEG-based evaluation of cognitive workload induced by acoustic parameters for data sonification. In: Proceedings of the 20th ACM International Conference on Multimodal Interaction, pp. 315–323 (2018)
6. Buiatti, M., Mognon, A.: ADJUST: An Automatic EEG artifact Detector based on the Joint Use of Spatial and Temporal features, A Tutorial (2014). https://www.nitrc.org/docman/view.php/739/2101/ADJUST%20Tutorial. Accessed 3 Aug 2020
7. Buscher, G., Dengel, A., Biedert, R., Elst, L.V.: Attentive documents: eye tracking as implicit feedback for information retrieval and beyond. ACM Trans. Interactive Intell. Syst. (TiiS) **1**(2), 1–30 (2012)
8. Chakladar, D.D., Dey, S., Roy, P.P., Dogra, D.P.: EEG-based mental workload estimation using deep BLSTM-LSTM network and evolutionary algorithm. Biomedical Signal Processing and Control **60**, 101989 (2020)
9. Debnath, R., Buzzell, G.A., Morales, S., Bowers, M.E., Leach, S.C., Fox, N.A.: The Maryland analysis of developmental EEG (made) pipeline. Psychophysiology **57**(6), e13580 (2020)

10. van Erp, J.B., Brouwer, A.M., Zander, T.O.: Using neurophysiological signals that reflect cognitive or affective state. Front. Neuroscience **9**, 193 (2015)

11. Gabard-Durnam, L.J., Mendez Leal, A.S., Wilkinson, C.L., Levin, A.R.: The harvard automated processing pipeline for electroencephalography (happe): standardized processing software for developmental and high-artifact data. Front. Neurosci. **12**, 97 (2018). https://www.frontiersin.org/article/10.3389/fnins.2018.00097

12. Groeneveld, R.A., Meeden, G.: Measuring skewness and kurtosis. J. R. Stat. Soc. Ser. D (Stat.) **33**(4), 391–399 (1984)

13. Groppe, D.M., Makeig, S., Kutas, M.: Identifying reliable independent components via split-half comparisons. Neuroimage **45**(4), 1199–1211 (2009)

14. Holm, A., Lukander, K., Korpela, J., Sallinen, M., Müller, K.M.: Estimating brain load from the EEG. Scientific World J. **9**, 639–651 (2009)

15. Hurst, H.E.: Long-term storage capacity of reservoirs. Trans. Am. Soc. Civ. Eng. **116**(1), 770–799 (1951)

16. Islam, M.K., Rastegarnia, A., Yang, Z.: Methods for artifact detection and removal from scalp EEG: a review. Neurophysiologie Clinique/Clin. Neurophysiol. **46**(4–5), 287–305 (2016)

17. Jeong, J.H., Yu, B.W., Lee, D.H., Lee, S.W.: Classification of drowsiness levels based on a deep spatio-temporal convolutional bidirectional LSTM network using electroencephalography signals. Brain Sci. **9**(12), 348 (2019)

18. Kuanar, S., Athitsos, V., Pradhan, N., Mishra, A., Rao, K.R.: Cognitive analysis of working memory load from EEG, by a deep recurrent neural network. In: 2018 IEEE International Conference on Acoustics, Speech and Signal Processing (ICASSP), pp. 2576–2580. IEEE (2018)

19. Lee, D.H., Jeong, J.H., Kim, K., Yu, B.W., Lee, S.W.: Continuous EEG decoding of pilots' mental states using multiple feature block-based convolutional neural network. IEEE Access **8**, 121929–121941 (2020)

20. Li, X., Song, D., Zhang, P., Zhang, Y., Hou, Y., Hu, B.: Exploring EEG features in cross-subject emotion recognition. Front. Neurosci. **12**, 162 (2018)

21. Lim, W., Sourina, O., Wang, L.: Stew: simultaneous task EEG workload data set. IEEE Trans. Neural Syst. Rehabil. Eng. **26**(11), 2106–2114 (2018)

22. Longo, L., Rusconi, F., Noce, L., Barrett, S.: The importance of human mental workload in web design. In: WEBIST, pp. 403–409 (2012)

23. Makeig, S., Bell, A.J., Jung, T.P., Sejnowski, T.J.: Independent component analysis of electroencephalographic data. In: Advances in Neural Information Processing Systems, pp. 145–151 (1996)

24. Martin, R.: Noise power spectral density estimation based on optimal smoothing and minimum statistics. IEEE Trans. Speech Audio Process. **9**(5), 504–512 (2001)

25. McKight, P.E., Najab, J.: Kruskal-wallis test. The corsini encyclopedia of psychology p. 1 (2010)

26. McKnight, P.E., Najab, J.: Mann-whitney u test. The Corsini encyclopedia of psychology p. 1 (2010)

27. Mognon, A., Jovicich, J., Bruzzone, L., Buiatti, M.: Adjust: an automatic EEG artifact detector based on the joint use of spatial and temporal features. Psychophysiology **48**(2), 229–240 (2011)

28. Nagabushanam, P., George, S.T., Radha, S.: EEG signal classification using LSTM and improved neural network algorithms. Soft Comput. 1–23 (2019)

29. Nussbaumer, H.J.: The fast Fourier transform. In: Fast Fourier Transform and Convolution Algorithms. SSINF, vol. 2, pp. 80–111. Springer, Heidelberg (1981). https://doi.org/10.1007/978-3-662-00551-4_4

30. Pincus, S.M.: Approximate entropy as a measure of system complexity. Proc. Nat. Acad. Sci. **88**(6), 2297–2301 (1991)
31. Reid, G.B., Nygren, T.E.: The subjective workload assessment technique: a scaling procedure for measuring mental workload. In: Advances in Psychology, vol. 52, pp. 185–218. Elsevier (1988)
32. Roy, Y., Banville, H., Albuquerque, I., Gramfort, A., Falk, T.H., Faubert, J.: Deep learning-based electroencephalography analysis: a systematic review. J. Neural Eng. **16**(5), 051001 (2019)
33. Schuster, M., Paliwal, K.K.: Bidirectional recurrent neural networks. IEEE Trans. Sig. Process. **45**(11), 2673–2681 (1997)
34. Taylor, L.P.: Chapter 20 - independent assessor audit guide. In: Taylor, L.P. (ed.) FISMA Compliance Handbook, pp. 239–273. Syngress, Boston (2013). https://www.sciencedirect.com/science/article/pii/B9780124058712000208
35. Urigüen, J.A., Garcia-Zapirain, B.: EEG artifact removal—state-of-the-art and guidelines. J. Neural Eng. **12**(3), 031001 (2015). https://doi.org/10.1088%2F1741-2560%2F12%2F3%2F031001
36. Vaid, S., Singh, P., Kaur, C.: EEG signal analysis for BCI interface: a review. In: 2015 Fifth International Conference on Advanced Computing and Communication Technologies, pp. 143–147. IEEE (2015)
37. Varshney, A., Ghosh, S.K., Padhy, S., Tripathy, R.K., Acharya, U.R.: Automated classification of mental arithmetic tasks using recurrent neural network and entropy features obtained from multi-channel EEG signals. Electronics **10**(9), 1079 (2021)
38. Wang, S., Gwizdka, J., Chaovalitwongse, W.A.: Using wireless EEG signals to assess memory workload in the n-back task. IEEE Trans. Hum. Mach. Syst. **46**(3), 424–435 (2015)
39. Wiebe, E.N., Roberts, E., Behrend, T.S.: An examination of two mental workload measurement approaches to understanding multimedia learning. Comput. Hum. Behav. **26**(3), 474–481 (2010)
40. Wilcox, R.R.: Introduction to Robust Estimation and Hypothesis Testing. Academic Press, Cambridge (2011)
41. Yang, S., Yin, Z., Wang, Y., Zhang, W., Wang, Y., Zhang, J.: Assessing cognitive mental workload via EEG signals and an ensemble deep learning classifier based on denoising autoencoders. Comput. Biol. Med. **109**, 159–170 (2019)
42. Young, M.S., Brookhuis, K.A., Wickens, C.D., Hancock, P.A.: State of science: mental workload in ergonomics. Ergonomics **58**(1), 1–17 (2015)
43. Zhang, P., Wang, X., Chen, J., You, W., Zhang, W.: Spectral and temporal feature learning with two-stream neural networks for mental workload assessment. IEEE Trans. Neural Syst. Rehabil. Eng. **27**(6), 1149–1159 (2019)
44. Zhang, Y., Liu, B., Ji, X., Huang, D.: Classification of EEG signals based on autoregressive model and wavelet packet decomposition. Neural Process. Lett. **45**(2), 365–378 (2017)
45. Zhao, R., Yan, R., Wang, J., Mao, K.: Learning to monitor machine health with convolutional bi-directional LSTM networks. Sensors **17**(2), 273 (2017)

Mental Workload Assessment in Military Pilots Using Flight Simulators and Physiological Sensors

Mario Henrique de Oliveira Coutinho da Silva[✉], Thiago Fontes Macêdo[✉],
Cinthia de Carvalho Lourenço[✉], Ivan de Souza Rehder[✉],
Ana Angélica da Costa Marchiori[✉], Mateus Pereira Cesare[✉],
Raphael Gomes Cortes[✉], Moacyr Machado Cardoso Junior[✉],
and Emilia Villani[✉]

Manufacturing Competence Center, Aeronautics Institute
of Technological, São José dos Campos 12228-900, Brazil
{coutinho,ITA,thiagomacedo,cinthia,ivan,anaangelica,cesare,
cortesrgc,moacyr,evillani}@ita.br

Abstract. This study evaluated the mental workload of military pilots during day and night conditions using night vision goggles (NVG) in a Flight Training Device, in order to rectify or ratify the fatigue correction factor used for flights using NVG. The experiment used basic military operational tasks measuring physiological data, specifically data on electrocardiography activity and galvanic skin response. Subjective data were gathered using NASA TLX and Psychomotor Vigilance Test methods. After collection, the data were subjected to treatment to correct possible errors during data acquisition and later analyzed in the domains of time and frequency. The analysis did not show a great change in mental workload between the day and night periods, which could be explained by the small sample, the small period between flights and the learning effect between day and night flight.

Keywords: Workload · Night vision goggles · Military operations · Flights

1 Introduction

The evaluation and measurement of the workload is not a new issue. It has been extensively discussed in the literature. The first studies and definitions date back to the end of the 20th century, concurrent with the human factors approach gained relevance in different safety areas. Historically, this period has been associated with risk management studies and the emergence of the Human Reliability Analysis (HRA) method, in the 1970s. The same decade brought the beginning of the passage from the Fordism model to Toyotism in the industrial sector, where workers ceased to perform a single mechanical function and became responsible for mastering a wider range of tasks.

In conceptual terms, [1] conceptualizing workload as the interaction between the subject and the demands of a particular work environment [2] proceeded with studies about workload, and reinforced that workload exists during the occurrence of any

L. Longo and M. C. Leva (Eds.): H-WORKLOAD 2021, CCIS 1493, pp. 99–115, 2021.
https://doi.org/10.1007/978-3-030-91408-0_7

work activity, emerging through factors internal and external to the operator, and the interrelated physical, cognitive and psychic demands arising from the activity [3].

However, it was only in the 21st century that the studies and practical applications of mental workload gained relevance, motivated by the growing technological advancement, in practically all areas of the globalized world, which substantially affected people's dynamics of life and work.

In the meantime, it is important to highlight the difference between the task load and the mental workload (MW). Task load is related solely to the demands of the job, while MW concerns a larger context, composed of the subjectivity and individuality of each worker when facing those demands.

According to [1], it is essential to understand that the MW is also characterized by the subjectivity with which each individual interprets the demands of the job, the obligations and constraints imposed on the worker. The MW comes as a consequence of the fact that the worker performs the task itself, taking into account all the complexity present in the work reality. In this sense, the mental load is not only derived from work, but also from other extrinsic factors of the task, such as: individual, sociocultural (intellectual capacity, age, level of education, professional training, learning, previous experience) and environmental (noise, heat and toxic) [4].

Nowadays, the complex systems environment has become a constant reality, reflecting significantly on the operators' mental workload. The operators, in turn, have an individual and limited capacity for mental resources, inherent to the human being, such as the capacity for attention and memorization. These resources are consumed to perform the activities coming from the system and the work itself, and people are sometimes subjected to excessive workloads that contribute to a society full of problems, such as depression and stress.

The aviation sector did not remain oblivious to these changes, on the contrary, it was one of the ones that most experienced this technological shift. The increase in world air traffic has resulted in stricter air traffic rules, requiring the aeronautical industry to develop more accurate and more complex air navigation systems, changing the cabin piloting tasks, moving from essentially manual tasks to management and monitoring focused tasks.

Therefore, the objective of the current study was to assess the workload demanded by military pilots, by physiological measurements and the application of questionnaires, providing a basis to evaluate the standards or regulations, as well as the development of training programs that focus on improving interactions between pilots and machines and thereby contribute to flight safety and to a better workload environment for the crews.

This work was organized in five sections. After this first section, a contextualization of the problem is presented in Sect. 2. Section 3 describes the methodology adopted, and Sect. 4 discusses the results. Finally, Sect. 5 draws some conclusions and discusses future works.

2 Military Aviation

Military Aviation was forced to follow the world's evolution, aiming to remain capable of fulfilling its essential function of guaranteeing air force support and supremacy. Aircraft development increasingly equipped with the latest technological devices, such as the migration of the analog panels to the Glass Cockpit and the four-axis autopilots in the helicopters.

However, in the midst of such an evolution something remained unchanged behind the joystick of airplanes or cyclical helicopters, the pilots, human beings subject to limited mental resources who have suffered from the significant increase in the workload, provenient from automation and the endless technological resources inserted in the cabin.

Adding to these new demands, the peculiarities of military flights are performed in conditions of low height, high speed, executing maneuvers that place the aircraft at the limit of its capabilities, which leads to a high demand for military systems management and operation.

It is noted, then, that technological advancement required a differentiated performance from the pilots, requiring specific skills and competences to obtain success. Otherwise, the excessive wear related to the mental workload of the aviator could cause failures or the occurrence of errors during the flight. The International Civil Aviation Organization [5] reinforces this aspect by validating the importance of incorporating the knowledge of Human Factors in the processes of development, acquisition and implementation of air traffic systems.

Extreme workloads increase the likelihood of human error. When in excess, errors arise due to the operator's inability to process high levels of information resulting from its internal and external conditions. When on a smaller scale, the operator tends to be complacent and not perform the task properly, also leading to error [6].

It is noteworthy that the technical skills developed by pilots, to fly safely, are not restricted only to physical conditions. Psychological factors, which interfere in the behavior, such as perception capacity, information processing, attention, agility of thought, decision making, risk management, cognitive control, personality, mental and emotional state, attitudes and humor are fundamental for the pilot to be able to make correct choices, directly or indirectly, in the face of unusual situations and/or ones that may generate stress and anxiety [5].

It is, therefore, essential the establishment of rules and procedures to aid the demands required from pilots, especially the military, so that they can adapt to the uncertainties of real workload requirements.

As well as civil aviation, which has in Brazilian Law No. 13475, of 28 August 2017, the determinations regarding workload limits, military aviation also has its laws, such as Operational Norm No. 1 (NOp nº 1), 2017, from the Army Aviation Command (CAvEx) and the NOPREP/SGV/01B of the Brazilian Air Force.

However, it was observed that the aforementioned standard requires an update and verification of the real suitability of its limits, since it was produced without scientific basis, taking as reference studies from other countries or the opinion from experts.

For validation purposes, this study assessed the proposed correction factor, in NOp nº 1/CAvEx, for the flight with night vision goggles (NVG), as shown in Table 1, performing the physiological measurements during flights in Flight Training Device (FTD) simulators. The Simulation Division of the Army Aviation Instruction Center of the Brazilian Army was chosen given the possibility of constant monitoring of activity in a controlled environment.

Table 1. Correction factors.

Type of flight	Correction factor used	Maximum specific flight effort
Daytime	1.0	8 HDR
IFR	1.4	5.7 HDR
VRF nighttime	1.4	5.7 HDR
Tatical flight	1.6	5 HDR
NVG	2.0	4 HDR
Enviroment QBN	3.1	2.5 HDR

Table 1, as already mentioned, was elaborated without an experimental scientific basis, based only on references from other Armed Forces and on the experience of the Brazilian Army Aviation Pilots. Its initial objective was to establish a limit on flight hours for crews, in order to avoid work overload and minimize risks to flight safety. Thus, the daytime flight was taken as the initial parameter (correction factor 1). The other flight types have a greater factor as the measure increases the complexity of the flight. For example, the flight with NVG in which a flight with an actual duration of 1 h, will be considered a total time of 2 h for planning purposes.

3 Proposed Method

The proposed method is based on measuring physiological responses and subjective responses regarding the changing in type of flight from day to night using NVG, aiming to rectify or ratify the correction factor proposed by NOp n° 1/CAvEx.

3.1 Characterization of the Experiment

This study was conducted at the Simulation Division of the Army Aviation Instruction Center (CIAvEx), in the city of Taubaté, Brazil, on October 26 and 27, 2020.

The Simulation Division had 06 (six) flight simulators, being 05 (five) Flight Training Device (FTD) and 01 (one) Full Flight Simulator (FFS), all with configurations and displays related to the aircraft AS-350, Esquilo, from Eurocopter.

In Brazil, flight simulators are certified by the National Civil Aviation Agency (ANAC) so that their hours can be counted as flight hours for pilots. This process is called qualification of Flight Simulation Training Devices (FSTD) and aims to sort the simulators in three categories according to their performance and realism: PCATD (Personal Computer Aviation Training Device); ATD (Aviation Training Device) and FSTD (Flight Simulation Training Device), as shown in Fig. 1.

For the current study, the FTD simulator was chosen due to its compatibility for flight with actual NVG, as opposed to the use of the simulated or fake NVGs used in the FFS of the facilite. Although the FTD had a level of realism of 4, for the purpose of this experiment, the differences regarding simulation realism and performance compared to the FFS level D were assumed negligible.

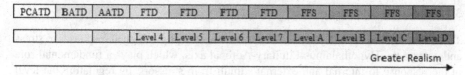

PCATD	BATD	AATD	FTD	FTD	FTD	FTD	FFS	FFS	FFS	FFS
			Level 4	Level 5	Level 6	Level 7	Level A	Level B	Level C	Level D

Greater Realism

Fig. 1. Degree of realism of the simulators.

3.2 Profile of Flights Performed

The flight planning allowed the execution in the same conditions, both during the day and night using NVG, making it possible to verify the difference in workload between the two executions.

The pilots performed a progression profile departing from Taubaté aviation base. After departure, a progression on flat terrain and in mountainous terrain was conducted, with variation in heading, altitude and speed, carrying out two procedures of Practical Reconnaissance of Landing Area (RPAP), two landings and three departures, one normal and two known as Takeoff in Campaign, totalizing approximately 45 min of flight.

To provide robustness and reliability to the execution of the experiment, throughout the flight, the crews were required to meet minimum operational efficiency requirements stipulated by the Brazilian Army, being without notice monitored by an experienced pilot. The parameters included maximum variation ranges for altitude, speed, and vertical/horizontal profile. The execution parameters control contributed to the maintenance of homogeneity in the performance of the flight execution in between day and night flight and among crews.

3.3 Sample of Crews

03 (three) crews from different Military Organizations (MO) were selected. One from the 1st Army Aviation Battalion (BAvEx), one from the 2nd BAvEx and one from CIAvEx. This crew selection attempted to ensure a thorough sample of flight and professional experience.

However, the small sample size (03 crews) was characterized as a limitation of the present study due to the fact that using real and operational crews from the Brazilian Army Aviation in the experiment was costly to the organization. The use of operational crews in an experiment makes them momentarily unavailable for operational employment in their respective Battalions, causing work overload for the other members of the Battalion, and it is also important to emphasize the high cost of the crews involved, as they all have, in addition to basic courses initial training for aviators, specializations in tactical flight, combat flight and flight with NVG.

The crews were composed, following the AvEx manuals, with two pilots and one or two flight mechanics, following the standardization of each OM. The pilots were officers from the Brazilian Army, trained at the Military Academy of Agulhas Negras and with a specialization in aviation from CIAvEx. The flight mechanics were enlisted militaries, trained and specialized in aviation by CIAvEX. After the beginning of the procedure, the replacement of any member of the crew was not allowed, in order to guarantee the homogeneity of the experiment.

3.4 Physiological Sensors Used

The Autonomic Nervous System (ANS) modulates the physiological responses to stress and acts on the Hypothalamus-Pituitary-Adrenal axis, which plays a fundamental role in the response to internal and external stimuli from stressors, by regulating the level of circulating glucocorticoids. Cortisol, for example, is one of these glucocorticoids secreted in response to stress, found in body fluids [12].

According to [13], the physiological measures stand on the assumption that when the mental workload levels change, there will be a corresponding response in the autonomic nervous system which can be reflected and measured in a number of physiological parameters.

Spontaneous heart rate variability has been related to three main factors originating from physiology: quasi-oscillatory fluctuations that are supposed to occur in blood pressure control, variable frequency oscillations due to thermal regulation and respiration [14].

Therefore, when subjected to high workload, the human body modifies its functioning by releasing hormones that interfere with its physiological characteristics, as well as emerging responses such as increasing heart rate and modifying the response of eyes.

The physiological measures, classified as physiological evaluations, analyze the physiological aspects of the operator during the workload application. Examples of tools used: heart rate, heart rate variability, endogenous blink rate, brain activity, electrodermal response, eye movements, papillary responses [7].

To identify, through physiological measures, the influence of the variation during the flight activity, from day to night flight with NVG, during the simulation, the following sensors were used:

- Galvanic Wireless Epidermal Response Sensor, TEA CAPTIV GSR (sample rate: 32 Hz), with the objective of measuring the electrical conductivity of the skin on the fingers of the volunteer pilot's left hand, allowing an estimate of sweat production, an important indicator of increased workload;
- Wireless Echocardiogram Strap, TEA CAPTIV T-Sens ECG (sample rate: 256 Hz), to monitor the heartbeat and, based on these, estimate the effects of the type of flight on the mental workload;
- Environment Temperature Sensor, TEA CAPTIV T-Sens Temperature (sample rate: 32 Hz), in order to monitor the change of temperature in the ambient and, after the tests, check if the temperature had any influence on the conductivity of the skin.

A compatibility test was performed to check the aforementioned physiological sensors with the pilot's flight equipment (glove, coveralls, helmet, etc.) of the CAvEx crews, finding no incompatibilities for daytime flight. However, this test in the night environment made the initially intended use of the Eye-Tracking Glasses unfeasible due its infrared emission on the NVG, which led to a blurred pilot's vision. Future studies are advisable to monitor eye movement and pupil dilation, factors that are highly influenced by variations in workload.

The measurements of the sensors were divided into 3 (three) phases: Rest, Operation and Restoration. The Rest Phase is a stage where the pilot is seated and stopped outside the aircraft and with the sensors all capturing their signals for 5 (five) minutes. The Operation Phase is the simulation itself. The Restoration Phase is similar to the Rest Phase but after the PVT test and the flight.

For each pilot and for each period, the results obtained during the Operation Phase were compared with those obtained during the Rest Phase, through a ratio between these numbers. This ratio indicates the change between the two phases (Rest and Operation). Posteriorly, a comparison was made between these ratios of the daytime and nighttime periods, thus allowing to obtain the variation between the aforementioned periods.

It was expected a change in the pilots' heart rate and skin conductance between rest's periods and during the flight. It was also expected that this change is bigger during the night than during the day, as the night requires a greater workload and the heart rate increases as the workload increases [8].

3.5 Questionnaires

Seeking robustness and to track variables not controlled in the experiment, an initial exploratory questionnaire was applied to the pilots, asking about the history and physical condition of the pilot on the day of the experiment. Other information such as experience and flight history were gathered in order to track individual variables that could influence the result of the military's performance during the programmed activity.

The subjective measures, which can be ascertained during or after the execution of the task, provide classifications about your perception of the mental load in real or simulated environments. There are two categories of subjective measures, one-dimensional or multidimensional, which depends on the dimension of the workload that will be evaluated [7].

The one-dimensional subjective measures can be measured continuously and in real time, following variations in mental workload. It does not depend on the participants' memory and provides only an overall score for the workload. For example, the Modified Cooper Harper Scale, is a one-dimensional measure that uses a decision tree flowchart to obtain subjective ratings of the operator's mental workload [7].

On the other hand, subjective multidimensional measures offer a diagnosis related to different dimensions of the mental workload. It is applied after the procedures, it is non-intrusive, has longer procedures, and is dependent on the worker's memory. However, it is a largely used tool, such as, NASA Task Load Index, NASA-TLX, which is a subjective, multidimensional classification tool [7].

There are a vast number of methods for subjective assessment of mental workload. The most commonly used is NASA Task Load Index (NASA-TLX) and the Subjective Workload Dominance Technique, SWORD [7].

In the current study, NASA-TLX and Psychomotor Vigilance Test (PVT) were used.

NASA TaskLoad Index (NASA-TLX). The NASA Task Load Index [9] is character-ized by being a multidimensional subjective classification tool. It has a weighted average of six workload subscales; the demands (requirements) imposed on the subject: mental, physical and temporal demands; and for having the subject's interaction with the task: effort, performance/achievement and level of frustration.

Psychomotor Vigilance Test (PVT). The Psychomotor Vigilance Test - PVT was used to check the subject's level of alertness and awareness, since this test stands out in relation to the study of sleep deprivation. In addition, the test obtains objective indicators of a behavioral nature.

For the test application, a tablet was used, considering that [10], only a computer is needed to perform the visual stimulation and capture the response time.

The applied methodology to obtain the PVT reaction time metric occurred as follows: the test was applied to the pilot before and after the flight in the simulator. The basic procedure of the psychomotor test was used, consisting of the presentation of visual stimuli and the monitoring of the subject's motor reaction using a tablet.

The presented result was counted in a spreadsheet and the difference between the pre-flight and post-flight results was verified in order to compare the subject's alert level differences between those flight conditions.

3.6 Sequence of Actions

For the correct assessment and validation of the mental workload gap, existing between daytime and NVG flights, the flights for each crew were performed on different days, reducing the influence of continued activities and the repetition of events in a short period of time.

On the first day, day flights were carried out, between 12:30 pm and 7:00 pm, and on the second day, the night flights occurred between 8:00 pm and 1:30 am, as shown in Table 2.

Table 2. Schedule of activities.

1st-day		2nd-day	
Briefing	Start of flight	Briefing	Start of flight
12:30 pm	1:30 pm	8:00 pm	8:45 pm
2:45 pm	3:45 pm	10:00 pm	10:45 pm
5:00 pm	6:00 pm	00:00 pm	00:45 pm

During the briefing phase, the following sequence was performed: presentation of the experiment, signature of the consent form, explanation of the NASA-TLX questionnaire, application of the PVT test, interview to track the activities of the day and pilots' flight experience, operational flight briefing and installation of the sensors.

The flight phase had a maximum duration of 45 min and was composed of two tactical corridors, variation of height groups, progression track in flat terrain and mountainous terrain, two Practical Land Area Reconnaissance (RPAP) and two landings.

After this phase, the application of the PVT test was followed, removal of the physiological sensors, application of the NASA-TLX questionnaire, and release of the crew. Figure 2 depicts the sequence of the experiment.

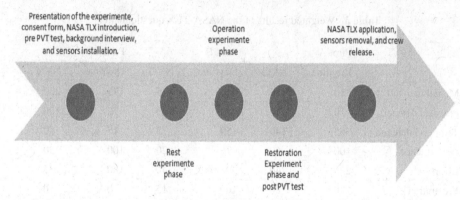

Fig. 2. Crew experiment timeline.

4   Results and Discussions

Once the experiment was finished, the data from the physiological sensors were collected and processed. The results were discussed and interpreted.

4.1   Preliminary Interview

In the preliminary interview, pilots were asked about their total flight experience and NVG flight experience. Pilot C, with 45 years of age, was the most experienced pilot, having around 3,500 h of flight, being 450 using NVG. Pilot A was 33 years old, with intermediate experience and 800 flight hours, being 90 using NVG. Pilot B was 28 years old, considered the least experienced, and had 340 flight hours, 40 with NVG.

In terms of fatigue, all pilots reported that they slept from 6 h to 8 h the night before the flight day and that their physical and health conditions were at normal levels before the beginning of the experiment.

For the NVG flight, during the following day, pilot A reported slight fatigue, pilot B reported fatigue slightly above and pilot C reported that he was rested. Pilot A showed a difference in the fatigue index [11], between daytime and NVG flight of 1.5, pilot B of 1.6 and pilot C of 0.4, which was a reflection of the daily routine and rest of each of the pilots between flights.

The experience and routine data were collected in order to track the fatigue conditions of each pilot before each experiment.

4.2   Nasa-Tlx

The weighted results of the NASA-TLX questionnaire are shown in Table 3 and 4.

The pilots had a small variation in the total weighted result between the day flight and the night flight with NVG, reaching a maximum reduction of 23%, in the case of the most experienced pilot and with less signs of fatigue (pilot C). Looking at the mental dimension, a tendency can be observed, even if still low, of an increase in mental demand reaching a maximum of 33%. The performance and frustration dimensions showed a

Table 3. Weighted results of the NASA-TLX questionnaire.

	Pilot A		Pilot B		Pilot C	
	Daytime	NVG	Daytime	NVG	Daytime	NVG
Mental demand	320	425	450	425	175	200
Physical demand	0	0	0	30	70	100
Temporal demand	65	140	50	75	15	50
Performance	100	60	75	20	100	30
Effort	225	240	300	340	180	35
Frustration	130	80	100	15	0	0
Total	56	63	63	60	36	27

more consistent behavior among the pilots, where all clearly improved their performance in the night flight with NVG, which is corroborated by the reduction in frustration rates.

As the pilots performed exactly the same tasks and activities during day and night flights with NVG, it appears that, looking at the variations in mental, performance and frustration dimensions, the effect of learning tasks predominated over a possible increase in workload from the use of the NVG during a night flight.

4.3 PVT Test

The results of the PVT Test are shown in Table 5, which refers to the difference between the average reaction time after and before each flight.

The PVT test has shown an increased reaction in time after the night flight with NVG for pilots A and B when compared to the day flight and a negligible reduction for pilot C.

Pilot C had practically no variation, which is corroborated by the more expressive result of reducing the total weighted mental load of the NASA-TLX questionnaire.

Table 4. Variation of NASA-TLX values between day and night flight with NVG for each pilot.

	Pilot A	Pilot B	Pilot C
Mental demand	33%	−6%	14%
Physical demand	0%	30%	43%
Temporal demand	115%	50%	233%
Performance	−40%	−73%	−70%
Effort	7%	13%	−81%
Frustration	−38%	−85%	0%
Total	13%	−7%	23%

Table 5. Results of the PVT test.

	Difference between after and before the day flight (ms)	Difference between after and before the night flight with NVG (ms)	Variation of results between day and night flight with NVG (ms)
Pilot A	−166	69	142%
Pilot B	−172	106	162%
Pilot C	74	62	−16%

Pilots A and B had a reduction in the reaction time indicating that the pilot rest (Pilot A - 1.5/Pilot B - 1.6/Pilot C - 0.4) had a clear effect in the reaction time.

4.4 GSR Sensor

From the wave generated by the GSR data, the mean [μS] and standard deviation [μS] were extracted. Figure 3 shows the main statistical characteristics of each pilot's operational phase signal during day and night flights.

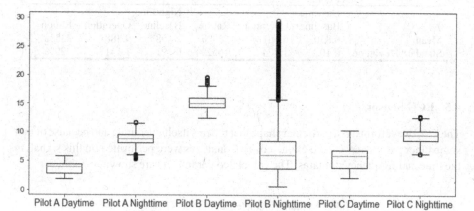

Fig. 3. Summary of statistical parameters of the operation's GSR signals for day and night flights.

In order to obtain values that may indicate the variation in the pilots' mental workload in each flight, both parameters (mean and standard deviation) were compared as shown in Tables 6, 7 and 8. The cells highlighted in green and with bold numbers represent an increase in the value, and in red and with italic numbers would indicate a decrease. The column "Ratio" shows the increase or decrease of parameter percentile.

These values showed that the variation between the Operation Phase and the Rest Phase in the night period, with NVG, is greater than the same variation in the daytime period. This indicates that pilots felt more tired or stressed during the night flight when compared to the same day flight. These values also show that less experienced pilots had a greater difference than more experienced pilots.

Table 6. Means and standard deviation of GSR Data Analysis from the pilot A.

	Pilot A					
	Daytime			Nighttime		
	Baseline	Operation	Ration	Baseline	Operation	Ration
Mean	2.741	3.664	34%	2.872	8.633	201%
Standard Deviation	0.356	0.943	165%	0.503	1.177	134%

Table 7. Means and standard deviation of GSR Data Analysis from the pilot B.

	Pilot A					
	Daytime			Nighttime		
	Baseline	Operation	Ration	Baseline	Operation	Ration
Mean	14.622	15.096	3%	2.847	6.799	139%
Standard Deviation	0.639	1.042	63%	0.960	4.439	362%

Table 8. Means and standard deviation of GSR Data Analysis from the pilot C.

	Pilot A					
	Daytime			Nighttime		
	Baseline	Operation	Ration	Baseline	Operation	Ration
Mean	0.850	5.601	559%	2.158	9.388	335%
Standard Deviation	0.107	1.874	1652%	0.191	1.141	499%

4.5 ECG Sensor

The ECG waveform has a particular shape that repeats itself over time, and because of that some other parameters can be extracted. Two analyzes were performed on this signal, in the time and frequency domains. The calculated parameters are shown in Table 9.

Table 9. Main parameters used in ECG analysis.

Parameter	Description	Unit
HR	General heart rate parameters (min, max, mean)	bpm
NNmean	Average value of NN intervals	ms
SDNN	Standard deviation of NN intervals	ms
RMSSD	Root mean square of successive NN interval differences	ms
pNN20	Ratio between NN20 and total number of NN intervals	%
pNN50	Ratio between NN50 and total number of NN intervals	%
LF/LH	Ratio between the LF e HF absolute values	

Due to the characteristics of the measuring equipment, the collection of ECG data suffered some interferences, which were corrected through the software. The correction consisted of finding peaks that were not as possible (below 300 ms and above 1200 ms), and correcting them using the moving average of the three previous peaks. The distribution of corrected NN intervals can be seen in Fig. 4.

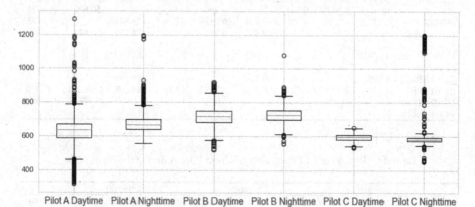

Fig. 4. Summary of statistical parameters of the operation ECG signals for day and night flights.

There are several free softwares available that analyze ECG data. Three were used in this article:

– Physionet: developed in Matlab, its latest version (1.0.0), released in 2018.
– PyHRV: developed in Python, its latest version (0.4.0), released in 2019.
– Kubios: its last free version (3.4.3), released in 2020.

To obtain values that may indicate the variation in the pilots' mental workload in each flight, the percentage relationship between the rest and operation phases of each calculated parameter was calculated. The result of this analysis can be seen in Tables 10, 11, 12, 13, 14 and 15.

The column "Ratio" in the Tables 10, 11, 12, 13, 14 and 15 showed that the pilots felt a lower mental workload during the NVG flight than during the daytime flight. This result goes against the initial hypothesis that flying NVG carries a higher mental workload than flying on the same day conditions. This result may be a consequence of the pilots' learning, since the flights were performed at an interval of approximately 30 h. Thus, it is possible to assume that the pilots tried to repeat the same flight performed during the day, reducing their mental fatigue, even under the effects of using NVG.

Table 10. Results of ECG data analysis from Pilot A during the day flight.

	Baseline			Operation			Ratio [%]		
	MatLab	PyHRV	Kubios	MatLab	PyHRV	Kubios	MatLab	PyHRV	Kubios
HR	82.427	83.506	82.761	93.719	99.019	93.633	13.700	18.577	13.137
NNmean	727.919	725.295	724.980	640.210	626.465	640.800	-12.049	-13.626	-11.611
SDNN	82.212	70.651	55.689	71.448	294.874	32.327	-13.093	317.370	-41.951
RMSSD	60.171	38.362	36.625	66.872	355.195	17.120	11.136	825.910	-53.256
PNN20		0.407	0.444		0.200	0.155		-50.806	-64.971
PNN50	0.141		0.125	0.034	0.083	0.016	-75.843		-87.172
LF/HF (Lomb Scargle)	3.829	0.489		0.833	0.455		-78.245	-6.864	
LF/HF (Welch)	4.660			0.882			-81.073		
LF/HF (Burg)	4.708			0.744			-84.199		
LF/HF (FFT)	4.910	4.109	4.125	0.805	57.572	10.195	-83.605	1301.261	147.169
LF/HF (Auto Regression)		0.567	4.612		0.649	10.154		14.499	120.189

Table 11. Results of ECG data analysis from Pilot A during the night flight.

	Baseline			Operation			Ratio [%]		
	MatLab	PyHRV	Kubios	MatLab	PyHRV	Kubios	MatLab	PyHRV	Kubios
HR	83.058	83.396	83.059	87.229	89.779	89.329	5.022	7.653	7.549
NNmean	722.383	722.183	722.370	687.841	672.960	671.680	-4.782	-6.816	-7.017
SDNN	45.338	45.250	35.373	60.707	59.247	45.420	33.897	30.932	28.403
RMSSD	20.955	20.966	20.741	28.025	38.034	21.297	33.740	81.405	2.681
PNN20		0.252	0.271		0.204	0.219		-19.227	-19.129
PNN50	0.031	0.031	2.657	0.071	0.043	0.035	126.401	37.623	-98.698
LF/HF (Lomb Scargle)	11.255	0.392		13.809	0.379		22.688	-3.203	
LF/HF (Welch)	11.397			8.873			-22.148		
LF/HF (Burg)	11.611			9.277			-20.100		
LF/HF (FFT)	11.383	9.091	10.715	7.836	9.184	18.958	-31.166	1.024	76.930
LF/HF (Auto Regression)		0.575	8.576		0.559	18.643		-2.720	117.378

Table 12. Results of ECG data analysis from Pilot B during the day flight.

	Baseline			Operation			Ratio [%]		
	MatLab	PyHRV	Kubios	MatLab	PyHRV	Kubios	MatLab	PyHRV	Kubios
HR	82.282	82.617	82.569	80.744	84.524	84.051	-1.869	2.309	1.795
NNmean	729.202	734.370	726.670	743.090	713.850	713.850	1.905	-2.794	-1.764
SDNN	80.874	75.973	64.870	48.190	52.966	34.677	-40.414	-30.283	-46.544
RMSSD	50.920	50.768	40.247	29.998	27.312	27.106	-41.088	-46.203	-32.651
PNN20		0.459	0.519		0.416	0.448		-9.299	-13.801
PNN50	0.109	0.102	0.107	0.082	0.070	0.063	-24.607	-30.988	-41.215
LF/HF (Lomb Scargle)	3.360	0.512		2.212	0.391		-34.179	-23.633	
LF/HF (Welch)	9.590			2.546			-73.447		
LF/HF (Burg)	8.908			2.646			-70.293		
LF/HF (FFT)	9.313	2.495	2.324	2.346	2.771	2.565	-74.811	11.059	10.370
LF/HF (Auto Regression)		0.541	3.284		0.558	2.647		3.227	-19.407

Table 13. Results of ECG data analysis from Pilot C during the night flight.

	Baseline			Operation			Ratio [%]		
	MatLab	PyHRV	Kubios	MatLab	PyHRV	Kubios	MatLab	PyHRV	Kubios
HR	89.266	89.772	94.132	82.536	83.138	83.293	-7.539	-7.390	-11.515
NNmean	672.145	674.017	637.400	726.951	724.597	720.350	8.154	7.504	13.014
SDNN	57.337	62.648	143.620	34.523	45.856	59.074	-39.789	-26.804	-58.868
RMSSD	25.315	47.369	43.298	21.874	26.153	28.308	-13.593	-44.788	-34.621
PNN20		0.282	0.355		0.321	0.349		14.119	-1.856
PNN50	0.057	0.061	0.063	0.034	0.040	0.039	-40.185	-33.790	-38.708
LF/HF (Lomb Scargle)	3.715	0.478		2.693	0.453		-27.519	-5.255	
LF/HF (Welch)	2.459			2.901			17.982		
LF/HF (Burg)	2.245			3.044			35.617		
LF/HF (FFT)	2.524	1.850	1.510	3.167	5.266	2.899	25.510	184.630	91.956
LF/HF (Auto Regression)		0.527	1.979		0.571	2.845		8.386	43.786

Table 14. Results of ECG data analysis from Pilot C during the day flight.

	Baseline			Operation			Ratio [%]		
	MatLab	PyHRV	Kubios	MatLab	PyHRV	Kubios	MatLab	PyHRV	Kubios
HR	93.027	93.515	93.054	100.264	101.602	101.490	7.780	8.647	9.066
NNmean	644.977	643.306	644.790	598.420	591.166	591.170	-7.218	-8.105	-8.316
SDNN	26.745	37.005	12.286	18.005	19.071	9.640	-32.678	-48.463	-21.535
RMSSD	10.616	39.321	7.719	6.490	5.172	5.062	-38.873	-86.847	-34.430
PNN20		0.024	0.013		0.001	0.001		-97.547	-95.562
PNN50	0.006	0.004	0.000	0.000	0.000	0.000	-100.000	-100.000	
LF/HF (Lomb Scargle)	3.923	0.465		16.550	0.550		321.882	18.152	
LF/HF (Welch)	12.842			8.884			-30.820		
LF/HF (Burg)	11.312			9.266			-18.088		
LF/HF (FFT)	12.372	1.046	7.048	9.254	12.338	10.318	-25.198	1079.433	46.407
LF/HF (Auto Regression)		0.531	6.267		0.627	11.675		18.205	86.308

Table 15. Results of ECG data analysis from Pilot C during the night flight.

	Baseline			Operation			Ratio [%]		
	MatLab	PyHRV	Kubios	MatLab	PyHRV	Kubios	MatLab	PyHRV	Kubios
HR	98.568	98.749	99.500	104.778	102.640	95.651	6.300	3.940	-3.868
NNmean	608.716	610.329	603.020	572.640	590.501	627.280	-5.927	-3.249	4.023
SDNN	60.175	51.117	20.001	13.332	78.958	49.564	-77.845	54.464	147.808
RMSSD	64.276	67.604	12.257	7.709	104.779	23.371	-88.007	54.989	90.675
PNN20		0.034	0.023		0.048	0.067		42.622	193.792
PNN50	0.011	0.028	0.014	0.002	0.047	0.033	-81.564	70.950	128.148
LF/HF (Lomb Scargle)	0.802	0.601		5.813	0.346		624.589	-42.525	
LF/HF (Welch)	1.637			4.128			152.162		
LF/HF (Burg)	1.531			4.629			202.380		
LF/HF (FFT)	1.687	0.309	3.495	4.372	0.712	20.374	159.178	130.164	482.880
LF/HF (Auto Regression)		0.494	1.369		0.461	19.122		-6.589	1296.888

5   Conclusion

This exploratory work investigated the use of different methods to measure workload, in order to use them as a subsidy for the assessment, validation and complementation of current flight standards, as well as for the proposal of new standards, related to the mental workload of military aviation pilots. For this purpose, an experiment was performed assessing and comparing the output of a set of methods in two different scenarios: day flight and night flight with NVG.

The workload is determined by the allocation of the mental resources required for the task achievement. In the impossibility of measuring directly this allocation, we used other indicators, based on physiological (ECG, GSR) and subjective methods (NASA-TLX, PVT test).

The GSR signals indicated that there was a change in fatigue, mental workload or both between the day flight and the NVG flight. On the other hand, the ECG signal does not point to a change in the pilots' mental workload. A possible explanation is that, given that the interval between flights was just over 30 h, the learning factor may have influenced the results. The only conclusion from the physiological data is that the flight with NVG generated more fatigue to the pilots than the day flight.

Regarding the subjective measures, NASA-TLX questionnaire has shown an inconclusive result, related to the variation in the mental workload, strengthening the idea that the learning effect had a significant influence on the final result.

However, an important item can be observed with this inconclusive result: the fact that the accomplishment of a day flight preceding the night favors the reduction of the mental effort of the pilots in the night flight with NVG, which is beneficial for flight safety.

On the other hand, the PVT test corroborated with the predicted in NOp n° 1/CAvEx, which results indicated the routine preceding the night flight have influence in the pilots' reaction time, making relevant the importance of well-rested and reduced working hours for crews employed on NVG flights.

It should be noted that, despite all technological developments, and the quality of the simulators used, there is a striking difference between the simulated flights and real flights, especially with the aircraft's reactions, weather conditions and the very feeling of safety of the aircraft crew while practicing flight in a simulator.

Due to the small sample, the short time between flights and the variations of results with different sensors, this study was not enough to rectify or ratify the problem issue related to NOv No. 1 of the CAvEx.

Thus, this work did not exhaust the proposed objective, becoming essential to continue the studies, expanding the sample and using the measurements obtained from actual flights, with different aircraft models and in the most diverse conditions of employability, such as: visual flight night, tactical flight, combat flight and in instrument conditions.

Acknowledgments. This study was financed in part by the Coordenação de Aperfeiçoamento de Pessoal de Nível Superior – Brasil (CAPES) – Financial Code 001.

References

1. Leplat, J., Cuny, X.: Introdução à Psicologia do Trabalho (Translation: Helena Domingos). Fundação Calouste Gulbenkian, Lisboa (1983)
2. Wisner, A.: A Inteligência no Trabalho. Textos Selecionados de Ergonomia, São Paulo (1994)
3. Corrêa, F.P.: Carga Mental e Ergonomia. Dissertation, Master in Production Engineering, Graduate Program in Production Engineering, UFSC, Florianópolis (2003)
4. Cardoso, M.S., Gontijo, L.A.: Evaluation of mental workload and performance measurement: NASA TLX and SWAT. G&P **19**, 873–884 (2012)
5. ICAO: Investigation of human factors in accidents and incidents, Circular 240 (1993)
6. Baumer, M.H.: Avaliação da Carga Mental de Trabalho em Pilotos da Aviação Militar. Dissertation, Master in Production Engineering, Graduate Program in Production Engineering, UFSC, Florianópolis (2003)
7. Jenkins, D.P., Stanton, N.A., Salmon, P.M., Rafferty, L.A., Walker, G.H., Baber, C.: Human Factors Methods: A Practical Guide for Engineering and Desing, vol. 2. Ashgate Publishing Limited (2013)
8. Borghini, G., Astolfi, L., Astolfi, A., Mattia, D., Babiloni, F.: Measuring neurophysiological signals in aircraft pilots and car drivers for the assessment of mental workload, fatigue and drowsiness. Neurosci. Biobehav. Rev. **44**, 58–75 (2014)
9. Hart, S.G., Staveland, L.E.: Development of NASA-TLX (task load index): results of empirical and theoretical research. In: Advances in Psychology, vol. 52, pp. 139–183. North-Holland (1988)
10. Basner, M., Dinges, D.F.: Maximizing sensitivy of the psychomotor vigilance test (PVT) to sleep loss. Sleep **34**(5), 581–591 (2011)
11. Health and Safety Executive. https://www.hse.gov.uk/research/rrhtm/rr446.htm. Accessed 18 Aug 2021
12. Sousa, M.B.C., Silva, H.P.A., Galvão-Coelho, N.L.: Stress response: I. Homeostasis and allostasis theory. Psychol. Stud. **20**(1), 2–11 (2015)
13. Midha, S., Maior, H.A., Wilson, M.L., Sharples, S.: Measuring mental workload variations in office work tasks using fNIRS. Int. J. Hum. Comput. Stud. **147**, 102580 (2021)
14. Perini, R., Veicsteinas, A.: Heart rate variability and autonomic activity at rest and during exercise in various physiological conditions. Eur. J. Appl. Physiol. **90**(3–4), 317–325 (2003). https://doi.org/10.1007/s00421-003-0953-9

Exploring the Influence of Information Overload, Internet Addiction, and Social Network Addiction, on Students' Well-Being and Academic Outcomes

Hasah H. AlHeneidi[1] and Andrew P. Smith[2(✉)]

[1] Psychological Researcher, Social Development Office, Kuwait City, Kuwait
[2] Centre for Occupational and Health Psychology, School of Psychology, Cardiff University, Cardiff CF10 3AS, UK
smithap@cardiff.ac.uk

Abstract. This study explored how students' main information problems during the information age, namely internet addiction, information overload, and social network addiction, influence holistic well-being and academic attainment. The participants were 226 university students, all UK based and regular internet users. They answered the Internet Addiction Test, Information Overload Scale, Bergen Social Media Addiction Scale, and the Wellbeing Process Questionnaire. Data were analysed with SPSS using correlation and linear regression analysis. The univariate analyses confirmed the negative impact of information overload, internet addiction and social media addiction on positive well-being but not academic attainment. However, multivariate analyses controlling for established predictors of well-being showed that the effects of information overload, internet addiction and social media addiction were largely non-significant, confirming other research using this analysis strategy. Future research should examine the type of internet use as well as the extent of it.

Keywords: Internet addiction · Information overload · Social media addiction · Well-being · Mental workload

1 Introduction

1.1 Mental Workload

The study of mental workload has received an escalating interest from researchers in various fields [1–3]. Various research approaches have been used to investigate workload [4, 5]. For a long time, mental workload has been researched primarily in psychology and other related areas [6, 7]. In addition to creating many primary mental workload measures [12–17], mental workload has been examined in laboratory settings and occupational frameworks [8–11]. Measures such as task parameters, physiological measures, and self-assessment measures such as the Subjective Workload Assessment Technique [4], the NASA Task Load Index [18], and the Workload Profile [19] have been widely used. The

© Springer Nature Switzerland AG 2021
L. Longo and M. C. Leva (Eds.): H-WORKLOAD 2021, CCIS 1493, pp. 116–135, 2021.
https://doi.org/10.1007/978-3-030-91408-0_8

emerging need to assess and measure workload perception in workers has led researchers to use single-item measures, which are strongly correlated with longer scales, and can efficiently predict the workers' well-being.

The present study examined factors that can be related to a holistic concept of mental workload. The first, information overload, can be considered as a chronic state of excessive mental workload, often reflecting input that has high demand or needs to be ignored. Excessive internet use may also lead to workload issues, with the person ignoring other activities while on the internet or thinking about internet content, such as messages on social media. The concepts of information overload, internet addiction, problematic internet use and social media addiction are now introduced. The aim of the present study was to examine the associations between these variables and subjective well-being. This was carried out using the well-being process model, which has established predictors that must be controlled when assessing the effects of specific risk factors (in this case, information overload and internet use). Details of this model are given after the sections on information overload, internet addiction and social media addiction.

1.2 Information Overload

Information overload (IO) is defined as the difficulty the information user experience in understanding a current issue or making a decision due to the high presence of information. Toffler first mentioned information overload in his book "Future Shock" [20] and defined it as a state of stress experienced when the given amount of information exceeds the limit of information user processing capacity [21]. Information overload is a form of cognitive barrier that blocks, limits, or hampers the information-seeking process and causes frustration to the information user [22], resulting in a flawed decision-making process, confusing the user and resulting in low work quality [23]. Previous studies have reported the psychological and economic consequences of information overload, resulting in severe implications at an individual and organisational level. The ongoing studies on information overload revealed that information overload costs the US economy annually US$900 billion [24], which results in work stress that triggers psychological and physical outcomes like depression, anxiety, heart disease and high blood pressure [25]. Recent information overload implications are attributed to the progressing use of and outgrowing reliability on different internet activities, which results in more distraction and continuous information flow. The heavy load of information results in confusing the user, affecting their ability to set priorities, or difficulty recalling information [26]. Attention is a limited cognitive resource that is defective in overload conditions [27]. Miller [28] hypothesised that there is a cognitive threshold, and when the information flow rises, it leads to a cognitive decline in processing the information.

Numerous studies have investigated and documented the psychological and economic consequences of information overload in the workplace. However, there is a lack of research about students' perceptions of information overload and its psychological consequences and association with well-being. There is also insufficient research on the combined effects of internet addiction, social media addiction and information overload.

1.3   Internet Addiction

The study of internet usage began in the mid-1990s. There has not been a single approved term that identifies problematic internet use, although research on the internet and information technology has progressed. Scientists have used different terms to measure internet addiction; "Pathological Internet Use" [29–31], "Problematic Internet Use" [32, 33], "Maladaptive Internet Use" [33, 34], Internet Behavior Dependence" [35], "Internet Dependence" [36, 37], "Internet Over-use" [38], "Misuse of the Internet" [39], and "Internet-related disorder" [40]. The different terms reflect the unrestricted use of the internet and the consequent abandonment of other responsibilities. Two primary models for conceptualising problematic internet usage symptoms have been developed, and they are detailed under the topics below.

1.4   Impulse-Control Disorder Model

Young [37] has conceptualised and created the Internet addiction diagnostic questionnaire based on impulse control disorder, using the DSM-IV as a basis for pathological gambling. Common disorder symptoms include failure to quit or to decrease time spent online, being mentally preoccupied with internet activates, having an intense desire to connect online, feeling a sense of loss of control, having symptoms of tolerance and withdrawal, and a failure to meet social and academic duties. Young's approach was supported by other researchers and hypothesised that problematic Internet use is a form of obsessive-compulsive disorder (OCD). Young characterised this as a repeated pathological behaviour of online activities that closely match some of the most typical symptoms of OCD, including uncontrollable and time-consuming behaviours [30]. However, Shapira et al.'s [41] findings with university students indicate that problematic internet use should only be classified as an impulse control disorder. Nevertheless, based on the DSM-IV diagnostic criteria, the provided model is supported by clinical cases and publications and can be quickly adopted.

1.5   Cognitive-Behavioural Model

Davis [29, 42] introduced the Cognitive-Behavioral model for problematic internet use, emphasising the psychological traits and personal cognitions that motivate pathological internet usage. He suggested that the individual's cognitions are triggering each abnormal and intensive behaviour and that PIU was caused by pre-existing psychological issues such as social anxiety, depression, poor self-esteem, or maladaptive cognitions. Davis divided problematic internet users into two categories. The first group, known as Generalised Problematic Internet Users (GPIU), were addicted to the internet itself rather than a specific internet activity. If other difficulties, such as poor work performance, are present, they display more significant internet addiction symptoms. According to Davis, pathological internet usage is caused by the "individual social context," which includes a lack of social support, isolation, and social shyness.

The other type is the Specified Problematic Internet Users (SPIU), who are drawn to a specific online activity, such as gambling or viewing social media content, and who may discontinue their internet addiction if they find a different source of the same material. Holden [43] agreed that most online addictive behaviours are comparable to offline addictive behaviours, including shopping, gambling, and pornography. Holden added that the internet combines all activities that an individual may become addicted to. Holmes' [44] findings confirmed Davis' hypothesis, which proposed that internet addiction resulted from psychological difficulties. Davis' model was further confirmed by the findings of Petrie and Gunn [45], who discovered that internet addiction was negatively correlated with positivity and extroversion and positively associated with depression. They concluded that internet addicts were most likely depressed and introverted.

1.6   Social Networks Addiction

In recent years, the usage of Social Network Services (SNS) has expanded, and it has become an integrated component of millions of people's everyday lives to share and connect with others. Individuals may communicate continually with others thanks to the development of speedy connection technology, smartphone usage, and a persistent internet connection [46]. Many people prefer smartphone-based SNS [47], and the advantages of smartphone-based SNS include the capability to connect at any time or place, feeling connected, and higher life satisfaction if the connection is managed [48, 49]. However, constant use of social media might have severe psychological and informational implications. Information overload, communication overload, and social fatigue may all be exacerbated by social media [21, 50–52].

1.7   Problematic Internet Use and Well-Being

A detailed review of problematic internet use and well-being literature can be found in our latest publications [53–55]. The key findings are summarised briefly below. Several studies have found that problematic internet use is linked to reduced psychological well-being [56–58]. Specific components of well-being, such as subjective vitality and happiness, have been proven to be lower in people who use the internet problematically [59].

Longitudinal studies of problematic internet use have revealed that negative outcome scores are higher [60, 61]. However, some studies have obtained conflicting outcomes [62]. The main problem with most studies on problematic internet use is that they do not account for other predictors of well-being outcomes. For example, Alheneidi and Smith [54] discovered that problematic internet use was related to lower well-being, but this impact was no longer significant when established well-being predictors were added to the analysis. These findings provide credibility to the cognitive-behavioural model of internet usage [29, 42], concentrating on the motivating psychological characteristics and personal cognitions behind problematic internet use.

1.8   The Well-Being Process

Well-being is challenging to define and involves many different factors. The "well-being process model" uses a comprehensive, holistic approach to well-being and provides a theoretical framework for developing a questionnaire that can be used in practice and policy. The initial study was founded on the Demands-Resources-Individual Effects (DRIVE) model, which was created to undertake occupational stress research [63–67]. Job features, perceived stress, personal traits such as coping techniques, and adverse outcomes were incorporated in this model (e.g. anxiety and depression). The model's next version [68–71] included positive qualities such as self-esteem, self-efficacy, and optimism, as well as a positive appraisal (e.g., job satisfaction) and outcomes (e.g. positive affect and happiness). Positive outcomes serve as the foundation for a wide range of approaches to subjective well-being. However, because they involve different CNS pathways, it is critical to incorporate both positive and negative components of well-being.

One initial concern was that the well-being process model required assessing numerous factors and using large scales, which resulted in a questionnaire that was extraordinarily long and unappealing to the participants. Short scales were constructed to address this issue, and they were significantly correlated with the longer scales from which they were formed [72–77]. The questionnaire has been adapted for use in student research [77]. Academic attainment and perception of workload, work efficiency, and course stress have been added to the outcome measures [78, 79]. Student stressors (e.g., too much academic work), social support, psychological capital (self-esteem, self-efficacy, and optimism), and negative coping methods are known determinants of student health (e.g. avoidance, wishful thinking and self-blame).

The present study's initial aim was to investigate whether internet addiction, social network addiction, and information and media overload from IT and media sources are linked to lower well-being and lower academic achievement. If the univariate analyses results were significant, multivariate analyses incorporating predictor variables of well-being and attainment would be performed to assess whether internet addiction, social network addiction and information overload had independent impacts or if they could be accounted for by other factors.

2   Measures

2.1   The Perceive Information Overload Scale

The information overload scale has been developed to measure the primary two sources that contribute to causing information overload, namely cyber-based and environment-based information overload. The Perceived Information Overload Scale was developed by Misra and Stokols [80] and had good internal consistency ($\alpha = .86$) and validity. The questionnaire consists of 16-items and is sub-divided into two subscales that measure environment-based and cyber-based information overload. The first part of the scale consists of nine items that assess the user's perception of information overload from cyber-based sources during the previous month, using a Likert scale of 5-points (0 = never and four = very often). Participants were asked how often they were overwhelmed by replying to emails/instant messages quickly; how often they felt overwhelmed with the amount of messages/emails or any social network notifications. The following part of the scale explores the environment-based information overload using seven items. The questions explore if the workplace demands exceed the participant's ability to function effectively, measuring how noisy and distracting their work and the home environment

are. The sum of the items reflects the participants' perception of the cyber-based information overload score and environment-based information overload score. Although
information overload is a form of stress, Misra and Stokols [80] found that the Perceived Information Overload Scale score and the Perceived Stress Scale score did not
overlap, which indicated that information overload scales measure different concepts
from perceived stress. Five previous studies investigated information overload and well-
being [81–85]. All the findings confirm the negative outcome of information overload
on well-being, although two studies showed a positive effect of information overload if
the internet connection is controlled.

2.2 Internet Addiction Test (IAT)

The IAT has been widely used and translated into many languages. Though numerous
internet addiction measures have been developed, the IAT has high face validity and
is a reliable instrument, and it is the first validated questionnaire to assess internet
addiction [86]. The measure was developed based on DSM-IV criteria of pathological
gambling, which identify behavioural addiction. Using 20 items, the IAT scale examines
the participant use of the internet for non-academic or non-job-related purposes during
the last month. Using a Likert scale, participants respond on a scale from $0 =$ not
applicable and $5 =$ always. For example, 'How often do you prefer the excitement of
the 'Internet to intimacy with your partner?' and 'How often do you try to hide how
long you have been online?'. The IAT identifies three types of internet users based on
their dependency on the internet: controlled internet users, problematic internet users,
and internet addicts.

- Scores from 31–49 reflect regular internet users who control their online activity.
- 50–79 points reflect occasional or frequent problematic internet use that might
  interfere with daily life flow.
- 80–100 points indicate heavy internet usage that is significantly affecting the
  participant's life.

2.3 Measuring Well-Being

Measuring well-being involves covering all the factors that contribute to well-being
outcomes. However, using multi-measures may result in negative features associated
with a lengthy questionnaire, like requiring high effort and time-consuming, which
results in a low response rate [87]. Therefore, short measures are ideal for measuring
well-being in empirical research. Perceived health [88] and quality of life [89] have been
successfully measured with single items, and this approach has been widely utilised.
Fisher et al. [87] found that single-item measures improve face validity and reduce
criteria contamination.

2.3.1 The Well-Being Process Questionnaire (WPQ)

The Wellbeing Process Questionnaire (WPQ) was created to explore worker and student
well-being [73, 75]. The concepts were measured using short scales correlated with more

lengthy versions of the measures [90]. As a result, a solid and reliable short questionnaire for assessing well-being was developed [91]. The nature of well-being suggested that one has to consider several variables [92]. Using short items to measure well-being is ideal as it saves time, cost and effort. The well-being outcome score can be calculated using the combined effects of positive well-being (e.g., life satisfaction and happiness) and negative well-being (e.g., depression, anxiety, and stress [73]). The WPQ can be used in conjunction with other multi-item measures and known predictors of control. The WPQ is adaptable and may be tailored to various populations. Williams, Smith, and colleagues have created a bank of questions used with various groups. The outcome of utilising the WPQ with a variety of samples, including nurses [73, 75, 76, 93], students [77], university staff [76], police officers [95], and train workers [95]. The established factors consistently predict well-being outcomes in all the WPQ studies, and the short questionnaire often has the same predictive validity as multi-item scales.

2.3.2   The Student WPQ

The Student WPQ is a multi-dimensional single-item measure of well-being that includes a stressor measure based on students' circumstances and characteristics developed from the Inventory of College Students' Recent Life Experiences (ICSRLE), such as developmental difficulties, social mistreatment, and time pressure [96]. Well-being variables based on the DRIVE model are measured in the student WPQ version, including negative coping, social support, and positive personality (self-efficacy, self-esteem and optimism). The WPQ questions are answered on a 10-point scale (0 = not at all, 10 = extremely). The items include questions about the student's social support, personality, positive and negative outcomes, coping style, life satisfaction, life stress, physical fatigue, and mental fatigue, as well as questions about the student's social support, personality, positive and negative outcomes, coping style, life satisfaction, life stress, physical fatigue, and mental fatigue [90]. The WPQ scales yield a clear picture of positive and negative well-being outcomes, as well as determinants of well-being. Well-being predictors are measured with short scales. The scores for depression, negative affect, and anxiety add up to a negative well-being score. The sum of the scores for life stress, physical fatigue, and mental fatigue is the negative appraisal score. The sum of positive effects scores and positive appraisal, represented by the life satisfaction score, gives an overall positive well-being score.

2.4   Bergen Social Media Addiction Scale (BSMAS)

This scale was used to see how a specific sort of internet addiction, social network addiction, affects well-being, which Young [31] identified as one of the addictive online activities like texting and emailing. The Social Media Addiction Scale is an adaption of the Bergen Facebook Addiction Scale (BFAS) and is a validated and reliable measure = .83 used to investigate the addiction of social media users [97]. Griffiths [98] proposed six potential addiction components for the scale: salience, tolerance, withdrawal, mood modulation, relapse, and conflict [97]. The social media scale consist of six items, answered on a 5-point Likert scale; ranging from 1–5, where (1) is very rarely and (5) is very often, regarding experiences during the past year, e.g., "How often during the last year have you felt an urge to use social media more and more?".

3   The Present Study

This study aimed to expand the findings on the effects of information overload and internet addiction on well-being in a university student sample. It also examined the effects of different types of internet use, focusing on social network addiction and its effects on the well-being and academic performance of a large sample of UK full-time students. In summary, this study aimed to investigate cross-sectional associations in 1) The prevalence of information overload (IO), internet addiction (IA) and Social Network Addiction (SNA) in a UK student sample; 2) The effects of Io, IA and SNA and other types on well-being and academic outcomes.

4   Methodology

4.1   Ethical Approval

The research received approval from the Ethics Committee at the School of Psychology, Cardiff University.

4.2   Sample Size Calculation

In determining the appropriate sample size, the Tabachnick and Fidell [99] formula was considered. Tabachnick and Fidell suggested the following formula for sample size consideration, considering the number of independent variables used in the regression analyses: $N \geq 50 + 8$ m (m = number of independent variables). A medium-size relationship between dependent and independent variable was assumed, with $\alpha = .05$, $\beta = .20$ and ten independent variables in the regression model, $N \geq 50 + (8)(10) = 130$. The formula suggested that a sample size of 130 would be appropriate.

4.3   Design

The present study was a cross-sectional online survey delivered through the Qualtrics platform.

4.4   Participants

Two hundred and twenty-six UK-based students, who were regular internet users, participated in the study by answering online questionnaires through Qualtrics. Each participant was paid five pounds for completing the questionnaires. Fifty per cent were male 50%, with an age range of 18–71 years (SD = 13.4). The mean number of hours spent at the University per was 30 h.

Consent forms, instructions and debrief forms were included with the questionnaires. The aim of the study was explained, and participants were given all relevant information.

4.5 The Survey

The questionnaires used included the Perceived Information Overload Scale, consisting of 16 items measuring cyber and environmental information overload [80]. The Internet Addiction Test consists of 20 items that examine the use of the internet for non-academic or non-job purposes during the last month items measuring addiction based on DSM-IV criteria of pathological gambling [31]. The Student WPQ [77] is a multi-dimensional scale of well-being that includes a measure of stressors based on students' circumstances and factors and measures other well-being predictors based on the DRIVE model: negative coping, social support, and positive personality (self-efficacy, self-esteem and optimism). The Bergen Social Media Addiction Scale (BSMAS), which consists of six items to assess social media addiction based on six addiction elements [97], was also used.

Demographic data were collected to measure general health, gender, age, sleep quality, height, weight and smoking. In addition, the academic outcomes were perceived course stress and work efficiency, with both measured using a 10-point scale.

4.6 Statistical Analysis

SPSS 20.00 was used to conduct all statistical analyses. Data met the assumption of normality. The reliability of the scales was tested using Cronbach alpha coefficients. Pearson correlations were conducted to evaluate the strength of the relationships among information overload, internet addiction, and the well-being total outcome and well-being factors using Cohen standards [100]. These initial correlations give an indication of the significance and size of bivariate associations. A correlation of 0.1 represents a small effect, one of 0.3 a medium-size effect, and one above 0.5 a large effect. The problem with univariate analyses is that they do not control for the influence of correlated attributes. For example, predictors of well-being may also be correlated with information overload and internet activity, and it is important to statistically adjust for these correlated attributes. Multiple linear regression and stepwise regression were conducted in order to assess the impact of information overload, internet addiction, SNA, and different internet use on the students' well-being. The initial analyses examined these variables alone. The 'Enter' variable selection method was chosen for the linear regression model. Multiple linear regression was conducted to predict the effects of different internet use on internet addiction, information overload, positive and negative well-being, and positive and negative appraisal. A total well-being outcome score was calculated by summing positive well-being, negative well-being, positive appraisal, and negative appraisal. Academic outcomes were also examined. Subsequent analyses included the established predictors of well-being and academic outcomes to determine whether any effects of information overload and internet activity remained significant.

5   Results

5.1 Internet Addiction, PIU and SNA Prevalence

The results were examined based on the thresholds for defining internet addiction, problematic internet usage, social network addiction and information overload. The following frequencies were obtained for the different categories:

- 0% were internet addicts
- 24.6% of the sample suffered from problematic internet use
- 28.8% were social network addicts
- 25.4% suffered from information overload "very often."

5.2 Pearson Correlation Analysis of Associations Between Information Overload, Internet Addiction, SNA, and Well-Being Variables

A Pearson correlation analysis was conducted using the information overload, internet addiction, SNA, and well-being variables. The results revealed a significant positive correlation between information overload and internet addiction ($r = 0.76$, $p < .0001$). The correlation coefficient between information overload and internet addiction indicated a large relationship. There was a significant positive correlation between information overload and total SNA ($r = 0.71$, $p < .0001$). The correlation coefficient between information overload and SNA indicated a large relationship. There was a significant positive correlation between information overload and negative appraisal ($r = 0.51$, $p < .0001$). The correlation coefficient between information overload and negative appraisal indicated a large relationship showing that as information overload increases, negative appraisal increases. There was a significant negative correlation between information overload and positive wellbeing ($r = -.18$, $p < .01$). The correlation coefficient between information overload and positive well-being was .18, indicating a small relationship. There was a significant positive correlation between information overload and negative well-being ($r = .45$ $p < .005$). The correlation coefficient between information overload and negative well-being was .45, indicating a moderate relationship as information overload increases negative well-being tends to increase.

There was a significant positive correlation between internet addiction and SNA ($r = 0.84$, $p < .0001$). The correlation coefficient indicated a large relationship. There was a significant positive correlation between internet addiction and total negative appraisal ($r = 0.41$, $p < .005$). The correlation coefficient between internet addiction and negative appraisal indicated a moderate relationship. There was a significant negative correlation between internet addiction and total positive wellbeing ($r = -0.14$, $p < .001$). The correlation coefficient between internet addiction and positive well-being indicated a small relationship. There was a significant positive correlation between internet addiction and negative wellbeing ($r = 0.40$, $p < .005$). The correlation coefficient between internet addiction and negative well-being indicated a moderate relationship confirming that as internet addiction increases, negative well-being increases.

There was a significant positive correlation between SNA and total negative appraisal ($r = 0.28$, $p < .005$). The correlation coefficient between SNA and negative appraisal indicated a small relationship. There was a significant negative correlation between SNA and positive well-being ($r = -0.14$, $p < .01$). The correlation coefficient between SNA and positive well-being was 0.14 indicating a small relationship. There was a significant positive correlation between SNA and negative well-being ($r = 0.28$, $p < .005$). The correlation coefficient between SNA and negative well-being indicated a small relationship. Information overload was positively correlated with course stress ($r = .33$, $p < .005$), with the size of the correlation indicating a small relationship between course stress and information overload. SNA was positively correlated with course stress ($r = .22$, $p < .01$), and a small association were indicated. SNA was negatively correlated with smoking (r = −.15, p < .02). Internet addiction was positively associated with course stress (r = .32, p < .0001), indicating that course stress would increase if internet addiction increased. Internet addiction was negatively correlated with smoking (r = −.183, p < .006), showing a small association. Internet addiction was negatively correlated with sleep quality (r = −.13, p < .01) which indicated a small association. Table 1 presents the results of the correlations.

Table 1. Pearson correlation matrix among information overload, internet addiction, SNA, and well-being outcomes and demographics

Variable	Information overload	SNA	Internet addiction	Well-being
Social support	.11	−.038	.020	.49**
Negative coping	.47**	.30**	.40**	.28**
Positive wellbeing	−.18**	−.13*	−.14*	−.40**
Negative wellbeing	.45**	.28**	.40**	.62**
Negative appraisal	.51**	.28**	.41**	.54**
Positive appraisal	.109	.057	.072	−.73**
Stressors	.69**	.63**	.63**	.53**
Positive personality	.15*	.07	.07	-.77**
Course stress	.33**	.22**	.32**	.44**

5.3 Information Overload, Internet Addiction and SNA Predicting Total Well-Being

To test the associations between information overload, internet addiction, SNA and the well-being outcome, a linear multiple regression was conducted. The results of the linear regression model were significant (F(3,227) = 28.43, p < .001, R2 = 0.27), indicating that approximately 27% of the variance in well-being outcome was explained by information overload, internet addiction and SNA. Information overload significantly predicted the wellbeing outcome (B = 0.40, t(227) = 5.59, p < .001). Similarly, internet addiction significantly predicted the wellbeing outcome (B = 0.29, t(227) = 2.56, p = .00), as did SNA (B = .46, t(227) = 4.51 p = .00). Table 2 summarises the results of the regression model. These results show that although internet addiction, information overload and SNA are correlated, they still have independent effects on well-being.

Stepwise regression was conducted to investigate the influence of the independent variables, information overload, internet addiction and SNA, on the well-being outcome after controlling for demographics and well-being covariates (stressors, social support, positive personality, and negative coping). The results indicated that the effects of information overload, internet addiction and SNA were not significant in predicting well-being; neither were the interaction variables of information overload* internet addiction, SNA*internet addiction or SNA*information overload.

Table 2. Results for multiple linear regression with information overload, Internet addiction and SNA predicting wellbeing outcome

Variable	B	SE	β	T	P
(Intercept)	19.64	2.78		7.06	.00
Information overload	.40	.07	.49	5.59	.00
Internet addiction	.29	.11	.30	2.56	.01
SNA	.46	.10	.28	4.51	.00

Note. F(3,227) = 28.43, p < .00, R2 = 0.27.

5.4 Information Overload, Internet Addiction and SNA Predicting Specific Appraisal and Outcome Measures

Stepwise regressions were conducted to investigate the influence of the independent variables, information overload, internet addiction and SNA, after controlling for demographics and well-being covariates (stressors, social support, positive personality, and negative coping) on the specific appraisal and outcome measures. The results indicated that the effects of information overload, internet addiction and SNA were not significant in predicting positive well-being, negative well-being or positive appraisal. The results indicated that only information overload was significant in predicting negative appraisal after controlling for demographics and well-being covariates ($B = 0.09, t(217) = 3.47, p < .001$). Internet addiction and SNA were not significant in predicting negative appraisal. The results of the last model of the stepwise regression are presented in Table 3.

5.5 Information Overload, Internet Addiction and SNA Predicting Academic Outcomes

Through a stepwise regression, the influence of information overload, internet addiction, and SNA on academic outcomes were examined, controlling for demographics and well-being covariates. No significant effects of information overload, internet addiction and SNA were obtained.

6 Discussion

Information overload, internet addiction, and SNA were all significantly associated with the total well-being outcome and specific appraisal and outcome measures. The regression results showed that information overload, internet addiction, and SNA had significant effects on the well-being outcome; however, after controlling for well-being covariates (stressors, social support, positive personality and negative coping), these effects were no longer significant. Further analyses investigated the effects of information overload, internet addiction and SNA on well-being components while controlling for demographics and well-being covariates, and information overload only influenced negative appraisal. The effects of internet addiction and SNA on different well-being

Table 3. Stepwise regression last model results information overload, Internet addiction and SNA predicting negative appraisal

Variable	B	SE	β	T	P
(Constant)	2.05	1.58		1.29	.19
Smoking	−.37	.45	−.04	−.81	.41
Student stress	.13	.09	.08	1.42	.15
Gender	.48	.44	.05	1.08	.27
Sleep quality	−.04	.35	−.01	−.11	.90
General health	−.25	.12	−.12	−1.95	.05
Stressors	.01	.02	.04	.55	.57
Social support	.09	.04	.13	1.93	.05
Positive personality	−.10	.05	−.15	−2.09	.03
Negative coping	.33	.04	.45	6.68	.00
Information overload	**.09**	**.02**	**.28**	**3.47**	**.001**
SNA	−.11	.06	−.17	−1.87	.069
Internet addiction	.03	.03	.09	.94	.34

components were not significant after controlling demographics and well-being covariates. The independent variables' influence on academic outcomes were also investigated, and the results showed no significant effect after controlling for well-being covariates and demographics. After controlling for demographics and established well-being predictors, information overload, internet addiction, and SNA did not affect positive well-being, positive appraisal, or negative appraisal. The impact of internet addiction and SNA on academic outcomes were explored, but no significant effect was found. These results confirm other research using similar analysis strategies [53–55, 101, 102], which showed that effects on well-being initially attributed to information overland and internet use can be accounted for by the established predictors of well-being (positive personality; coping; social support, and student stressors). Such results show that it is important to use a multivariate approach, as univariate analyses do not consider the effects of correlated attributes. This is now an established approach in well-being research and should be applied to studies of mental workload, especially those using subjective reports. It is now important to determine whether similar effects are observed when objective outcomes are used. Indeed, many approaches to mental workload can be applied to the well-being area, which, up to now, has focused solely on subjective well-being rather than considering other indicators. When one moves to objective outcomes, the term well-being is often replaced by other concepts. For example, when objective signs of illness are observed, the topic is usually referred to as health. Similarly, in the work domain, changes in absenteeism, presenteeism, accidents and injuries are referred to as health and safety outcomes.

As well as examining different outcomes, further research is required to study samples that have a more extended experience of the issues examined here (e.g. workers) to determine the effect that age and occupation may play in various internet use, internet addiction and SNA on employees' well-being. It is also essential to examine the type of activity carried out on the internet. For example, interference from internet activity may be a more critical variable than internet use per se [53, 55, 101, 102]. Research can, therefore, continue with the present approach but manipulate samples and outcomes in order to determine whether information overload and internet activity do influence well-being. Alternatively, subjective well-being can be replaced with other outcomes which may be less affected by the other types of independent variables that have become the established predictors of well-being.

7 Limitations

The present research needs to be extended by using longitudinal studies, preferably involving interventions. In addition, more precise information on internet use needs to be obtained, and a diary methodology may be appropriate. Objective measures should also be used to complement the subjective reports. As discussed above, wider approaches, such as those used in studies of mental workload, may help to develop the area.

8 Conclusions

The results from the present study show that information overload, internet addiction, and social media addiction, when viewed in isolation, may affect well-being. However, these effects were not observed when other established predictors of well-being were statistically controlled. These results confirm other recent research and suggest that further investigation of the type of internet usage, not just the extent of it, is required. It will also be interesting to see whether a paradigm shift, based on the methodology of mental workload, identifies clearer effects of information overload and internet use than those observed in studies of subjective well-being.

Conflict of Interest. The authors of this article declare no conflict of interest.

References

1. Longo, L., Leva, M.C. (eds.): Human Mental Workload: Models and Applications. H-WORKLOAD 2017. Communications in Computer and Information Science, vol. 726, pp. 251–263. Springer, Cham (2017). https://doi.org/10.1007/978-3-030-32423-0
2. Longo, L., Leva, M.C. (eds.): Human Mental Workload: Models and Applications. H-WORKLOAD 2018. Communications in Computer and Information Science. Springer, Cham (2019)
3. Longo, L., Leva, M.C. (eds.): Human Mental Workload: Models and Applications. H-WORKLOAD 2019. Communications in Computer and Information Science. Springer, Cham (2019)

4. Reid, G.B., Nygren, T.E.: The subjective workload assessment technique: a scaling procedure for measuring mental workload. Adv. Psychol. **52**, 185–218 (1988)
5. Stassen, H.G., Johannsen, G., Moray, N.: Internal representation, internal model, human performance model and mental workload. Automatica **26**(4), 811–820 (1990)
6. De Waard, D.: The Measurement of Drivers' Mental Workload. University of Groningen The Traffic Research Centre VSC (1996)
7. Hart, S.G.: Nasa-task load index (NASA-TLX); 20 years later. In: Human Factors and Ergonomics Society Annual Meeting. vol. 50. Sage Journals (2006)
8. Smith, A.P., Smith, K.: Effects of workload and time of day on performance and mood. In: Megaw, E.D. (ed.) Contemporary Ergonomics, pp. 497–502. Taylor & Francis, London (1988)
9. Evans, M.S., Harborne, D., Smith, A.P: Developing an objective indicator of fatigue: an alternative mobile version of the Psychomotor Vigilance Task (m-PVT). Presented at: H-WORKLOAD 2018: International Symposium on Human Mental Workload: Models and Applications, Amsterdam, The Netherlands, 20–21 September 2018. Longo, L., Leva, M.C. (eds.): H-WORKLOAD 2018, CCIS 1012, pp. 147–159, 2019. Springer Nature, Cham (2019)
10. Smith, A.P., Smith, H.N.: Workload, fatigue and performance in the rail industry. In: Longo, L., Leva, M.C. (eds.) Human Mental Workload: Models and Applications. H-WORKLOAD 2017. Communications in Computer and Information Science, vol. 726, pp. 251–263. Springer, Cham (2017)
11. Fan, J., Smith, A.P.: Mental workload and other causes of different types of fatigue in rail staff. In: Longo, L., Leva, M.C. (eds.) H-WORKLOAD 2018. CCIS, vol. 1012, pp. 147–159. Springer, Cham (2019). https://doi.org/10.1007/978-3-030-14273-5_9
12. Cortes Torres, C.C., Sampei, K., Sato, M., Raskar, R., Miki, N.: Workload assessment with eye movement monitoring aided by non-invasive and unobtrusive micro-fabricated optical sensors. In: Adjunct Proceedings of the 28th Annual ACM Symposium on User Interface Software & Technology, pp. 53–54 (2015)
13. Yoshida, Y., Ohwada, H., Mizoguchi, F., Iwasaki, H.: Classifying cognitive load and driving situation with machine learning. Int. J. Mach. Learn. Comput. **4**(3), 210–215 (2014)
14. Wilson, G.F., Eggemeier, T.F.: Mental workload measurement. In: Karwowski, W. (ed.) International Encyclopedia of Ergonomics and Human Factors, 2nd edn., vol. 1, Chap. 167. Taylor & Francis, London (2006)
15. Young, M.S., Stanton, N.A.: Mental workload. In: Stanton, N.A., Hedge, A., Brookhuis, K., Salas, E., Hendrick, H.W. (eds.) Handbook of Human Factors and Ergonomics Methods, Chap. 39, pp. 1–9. CRC Press, Boca Raton (2004)
16. Young, M.S., Stanton, N.A.: Mental workload: theory, measurement, and application. In: Karwowski, W. (ed.) International Encyclopedia of Ergonomics and Human Factors, 2nd edn., vol. 1, pp. 818–821. Taylor & Francis, London (2006)
17. Moustafa, K., Luz, S., Longo, L.: Assessment of mental workload: a comparison of machine learning methods and subjective assessment techniques. In: Longo, L., Leva, M.C. (eds.) H-WORKLOAD 2017. CCIS, vol. 726, pp. 30–50. Springer, Cham (2017). https://doi.org/10.1007/978-3-319-61061-0_3
18. Hart, S.G., Staveland, L.E.: Development of NASA-TLX (Task Load Index): Results of empirical and theoretical research. Adv. Psychol. **52**(C), 139–183 (1988)
19. Tsang, P.S., Velazquez, V.L.: Diagnosticity and multi-dimensional subjective work- load ratings. Ergonomics **39**(3), 358–381 (1996)
20. Toffler, A.: Future Shock. Bantam Books, New York (1970)
21. Eppler, M.J., Mengis, J.: The concept of information overload: a review of literature from organisation science, accounting, marketing, and related disciplines. Inf. Soc. **20**(5), 325–344 (2004)

22. Chewning, E.G., Jr., Harrell, A.M.: The effect of information load on decision makers' cue utilisation levels and decision quality in a financial distress decision task. Account. Organ. Soc. **15**(6), 527–542 (2009)

23. Savolainen, I., Kaakinen, M., Sirola, A., Oksanen, A.: Addictive behaviors and psychological distress among adolescents and emerging adults: a mediating role of peer group identification. Addict. Behav. Rep. **7**, 75–81 (2018)

24. Spira, J., Burke, C.: Intel's war on information overload: Case study. Basex (2009). http://iorgforum.org/wp-content/uploads/2011/06/IntelWarIO.BasexReport1.pdf

25. Guarinoni, M., et al.: Occupational health concerns: stress-related and psychological problems associated with work. European Parliament's Committee on Employment and Social Affairs, Brussels (2013)

26. Schick, A.G., Gorden, L.A., Haka, S.: Information overload: a temporal approach. Account. Organ. Soc. **15**(3), 199–220 (1990)

27. McLeod, S.A.: Selective attention (2008). http://www.simplypsychology.org/attention-models.html

28. Miller, G.A.: The magical number seven, plus or minus two: some limits on our capacity for processing information. Psychol. Rev. **63**(2), 81–97 (1956)

29. Davis, R.: A cognitive-behavioral model of pathological Internet use. Comput. Hum. Behav. **17**(2), 187–195 (2001). https://doi.org/10.1016/s0747-5632(00)00041-8

30. Shapira, N.A., Goldsmith, T.D., Keck, P.E., Khosla, U.M., McElroy, S.L.: Psychiatric features of individuals with problematic internet use. J. Affect. Disord. **57**, 267–272 (2000)

31. Young, K.S.: Internet addiction: the emergence of a new clinical disorder. Cyberpsychol. Behav. **1**(3), 237–244 (1998). https://doi.org/10.1089/cpb.1998.1.237

32. Caplan, S.E.: Problematic Internet use and psychosocial well-being: development of a theory-based cognitive–behavioral measurement instrument. Comput. Hum. Behav. **18**(5), 553–575 (2002). https://doi.org/10.1016/s0747-5632(02)00004-3

33. Davis, R.A., Flett, G.L., Besser, A.: Validation of a new scale for measuring problematic internet use: Implications for pre-employment screening. Cyberpsychol. Behav. **5**(4), 331–345 (2002). https://doi.org/10.1089/109493102760275581

34. Kubey, R.W., Lavin, M.J., Barrows, J.R.: Internet use and collegiate academic performance decrements: early findings. J. Commun. **51**(2), 366–382 (2001)

35. Hall, A.S., Parsons, J.: Internet addiction: college student case study using best practice in cognitive behavior therapy. J. Ment. Health Couns. **23**(4), 312–327 (2001)

36. Scherer, K.: College life online: healthy and unhealthy Internet use. J. Coll. Stud. Dev. **38**(6), 655–665 (1997)

37. Young, K.S.: Psychology of computer use: XL. addictive use of the internet: a case that breaks the stereotype. Psychol. Rep. **79**(3), 899–902 (1996)

38. Whang, L.S., Lee, S., Chang, G.: Internet over-users' psychological profiles: a behavior sampling analysis on Internet addiction. Cyberpsychol. Behav. **6**(2), 143–150 (2003)

39. Greenfield, D.N., Davis, R.A.: Lost in cyberspace: the web @ work. Cyberpsychol. Behav. **5**(4), 347–353 (2002)

40. Pratarelli, M.E., Browne, B.L.: Confirmatory factor analysis of Internet use and addiction. Cyberpsychol. Behav. **5**(1), 53–64 (2002)

41. Shapira, N.A., et al.: Problematic Internet use: proposed classification and diagnostic criteria. Depress. Anxiety **17**, 207–216 (2003)

42. Davis, R.: Psychological implications of technology in the workplace. Cyberpsychol. Behav. **5**(4), 277–278 (2002). https://doi.org/10.1089/109493102760275545

43. Holden, N.: Knowledge management: raising the spectre of the cross-cultural dimension. Knowl. Process. Manag. **8**, 155–163 (2001). https://doi.org/10.1002/kpm.117

44. Holmes, D.L.: Virtual Politics: Identity and Community in Cyberspace. Sage, London (2001)

45. Petrie, H., Gunn, D.: "Internet addiction": the effects of sex, age, depression, and introversion. Paper presented at the British Psychological Society Conference, London (1998)

46. Choi, S.B., Lim, M.: Effects of social and technology overload on psychological well-being in young South Korean adults: the mediatory role of social network service addiction. Comput. Hum. Behav. **61**, 245–254 (2016). https://doi.org/10.1016/j.chb.2016.03.032

47. Kwon, M., Kim, D.J., Cho, H., Yang, S.: The smartphone addiction scale: development and validation of a short version for adolescents. PLoS ONE **8**(12), e83558 (2013). https://doi.org/10.1371/journal.pone.0083558

48. Ellison, N.B., Steinfeld, C., Lampe, C.: The benefits of Facebook "friends:" Social capital and college students' use of online social network sites. J. Comput.-Mediat. Commun. **12**, 1143–1168 (2007). https://doi.org/10.1111/j.1083-6101.2007.00367.x

49. Valenzuela, S., Park, N., Kee, K.F.: Is there social capital in a social network site? Facebook use and college students' life satisfaction, trust, and participation. J. Comput.-Mediat. Commun. **14**, 875–901 (2009). https://doi.org/10.1111/j.1083-6101.2009.01474.x

50. Jones, Q., Gilad, R., Sheizaf, R.: Information overload and the message dynamics of online interaction spaces: a theoretical model and empirical exploration. Inf. Syst. Res. **15**(2), 194–210 (2004)

51. Lee, A.R., Son, S.M., Kim, K.K.: Information and communication technology overload and social networking service fatigue: a stress perspective. Comput. Hum. Behav. **55**, 51–61 (2016)

52. Soto-Acosta, P., Molina-Castillo, F.J., Lopez-Nicolas, C., Colomo-Palacios, R.: The effect of information overload and disorganisation on intention to purchase online: the role of perceived risk and internet experience. Online Inf. Rev. **38**(4), 543–561 (2014). https://doi.org/10.1108/OIR-01-2014-0008

53. Alhenieidi, H., Smith, A.P.: Effects of perceptions of information overload, noise and environmental demands on wellbeing and academic attainment. In: Longo, L., Leva, M.C. (eds.) H-WORKLOAD 2020. CCIS, vol. 1318, pp. 87–96. Springer, Cham (2020). https://doi.org/10.1007/978-3-030-62302-9_6

54. Alheneidi, H., Smith, A.P.: Perceptions of noise exposure, information overload and the well-being of workers. In: ICBEN (2021)

55. Pereira, G.: and. In: Schweiger, G. (ed.) Poverty, Inequality and the Critical Theory of Recognition. PP, vol. 3, pp. 83–106. Springer, Cham (2020). https://doi.org/10.1007/978-3-030-45795-2_4

56. Alavi, S.S., Maracy, M.R., Jannatifard, F., Eslami, M.: The effect of psychiatric symptoms on the Internet addiction disorder in Isfahan's university students. J. Res. Med. Sci. **16**(6), 793–800 (2011)

57. Cardak, M.: Psychological well-being and internet addiction among university students. Turkish Online J. Educ. Technol. **12**(3), 134–141 (2013)

58. Casale, S., Lecchi, S., Fioravanti, G.: The association between psychological well-being and problematic use of Internet communicative services among young people. J. Psychol. Interdiscipl. Appl. **149**, 480–497 (2015). https://doi.org/10.1080/00223980.2014.905432

59. Akin, A.: The relationships between Internet addiction, subjective vitality, and subjective happiness. Cyberpsychol. Behav. Soc. Netw. **15**, 404–410 (2012). https://doi.org/10.1089/cyber.2011.0609

60. Chen, S.: Internet use and psychological well-being among college students: a latent profile approach. Comput. Hum. Behav. **28**, 2219–2226 (2012). https://doi.org/10.1016/j.chb.2012.06.029

61. Muusses, L.D., Finkenauer, C., Kerkhof, P., Billedo, C.J.: A longitudinal study of the association between compulsive internet use and well-being. Comput. Hum. Behav. **36**, 21–28 (2014). https://doi.org/10.1016/j.chb.2014.03.035

62. Kutty, N., Sreeramareddy, C.: A cross-sectional online survey of compulsive internet use and mental health of young adults in Malaysia. J. Fam. Community Med. **21**(1), 23–28 (2014). https://doi.org/10.4103/2230-8229.128770

63. Mark, G.M., Smith, A.P.: Stress models: a review and suggested new direction. In: Houdmont, J., Leka, S. (eds.) Occupational Health Psychology: European Perspectives on Research, Education and Practice, pp. 111–144. Nottingham University Press, Nottingham (2008)

64. Mark, G., Smith, A.P.: Effects of occupational stress, job characteristics, coping and attributional style on the mental health and job satisfaction of university employees. Anxiety Stress Coping **25**, 63–78 (2011)

65. Mark, G., Smith, A.P.: Occupational stress, job characteristics, coping and mental health of nurses. Br. J. Health. Psychol. **17**, 505–521 (2012)

66. Mark, G., Smith, A.P.: A qualitative study of stress in university staff. Adv. Soc. Sci. Res. J. **5**(2), 238–247 (2018)

67. Mark, G., Smith, A.P.: Coping and its relation to gender, anxiety, depression, fatigue, cognitive difficulties and somatic symptoms. J. Educ. Soc. Behav. Sci. **25**(4), 1–22 (2018)

68. Smith, A.P.: A holistic approach to stress and well-being. Occup. Health (At Work) **7**(4), 34–35 (2011)

69. Smith, A.P., Wadsworth, E.: A holistic approach to stress and well-being. Part 5: what is a good job? Occup. Health (At Work), **8**(4), 25–27 (2011)

70. Smith, A.P., Wadsworth, E.J.K., Chaplin, K., Allen, P.H., Mark, G.: The Relationship Between Work/Well-Being And Improved Health and Well-Being. IOSH, Leicester (2011)

71. Wadsworth, E.J.K., Chaplin, K., Allen, P.H., Smith, A.P.: What is a good job? Current perspectives on work and improved health and wellbeing. Open Health Saf. J. **2**, 9–15 (2010)

72. Williams, G.M., Smith, A.P.: Using single-item measures to examine the relationships between work, personality, and well-being in the workplace. Posit. Psychol. **7**, 753–767 (2016)

73. Williams, G.M., Smith, A.P.: A holistic approach to stress and well-being. Part 6: the well-being process questionnaire (WPQ Short Form). Occup. Health (At Work), **9**(1), 29–31 (2012)

74. Williams, G.M., Smith, A.P.: Diagnostic validity of the anxiety and depression questions from the wellbeing process questionnaire. J. Clin. Transl. Res. **10** (2018)

75. Williams, G.M., Pendlebury, H., Smith, A.P.: Stress and well-being of nurses: an investigation using the demands-resources- individual effects (DRIVE) model and well-being process questionnaire (WPQ). Jacobs J. Depress. Anxiety **1**, 1–8 (2017)

76. Williams, G., Thomas, K., Smith, A.P.: Stress and well-being of university staff: an investigation using the Demands-Resources- Individual Effects (DRIVE) model and Well-being Process Questionnaire (WPQ). Psychology **8**, 1919–1940 (2017)

77. Williams, G.M., Pendlebury, H., Thomas, K., Smith, A.P.: The student well-being process questionnaire (Student WPQ). Psychology **8**, 1748–1761 (2017)

78. Smith, A.P., Firman, K.L.: Associations between the well-being process and academic outcomes. J. Educ. Soc. Behav. Sci. **32**(4), 1–10 (2019)

79. Smith, A.P.: Student workload, wellbeing and academic attainment. In: Longo, L., Leva, M.C. (eds.) H-WORKLOAD 2019. CCIS, vol. 1107, pp. 35–47. Springer, Cham (2019). https://doi.org/10.1007/978-3-030-32423-0_3

80. Misra, S., Stokols, D.: Psychological and health outcomes of perceived information overload. Environ. Behav. **44**(6), 737–759 (2011)

81. LaRose, R., Connolly, R., Lee, H., Li, K., Hales, K.D.: Connection overload? A cross cultural study of the consequences of social media connection. Inf. Syst. Manag. **31**(1), 59–73 (2014)

82. Lee, H., Connolly, R., Li, K., Hales, K., LaRose, R.: Impacts of social media connection demands: a study of Irish college students (2013). https://aisel.aisnet.org/amcis2013/Social TechnicalIssues/GeneralPresentations/6/

83. Saunders, C., Wiener, M., Klett, S., Sprenger, S.: The impact of mental representations on ICT-Related overload in the use of mobile phones. J. Manag. Inf. Syst. **34**(3), 803–825 (2017)

84. Sonnentag, S.: Being permanently online and being permanently connected at work: a demands–resources perspective. In: Permanently Online, Permanently Connected, pp. 258–267. Routledge (2017)

85. Swar, B., Hameed, T., Reychav, I.: Information overload, psychological ill-being, and behavioral intention to continue online healthcare information search. Comput. Hum. Behav. **70**, 416–425 (2017)

86. Widyanto, L., McMurran, M.: The psychometric properties of the internet addiction test. Cyberpsychol. Behav. Impact. Internet Multimedia Virtual Reality on Behavior and Society, 7(4), 443–50 (2004) doi. 443–50. https://doi.org/10.1089/cpb.2004.7.443

87. Fisher, M., Knobe, J., Strickland, B., Keil, F.: The influence of social interaction on intuitions of objectivity and subjectivity. Cogn. Sci. **41**(4), 1119–1134 (2016). https://doi.org/10.1111/cogs.12380

88. Bowling, A.: Mode of questionnaire administration can have serious effects on data quality. J. Public Health **27**(3), 281–291 (2005). https://doi.org/10.1093/pubmed/fdi031

89. de Boer, A., van Lanschot, J., Stalmeier, P., et al.: Is a single-item visual analogue scale as valid, reliable and responsive as multi-item scales in measuring quality of life? Qual Life Res **13**, 311–320 (2004). https://doi.org/10.1023/B:QURE.0000018499.64574.1f

90. Williams, G.: Researching and developing mental health and well-being assessment tools for supporting employers and employees in Wales (Doctoral dissertation). Cardiff University, Wales (2014)

91. Williams, G., & Smith, A.P. (2016). Using single-item measures to examine the relationships between work, personality, and well-being in the workplace. Psychology **7**(6), 753–767 (2016). https://doi.org/10.4236/psych.2016.76078

92. Diener, E., Lucas, R. Personality, and subjective well-being. In: Kahneman, D., Diener, E., Schwarz, N. (eds.) Well-being: The Foundations of Hedonic Psychology, pp. 213–229. Russell Sage Foundation, New York (1999)

93. Williams, G., Smith, A.P.: Measuring well-being in the workplace: Single item scales of depression and anxiety. In Anderson, N. (ed.) Contemporary Ergonomics and Human Factors 2013, pp. 87–94. CRC Press, Boca Raton (2013)

94. Galvin, J., Smith, A.P.: Stress in UK mental health training: a multi-dimensional comparison study. Br. J. Educ. Soc. Behav. Sci. **9**(3), 161–175 (2015). https://doi.org/10.9734/bjesbs/2015/18519

95. Williams, G., Thomas, K., Smith, A.P.: Stress and well-being of university staff: an investigation using the demands-resources- individual effects (DRIVE) model and well-being process questionnaire (WPQ). Psychology 8, 1919–1940 (2017). https://doi.org/10.4236/psych.2017.812124

96. Nelson, K.V., Smith, A.P.: Occupational stress, coping and mental health in Jamaican police officers. Occup. Med. **66**(6), 488–491 (2016)

97. Fan, J., Smith, A.P.: Positive well-being and work-life balance among UK railway staff. Open J. Soc. Sci. **5**(6), 1–6 (2017)

98. Kohn, A.: The Brighter Side of Human Nature: Altruism and Empathy in Everyday Life. Basic Books, New York (1990)

99. Andreassen, C., Torsheim, T., Brunborg, G., Pallesen, S.: Development of a Facebook addiction scale. Psychol. Rep. **110**(2), 501–517 (2012)

100. Griffiths, M.: Internet addiction: time to be taken seriously? Addict. Res. **8**(5), 413–418 (1996)
101. Tabachnick, B., Fidell, L.: Using Multivariate Statistics, 6th edn. Allyn and Bacon, Boston (2014)
102. Cohen, J.: Statistical Power Analysis for the Behavior Sciences, 2nd edn. West Publishing Company, St. Paul, MN (1988)
103. Alheneidi, H., Smith, A.P.: Effects of internet use on well-being and academic attainment of students starting university. Int. J. Hum. Soc. Sci. Educ. **7**(5), 20–34 (2020) https://doi.org/10.20431/2349-0381.0705003, www.arcjournals.org
104. AlHeneidi, H.: The influence of information overload and problematic internet use on adults' well-being. Unpublished doctoral dissertation. Cardiff University (2019)

Examining Cognitive Workload During Covid-19: A Qualitative Study

Robert Houghton(✉), Dalia Lister, and Arnab Majumdar

Centre for Transport Risk Management, Department of Civil and Environmental Engineering, Imperial College London, United Kingdom, South Kensington Campus, London SW7 2AZ, UK
r.houghton18@imperial.ac.uk

Abstract. Covid-19 has caused a shift in the working environment, with people mandated to work from home where possible in the UK since March 2020. Cognitive workload is sensitive to environmental changes, so it's possible that in moving from the office to working from home, people's cognitive workload has been impacted. The research outlined presents findings from 11 interviews with office workers on whether their cognitive workload has been impacted due to changes in the working environment, consequence of Covid-19. Thematic analysis identified three themes that impact cognitive workload: The home environment, differing distractions and no longer having to commute. The paper finishes with a discussion of these themes in relation to cognitive workload and Covid-19 literature, as well as some recommendations on how employers should be flexible with employees to optimise workload.

Keywords: Cognitive workload · Covid-19 · Working from home

1 Introduction

The Covid-19 pandemic has caused a major shift both in the way people work and where they do so. Prior to the onset of the pandemic, the majority of people commuted to work in major conurbations, typically cities and towns, using either private or public transport, and worked in office spaces following a schedule typically between 9am to 5pm. However, the pandemic led many countries to enforce lockdowns and that required people to work from home (WFM), and therefore employees were no longer required to commute to an office space, but instead had to WFH and communicate digitally with colleagues.

Cognitive workload (CWL) is used to describe the working memory and cognitive resources of an individual required to carry out any form of work. Whilst the official definition of CWL has been debated within the field of ergonomics, the most appropriate definition comes from [1] who define CWL as 'the level of attentional resources required to meet both objective and subjective performance criteria, which may be mediated by task demands, external support, and past experience'.

© Springer Nature Switzerland AG 2021
L. Longo and M. C. Leva (Eds.): H-WORKLOAD 2021, CCIS 1493, pp. 136–150, 2021.
https://doi.org/10.1007/978-3-030-91408-0_9

1.1 Cognitive Workload and Working from Home

WFH recognises the need for new aspects to be considered when examining an individual's CWL, e.g. office buildings tend to be designed for prolonged work, whereas the home environment may be unsuitable to complete work. In this paper, work is defined as a mixture of virtual meetings with colleagues and clients, with all other work tasks being computer mediated. Work should also be relatively easy to complete from home and the tasks should be similar to that of when people worked in the office as defined by [2]. Furthermore, prolonged work refers to working between March 2020 and June 2021, with WFH mandatory across the UK.

The home environment can introduce distractions such as noise and caring for children that may negatively impact CWL. When an employee is working in the office, the distractions that they experience are limited to whatever occurs in the office environment. One of the main differences between working at an office and WFH is that the distractions are no longer limited to the office environment. The distractions that can occur when an individual is 'at work', but at home, vary between employees and their respective personal lives and home-working environments. [3] assessed the main advantages and disadvantages that were experienced when WFH during the pandemic. The authors differentiated between those with and without children under the age of 12 and found that 67% of those with children under the age of 12 cited the increased household and caring responsibilities as the main disadvantage of WFH. Conversely, the biggest disadvantage stated by 64% of those without children under the age of 12 was social isolation and [3] demonstrates how such children generally cannot care for themselves and therefore possibly intrude on an individual's work schedule.

[4] found that one of the main advantages of WFH was the improvement in productivity, facilitated by being able to organise one's own time and the absence of distractions from colleagues. This is contrary to the expectation that there are more distractions present in the home environment than the workplace, but it is important to remember that [4] is based on pre-pandemic conditions. However, this finding also holds true whilst working during Covid-19, as both [5] and [6] noted that increased autonomy in the home environment enabled better productivity due to the increased job control for teleworkers working during the Covid-19 pandemic. Furthermore [7] highlighted the complicated situation for teleworkers with poor work-life boundaries and less control over when they worked, experienced increased distractions and higher levels of burnout. Thus, it's important to investigate to whether teleworkers' increased job control from WFH helps in optimising their workload and productivity.

Finally, a major source of distraction that is present both at home and in the workplace is the smartphone and the accompanying social media. [4] notes the lack of research available on how distractions from self-interruptions (i.e. checking one's phone) can affect focus, productivity and CWL. Research has been conducted on the implications of blocking distractions in the workplace on focus and productivity. [8] found that people were susceptible to getting distracted when they were bored and possibly experiencing cognitive underload. Cognitive underload occurs when task demands require very little to no cognitive resources or, the participant has excess cognitive resources to utilise against task demands. Cognitive underload often results in reduced attention, slower response times and task disengagement, thus being more susceptive to distraction [1].

On the other hand, when they experienced higher workload, they were less distracted; but when they did take proper breaks, they were able to return to their work more refreshed and better able to concentrate. Similarly [9] found individuals will engage in multitasking during remote meetings if they feel themselves becoming bored or cannot constantly attend meetings during teleworking.

Additionally, [8] found WFH may lead to increased teleworking, where latency problems and issues with clarity meant individuals find it harder to process social cues, having to spend greater effort to attend a virtual interaction in contrast to one involving physical presence in real life. This in turn means more cognitive resources are spent on social processing as opposed to the task itself, leading to a prolonged increase in CWL [10]. While this may pose few problems when individuals can choose when to schedule virtual interactions, the increased need to WHF and social distance requirements, mean the need to pursue this further.

Finally, WFH may have brought additional benefits through the absence of a commute. A Department of Transport report states that the average commute in Britain is around 25 min, however if one travels by car, bus or rail, the average is typically 50 min. Furthermore approximately 90% of British workers commute via one of these three modes, with car travel being the overwhelming favourite. A lack of commute appears to offer certain benefits in that individuals can re-purpose their commuting time towards completing extra work; spending more time with their families; or exercising [11]. However, the advantages of a commute to mental health have only been fully appreciated through experiencing a working day with no commute. A pre-pandemic article by Refinery 29 claimed that a commute can set the tone for a working day [12]. The article "Why You Find Your Commute So Exhausting" noted that commuting time is essential to decompressing after a long day and can contribute greatly to maintaining positive mental health [8]. After realising the need to create a boundary to a working day, some individuals have incorporated 'fake commutes' into their day by going on short walks at the beginning and ends of the day [11].

In summary, the home environment, whilst offering more flexibility in planning an individual's work and potentially increasing autonomy and removing spontaneous workplace distractions, may also add distractions such as the need to care for children and allowing people to easily interact with social media and smartphone apps that may become an additional source of distraction. Furthermore the home environment requires only virtual interactions with colleagues that may be detrimental to optimising CWL throughout the day, and finally it's possible individuals may gain additional benefits in managing their work and home life balance as they no longer need to commute, which inadvertently assists in managing CWL. However, to date there has been no study that explores the impact on CWL resulting from the shift to the home environment from the office. Thus, this paper aims to investigate both whether CWL has been impacted by homeworking, and if so, what is the impact of prolonged virtual interaction, a lack of commute and home distractions impact cognitive workload.

2   Methods

2.1   Participants

Eleven participants, defined as office workers, were identified to meet the following criteria set out by the authors:

- Participants worked 12 days or less per month from home prior to the pandemic
- Worked daily in an office before the pandemic; and
- Carried out face to face meetings (with colleagues and/or clients) regularly before the pandemic; and
- Has had minimal experience of working from home; and
- Worked from home throughout the COVID-19 pandemic.

Participants were selectively sampled from the authors' network of colleagues' and acquaintances to build a diverse and balanced sample as possible. All participants were interviewed. Nine interviews were carried out initially, and analysed, with a further two being conducted once the coding scheme had reached fully maturity to assess for data saturation (see details below). The final two interviews generated no new codes, suggesting saturation point was researched [13].

2.2   Demographics

The average age of the sample was 32 years old and consisted of six females and five males. Additionally, three participants had children over the age of 12, and two had children aged 12 or under. This was an important consideration regarding possible distractions as mentioned in [2] relating to children. All interviews took place between March and April 2021, in order to provide a year's experience of WFH for reflection. All participants lived and worked in London, thus being geographically constrained. Participants worked a range of occupations that would be considered as "White Collar" including Law, Finance, Journalism, Accounting, and Marketing.

2.3   Data Collection

Data was collected via semi-structured interviews over Zoom to enable a rich exploration of the impacts of CWL during WFH when compared to working in the office. Interviews were the preferred data collection method due to their ability to gather rich data and highlight possible aspects of working that can be perceived as sensitive [14]. The interviews were approximately one hour in duration and were conducted solely by DL to ensure consistency across interviews.

2.4   Data Analysis

Analysis was conducted out using Thematic Analysis, in accordance to the guidance set out by [15] as well as certain considerations from [16]. Thematic analysis was chosen for several reasons. Firstly, [15] is the seminal paper on Thematic Analysis and outlines the process very well, which is further strengthen using the process described in [16]. Thematic analysis was deemed most appropriate as the study was not concerned with assessing the linguistics used in association with cognitive workload or interested in assessing the life course of participants. The authors took a combined approach in regard to inductive and deductive coding and thematic development, as described in [17]. The research process followed the 6 processes in [15], as outlined in Table 1.

Table 1. Description of the Thematic analysis process taken in the present study in relation to the steps outlined in Braun and Clarke (2006)

Phase of thematic analysis	Current study's description
1. Familiarizing yourself with your data:	All data was transcribed verbatim, then read by DL and RH, to familiarise themselves with the data
2. Generating initial codes	Codes were individually generated, mainly through DL, RH coded several transcripts separately to assess the robustness of the coding scheme generated. Codes were then reviewed, and a final initial coding scheme was used for the remainder of the data set
3. Searching for themes	Once all the datasets were coded, codes were reviewed in relation to each in to generate themes and subthemes
4. Reviewing themes	Once all themes and subthemes were generated, their content was reviewed in relation to the codes in that each theme felt consistent in itself and that codes did not bleed across multiple themes, resulting in a thematic map
5. Defining and naming themes	Themes were then named and defined in accordance to their content, their relationships with other themes and how well they tell the story in answering the research questions
6. Producing the paper	Selection of extracts from each theme has been selected for this paper to demonstrate to the reader how the analysis relates back to the research questions

3   Results

The thematic analysis generated major three themes in relation to cognitive workload:

1. From F2F to technology - changing work-based impacts CWL
2. Changing breaks and distractions impacts CWL
3. The lack of commute impacts CWL

These themes are discussed in turn.

3.1   Theme 1: From F2F to Technology - Changing Work-Based Impacts CWL

This theme captures how participants felt the prolonged digital working may have impacted their cognitive workload and has been split into two categories.

3.2   Technological Interaction Increases Cognitive Workload

This category captures how a participant felt while interacting via services such as Microsoft Teams, Zoom and Skype. These services increased cognitive workload due to the difficulties associated with processing social cues, with one participant describing how online communication is not as natural as communicating in person, resulting in a greater level of concentration:

'I think that online meetings are much less, you know, they flow much less. You know, they're a bit contrived and takes quite a lot of concentration. And, you know, I don't think there's no fluidity to it.'

Similar sentiments were also echoed by another participant:

'I have had to, i think, devote much higher levels of attention in order to engage people'

This is also associated with participants highlighting that communicating virtually results in lower attention spans and the ease of "tuning out" of a conversation, which will also likely result in increasing an individual's cognitive workload:

'If I was there in person, I would probably have more sort of attention and focus than I probably will do now, because just because, quite difficult to keep attention for that long. When something's does not sort of in person or in real life.'

and:

'I would say yes, a different way of answering it, it's much easier to tune out. so, it's very easy to tune out, So yes to stay tuned in, yes it's is hard work'

3.3   Home Environments Help Optimise Cognitive Workload (CWL)

Participants outlined that the home environment impacted CWL in both a positive and negative sense. Firstly, WFH helps offset high CWL by allowing participants to work in an environment which they can optimise for their own comfort. For example, one participant discussed the slower pace of the day which helped him/her to focus in greater depth on their own work tasks:

'I've spent less negative energy on, you know, having to get up, get dressed, put on makeup, like use the mental energy of like what am I going to wear today, I don't have to think about any of that. Yeah, way more capacity to actually think about the work that I'm doing.'

Similarly:

If I have like an equally as hard task now, I can be doing like doing so in like trackies, you know, sitting cross legged you know doing the right one. And that probably does impact sort of how you do the tasks that you're doing.'

Additionally, participants associated the optimised CWL with increases to productivity, with one participant stating:

'like I noticed that when I do my morning routines, my productivity and like my mental cognitive resources are massively improved'

Additionally another stated:

'For example, in terms of productivity, i can actually get more done and do it more quickly at home which is obviously a positive'

When queried about how WFH has increased productivity, participants noted that it gave them more autonomy over their schedule as well as when and how they work:

'For example, in terms of productivity, I can actually get more done and do it more quickly at home which is obviously a positive'

Furthermore:

'I feel like it's made it better, because I can work on like, on, on my own schedule, so like, I know that if I'm going to be tired at like three, I'll do tasks that don't, like, yeah, whereas like in the morning I know that I like work well, so like, I'll do like they're like tasks that I know or like require more like brain power'

However, WFH can also contribute to the experience of more cognitive underload, given the isolation and monotony, resulting in a reduced job satisfaction. (i.e. the degree to which people like or dislike their job [18]) and a detachment from work. One participant highlighted:

There's days where it affects my mood like my sense of satisfaction from the job, because it feels very isolating and you don't. You don't celebrate the wins with anyone know, find mutual support in the in the down moments of the losses. And so I think it's felt at times quite draining and also quite repetitive, in a sort of very monotonous way, because there's no change yet, you're on your own'.

Similarly, another participant stated:

'It's just the lack of social interaction. I mean, I think, as humans, we're social beings and I think being stuck in in a, in an eight-by-eight room all day isn't conducive necessarily to mental health and I think or necessarily productivity…you can't, you can't replicate the tangibility of social interaction on the computer, over, over yeah over zoom or over teams'

Participants often associated underload with monotony due to a lack of dynamism and social interaction in their environments:

'it's quite monotonous you know we are Doing the same thing. We're looking at the same charts and, you know, it doesn't really feel like there's a lot of progress. We know we're not traveling. Right. So you know, a lot of the, you know, not fun but exciting parts of our work has gone, we're not meeting interacting with people outside of our institution'

And:

'in a sort of very monotonous way, because there's no change yet, you're on your own, and the nature of the role is that it's social, and it's missing that completely. So pre COVID For example, you'd go out a lot. It's not just desk base Yeah, travel, you meet people you're out for lunch, you go to events you're in, you entertain that's all been stripped away, it's just you and your laptop. Yeah and that's quite a monotonous experience'

Furthermore, participants also associated the lack of an office atmosphere with perceptions of cognitive underload with one stating:

'I probably have experienced more cognitive underload, and I don't know if that's just because sort of like, there's a bit of disassociation that comes with working from home, that you're not like directly with people or like in the office, and so I think sometimes'

Another echoed a similar sentiment:

'the lack of atmospheric cues around you that tell you when you're with other people working in a team, what mode of cognitive overload and underload you need to shift into depending on how you're like group work is progressing in a certain towards a certain deadline. That was really difficult not to have.'

3.4   Theme 2: Changing Distractions Impacts CWL

This theme captures the differences between distractions at home to those in the office. Furthermore, every participant said that colleagues were a distraction in the office, and whilst conversations with them were a source of positive social interaction, they were also intensive, noisy and negatively impact CWL:

'from the team like coming in for a chat, which are often really nice but sometimes you know they take quite a lot of time out of the day'

and:

Mainly other people's conversations. You know, if someone's having a conversation about something, but it's, you know'

Furthermore, participants reported that more often than not, they became distracted during underload, mainly relating this to a state of boredom:

But when it's under load, that's when I struggled to stay concentrated on my work.'

Whilst WFH, several participants report their smartphone being the largest distraction:

'At home it is a lot more about my phone. Because at work if I was on my phone people could see and I think I feel self-conscious about being on it, but at home being on my phone, browsing on the internet'

And additionally:

My phone is my biggest distraction.'

It is likely that mobile phones become a distraction in the home environment as there is no social pressure nor any organisational rules that limit their use, as there would be in the workplace. Office atmosphere or work culture appears to possibly help people regulate and re-focus on their own work, with one participant stating:

'I find it I find it easier to come back after being distracted in the office, but not when I was working at home, because I think in the office like you're going from that distraction back into a fixed work environment and there are two people sitting on either side of you'

Additionally, one participant described how the office only offered discrete distractions whereas multiple and simultaneous distractions were present in the home environment. *'you have a cigarette, you have a coffee you talk by the water fountain… but there's not that a wide array of variety of exciting things you can do when you're at home that the, the distractions are infinite'*.

Understanding whether children were a distraction was hard to assess, as only one participant with children reflected with considerable depth in their responses. However other participants with children of their own or siblings around late high school to early college years did not report them being a distraction. Hence, it's likely that either only young children, or those who cannot really teach themselves, were really a distraction, with one participant highlighting the difficulty of home-schooling their children:

'So now that the children are at school, I actually do prefer it. When i was homeschooling, I really hated it'.

3.5   Theme 3: The Lack of Commute Impacts Cognitive Workload

This theme captures how a lack of commute impacts cognitive workload both positively and negatively, see table two for a summary of the findings (Table 2).

All but two of the participants stated that the lack of a commute affected them positively, with one stating:

Table 2. Summary of impacts on cognitive workload stemming from no Commute

Positive impacts	Negative impacts

• Able to complete more work in the time saved not commuting
• Less time spent travelling to and from meetings, therefore more efficient and able to complete more work
• Cognitive resources and energy saved by not commuting:
  – Less drained,
  – Less stressed,
  – Less wasted negative energy
• More time for oneself for:
  – Exercise,
  – Socialising,
  – Relaxing
	• Miss period of refresh and decompressing on commute
	• Expected to complete more work because not commuting
	• Evening transition is hard without commute to separate work from home
	• Cognitive resources not refreshed by the commute:
	  – Reduced cognitive resources at start of the day

'I've got three and a half hours to go for a walk, to do exercise, cook for myself to not be in a disgusting tube. Yeah, massively, massively benefited'

And another stated:

And I definitely would usually sort of have this like hectic start to the day where I would always be like running late, no matter what. If you were doing something lots of work… like all of that just means that not having to think about all of that sort of just takes the stress away.'

The amount of time that is released by not having to commute enables individuals to better optimise their working day, being both more productive and efficient, as well as having more time to enjoy leisure related activities. However, six of those interviewed did introduce some sort of boundary activity such as moving locations in the house and completing non-work-related tasks in an effort to separate work and home life, for example instead of commuting, one participant introduced a morning routine of exercise instead to separate home and work:

'like I noticed that when I do my morning routines, my productivity and like my mental cognitive resources are massively improved like days where I don't do or days when I have a lie in, like my actual work performance decreases massive so yeah'

4 Discussion

The paper outlines findings from a set of eleven interviews exploring how cognitive workload may be impacted to prolonged virtual working due to WFH, in particular, assessing the impact distractions and the need to no longer commute have on CWL.

4.1 Home Cannot Entirely Replace the Office

Participants expressed more intense feelings of underload when WFH. In virtual interaction, office workers resumed a more passive state and found it harder to focus. Participants reported that continued virtual interaction compared increased workload due to the need to attend more to the conversation and prolong concentration in order to keep informed in the meeting due to latency issues and lack of social cues. The findings of the present study support and extend the results in [19], who found extended teleconferencing created a higher workload due to difficulties processing social cues. However, the present study also found prolonged virtual interaction resulted in a loss of attention, possibly due prolonged virtual communication being somewhat similar to a vigilance task, in that it requires sustained attention [20]. Additionally, the results support findings from [9] in that Employers should only ask for meetings when absolutely necessary if staff are WFH, or spread meetings throughout the week to mitigate the negative effects of prolonged virtual interaction.

Participants experienced lower attention and more extreme underload when working on monotonous tasks due to isolation from colleagues, leading to periods of sustained underload. Participants stated that WFH helped to moderate the impact of high workload in that the home environment adds many freedoms and more autonomy to optimise workload [21]. This finding contributes to research by [5] and [6] who also found during the Covid-19 pandemic, participants in both interviews and questionnaires stated increased productivity, in that it helps explain why productivity can increase. WFH means individuals are no longer monitored or observed and are free of expected work hours in the office. This means individuals can use this increased control over how and when they work to ensure they are working effectively, doing the tasks when they are best suited to complete them, and taking breaks when necessary. However, the home environment can also induce a level of cognitive underload, which is seen to negatively impact participants [1]. The present study found that WFH often lacked rapid change, spontaneous interaction and lack of social interaction which resulted in perceptions of monotony and isolation that created feelings of cognitive underload. Whilst there is little research on cognitive underload outside of safety critical environments, the current findings are supported by prior research on cognitive underload, where it has been present in contexts such as long haul driving and highly automated environments that lack regular change in the work environment [22] and [23]. It's interesting in the present study that cognitive underload was associated with a lack of social interaction and isolation, which has yet to be seen in the current body of underload literature. It is possible this is a finding that is purely constrained to WFH during the Covid-19 pandemic, due to the need to socially distance, thus individuals cannot socialise out of work in they way they may have done previously, and socialising via digital medium may not result in the same satisfaction [24].

Regarding practical recommendations in relation to the effects of WFH on CWL, employers should allow participants to be flexible in their work environment and choose the right balance of office to WFH in order to maximise the moderating impacts against high workload, whilst mitigating against effects of sustained underload.

4.2   Distractions at Home and the Office

Participants universally found colleagues to be a distraction, due to creating additional time pressure as colleague interactions can be time intensive, noisy and conversations of the office were distracting. Furthermore, five participants stated they were distracted when they were bored, which was more likely to occur during underload, being consistent with research by [8]. It's possible that becoming distracted during underload are participants' attempts to self-regulate and seeking a source of additional stimulation, which is supported in an in-depth review of boredom in occupational settings [25].

Furthermore, the home environment offers many more types of distractors and lacks the norms and social pressure of not being on your phone or social media in the workplace. It's likely that participants can re-engage with their work more easily in the office as the distractions there are time limited e.g. the duration of a cigarette or coffee break, whereas at home additional autonomy may increase the distraction indefinitely, such as scrolling through social media. Participants gave varied responses when questioned as to which environment was more distracting. Five participants stated that they were more distracted at home but caveated this with statements about also feeling less inspired without their colleagues' present. Again, this supports the notion that employers should really ensure participants can get a mix of interaction types, to help negate the wide array of distractions at home.

The interviews also found participants felt family members especially young children were a distraction, in that children were required to conduct school from home, and parents assisted in some teaching during this period. This type of distraction likely increased cognitive workload as parents have an additional response during work hours, looking after their children, which increases a burden in relation to those times when parents can really work efficiently without the need to assist children. This finding supports research by [21] who found individuals with dependents have somewhat lower job satisfaction due to other commitments. Additionally, the findings on distraction partially support research by [5] in that they also found other employees to be a large source of distraction in the workplace due to both noise and time impact. [5] Also state WFH should reduce distractions compared to the office environment due to the absence of negative distractors. However WFH also offers an equal if not greater number of distractors due home distractions are not time limited, e.g. you can check your phone whenever you want, and also the presence of children who are not yet mature enough to care for themselves, at least during work hours appears to be a huge source of distraction, albeit our small sample size.

4.3   To Commute or not to Commute

Most participants cited that not having to commute freed up a lot of their time to create a work schedule that suited them. This supports the findings of [21] and [5] in that the Covid-19 pandemic reduces the need to commute and attend the office and allows individuals greater autonomy, giving them mastery over their own work schedule. Not having to commute also allows time for non-work related activities that people enjoy and increasing personal well-being which supports research by [12] and [5] who found commuting daily is exhausting, time intensive and impacts personal satisfaction in general. However, not having a commute can also have disadvantages, mainly the difficulty separating home and work life balance, with six participants introducing some sort of boundary activity to try separate home and work activities in their own homes.

Additionally, this may bleed into affecting CWL since participants struggle to switch off, work longer hours than they should or develop ineffective work schedules, as well as not benefitting from refreshment periods of the commute to buffer work and home environments [26, 27]. [27] Notes that flexible work schedules are only beneficial when an individual also has the flexibility at home to match both home and work schedules, since if one supersedes the other, then individuals face work-home conflict.

Not having to commute helps promote balance between home and work schedules, however some participants in the present study discussed employers increasing expectations of work output, due to the absence of the commute. The extra time should not be used for more work, rather used either to relax, complete necessary non-work-related tasks such as caring or assisting any dependents, and to optimise their own workload so they can work productively. This is in line with [26] whose findings highlight that when work and home schedules are in equilibrium, people's general well-being improves. Hence, it's important any extra time freed up not having to commute is used to promote well-being and personal productivity, rather than to complete more work, if participants are already completing their mandated and possibly more work hours.

4.4 Limitations

The study had several limitations, mainly relating to the sample, the size compared to some other studies now examining the effects of covid-19 on home working is relatively small. For example [21] collected data from over 500 participants across several time points, and whilst mainly quantitative in nature, they did manage to gather some qualitative data. Hence the findings could be made more robust by including more participants and resampling with the same questions to understand whether the findings outlined in this study have changed due to time.

Furthermore, the sample was constrained in both its geography, in that all participants worked and lived in the London area, and in profession, in that all participants worked in relatively high performing jobs such as in Law, Finance and Journalism. Whilst saturation point was reached the sample is somewhat homogenous, and thus more research is needed to assess whether these findings are only relevant to those who are working in stable and well-paying jobs, as individuals who work in other locations and in other sectors may have differing experiences relating to non-commuting, distraction, and home working on cognitive workload. However, the results of the study still offer merit in that the findings could be applied to similar large scale urban areas with a high presence of white-collar workers such as New York, Paris, Sydney and, Tokyo in that these localities often require participants to commute on busy public transport in order to work.

4.5 Conclusion

This paper discusses findings from a set of interviews assessing the impact of WFH on individuals' cognitive workload. What is clear from the interviews is that any employer should allow participants to choose their own schedule of when they would like to work from the office and when from home, if possible. By allowing people to optimise their own workload and thereby prevent the onset of a monotonous environment, entailing constant digital interaction in which a participant's attention is driven to its limits. Employers considering the world of work beyond Covid-19 restrictions should be flexible when their employees have dependents and should allow any time not spent commuting to assist in this endeavour. Finally, there is a need to further explore the interaction between distraction and workload, as within the present study distractions were possibly an outcome of underload and yet increased an individual's cognitive workload. This was certainly the case if that particular distraction intruded on the individuals work schedule, such as care commitments.

References

1. Young, M.S., Brookhuis, K.A., Wickens, C.D., Hancock, P.A.: State of science: mental workload in ergonomics. Ergonomics **58**, 1–17 (2015)
2. Qvortrup, L.: From teleworking to Networking: Definitions and Trends. In: Teleworking, pp. 41–59. Routledge (2002)
3. Rubin, O., Nikolaeva, A., Nello-Deakin, S., te Brömmelstroet, M.: What can we learn from the COVID-19 pandemic about how people experience working from home and commuting. Centre for Urban Studies, University of Amsterdam, pp. 1–9 (2020)
4. Nakrošienė, A., Bučiūnienė, I., Goštautaitė, B.: Working from home: characteristics and outcomes of telework. Int. J. Manpower (2019)
5. Wöhrmann, A.M., Ebner, C.: Understanding the bright side and the dark side of telework: An empirical analysis of working conditions and psychosomatic health complaints. New Technology, Work and Employment (2021)
6. Wang, B., Liu, Y., Qian, J., Parker, S.K.: Achieving effective remote working during the COVID-19 pandemic: a work design perspective. Appl. Psychol. **70**(1), 16–59 (2021)
7. Carvalho, V.S., Santos, A., Ribeiro, M.T., Chambel, M.J.: Please, do not interrupt me: work–family balance and segmentation behavior as mediators of boundary violations and teleworkers' burnout and flourishing. Sustainability **13**(13) (2021)
8. Mark, G., Iqbal, S., Czerwinski, M.: How blocking distractions affects workplace focus and productivity. In: Proceedings of the 2017 ACM International Joint Conference on Pervasive and Ubiquitous Computing and Proceedings of the 2017 ACM International Symposium on Wearable Computers, pp. 928–934 (2017)
9. Cao, H., et al.: Large scale analysis of multitasking behavior during remote meetings. In: Proceedings of the 2021 CHI Conference on Human Factors in Computing Systems, pp. 1–13 (2021)
10. Ferran, C., Watts, S.: Videoconferencing in the field: a heuristic processing model. Manage. Sci. **54**(9), 1565–1578 (2008)
11. Jacobs, E., Warwick-Ching, L.: Feeling the strain: stress and anxiety weigh on world's workers. Financ. Times (2021)
12. Truong, K.: Why you find your commute so exhausting refinery, 29 (2019). https://www.refinery29.com/en-gb/commuting-affects-mental-health
13. Majid, M.A., Othman, M., Mohamad, S.F., Abdul Halim Lim, S.: Achieving data saturation: evidence from a qualitative study of job satisfaction. Soc. Manage. Res. J. (SMRJ) **15**(2), 65–67 (2018)
14. Barriball, K.L., While, A.: Collecting data using a semi-structured interview: a discussion paper. J. Adv. Nurs. Inst. Subscription **19**(2), 328–335 (1994)

15. Braun, V., Clarke, V.: Using thematic analysis in psychology. Qual. Res. Psychol. **3**(2), 77–101 (2006)
16. Erlingsson, C., Brysiewicz, P.: A hands-on guide to doing content analysis. Afr. J. Emerg. Med. **7**(3), 93–99 (2017)
17. Fereday, J., Muir-Cochrane, E.: Demonstrating rigor using thematic analysis: a hybrid approach of inductive and deductive coding and theme development. Int. J. Qual. Methods **5**(1), 80–92 (2006)
18. Spector, P.E.: Job Satisfaction: Application, Assessment, Causes, and Consequences. vol. 3. Sage (1997)
19. Tentama, F., Rahmawati, P., Muhopilah, P.: The effect and implications of work stress and workload on job satisfaction. Int. J. Sci. Technol. Res. **8**(11), 2498–2502 (2019)
20. Warm, J.S., Parasuraman, R., Matthews, G.: Vigilance requires hard mental work and is stressful. Hum. Factors **50**(3), 433–441 (2008)
21. Syrek, C., Kühnel, J., Vahle-Hinz, T., de Bloom, J.: Being an accountant, cook, entertainer and teacher—all at the same time: Changes in employees' work and work-related well-being during the coronavirus (COVID-19) pandemic. Int. J. Psychol. (2021)
22. McWilliams, T., Ward, N.: Underload on the road: measuring vigilance decrements during partially automated driving. Front. Psychol. **12**, 1113 (2021)
23. Saxby, D.J., Matthews, G., Warm, J.S., Hitchcock, E.M., Neubauer, C.: Active and passive fatigue in simulated driving: discriminating styles of workload regulation and their safety impacts. J. Exp. Psychol. Appl. **19**(4), 287 (2013)
24. Costa, R.M., Patrão, I., Machado, M.: Problematic internet use and feelings of loneliness. Int. J. Psychiatr. Clin. Pract. **23**(2), 160–162 (2019)
25. Cummings, M.L., Gao, F., Thornburg, K.M.: Boredom in the workplace: a new look at an old problem. Hum. Factors **58**(2), 279–300 (2016)
26. Allen, T.D., Merlo, K., Lawrence, R.C., Slutsky, J., Gray, C.E.: Boundary management and work-nonwork balance while working from home. Appl. Psychol. **70**(1) (2021)
27. Hill, E.J., Erickson, J.J., Holmes, E.K., Ferris, M.: Workplace flexibility, work hours, and work-life conflict: finding an extra day or two. J. Fam. Psychol. **24**(3), 349 (2010)

The Relationship Between Workload, Fatigue and Sleep Quality of Psychiatric Staff

Jialin Fan[1][(⊠)] [iD], Juqing Liu[1], and Andrew P. Smith[2] [iD]

[1] School of Psychology, Shenzhen University, L3-1236, South Campus, 3688 Nanshan Road, Shenzhen 518000, China
FanJL@szu.edu.cn

[2] Centre for Occupational and Health Psychology, School of Psychology, Cardiff University, 63 Park Place, Cardiff CF10 3AS, UK
SmithAP@cardiff.ac.uk

Abstract. The present research investigated the relationship between workload, fatigue, and sleep quality of physicians and nurses in psychiatric hospitals by conducting a cross-sectional survey and a diary study. Both studies were conducted in China in early 2021, investigating the effect of workload on fatigue and sleep quality among psychiatric staff in a real-life setting. Study 1 was a cross-sessional survey, investigating 334 responses from physicians and nurses in five psychiatric hospitals, and Study 2 was a diary study examining the association between workload, fatigue and sleep quality in the working week of 48 psychiatric staff. The findings from the first study showed that the staff reported a high workload, and fatigue and poor sleep quality were very prevalent. Workload was the strongest predictor of fatigue. In the diary study, workload and fatigue increased over the week, and sleep quality declined. This research has identified the importance of studying workload and its effects on psychiatric staff.

Keywords: Workload · Occupational fatigue · Sleep quality · Psychiatric staff · Diary study

1 Introduction

1.1 Mental Workload

Mental workload has been widely studied in both laboratory [1, 2] and occupational settings [3–5]. Workload is a multi-dimensional concept involving time, task input load, operator effort, performance or other outcomes [6]. Wickens [7] stated that workload is defined by human's limited resources available for mental processing. It is considered as a mental construct of an "intervening variable" [8], reflecting the interaction of mental demands imposed on operators by tasks they are involved in [9]. Despite no clearly defined definition of mental workload, it is commonly accepted as 'the volume of cognitive work necessary for an individual to accomplish a task over time' [10–12].

Mental workload can be assessed by using self-report measures, task variables and physiological outcomes. Although fundamental research often requires comparing subjective and objective workload, the subjective measure can generally be considered

© Springer Nature Switzerland AG 2021
L. Longo and M. C. Leva (Eds.): H-WORKLOAD 2021, CCIS 1493, pp. 151–164, 2021.
https://doi.org/10.1007/978-3-030-91408-0_10

sufficient [9, 10]. The NASA-Task Load Index (NASA-TLX) and the Subject Work-load Assessment Technique are well-known self-assessment tools for mental workload. Recently, the single-item measure of workload was also confirmed to be reliable and valid, and it was able to predict fatigue and wellbeing of workers and students [13–15].

Compared with different occupational groups, healthcare workers reported higher workloads and higher levels of effort [16]. The workload of physicians and nurses was a combination of time spent, mental effort and judgment, technical skill and physical effort, and perceived psychological stress while providing medical services [17]. Several previous studies [18–20] found that mental workload was the highest valued dimension among healthcare workers when using the NASA-TLX to measure multi-dimensional workload in a hospital. The continually evolving human-system interactions in healthcare require learning, processing new data inputs, and substantial adaptation by staff, leading to further mental costs [20]. As in general hospitals, physicians and nurses in psychiatric hospitals work under a high mental workload. However, there is very little relevant literature focused on psychiatric staff.

1.2 Occupational Fatigue

Occupational Fatigue is a common problem among workers. It represents a state of "extreme tiredness and reduced functional capacity experienced during or at the end of the workday" [21]. Fatigue's consequences mainly include impaired cognitive and skilled performance, negative mood, low wellbeing, physical and mental ill-health. In an occupational setting, fatigue can be considered the outcome of high workload, overtime work, low job support and control, shiftwork, poor work environment, or the combined effect of these factors [13, 22].

Healthcare workers usually experience heavy workloads and shiftwork and, thus, suffer from high occupational fatigue. They report higher mental fatigue than physical fatigue [23]. The central role of fatigue in impairing their work performance has been supported by research using subjective measures, objective measures, or both [23–26]. In China, healthcare workers were listed as one of the most vulnerable work populations to occupational fatigue, followed by taxi drivers and police officers [27]. Existing literature on healthcare workers in China shows that fatigue is associated with workload and shift schedules and results in psychological withdrawal [28]. A study among surgery nurses showed that perceived fatigue was higher when working with a high workload [29].

Compared with general hospitals, physicians and nurses in psychiatric hospitals have a higher fatigue risk [30]. They have specific work characteristics, work environment, and service targets, which increases their psychological load [31]. Dong et al. [32] found that the fatigue phenomenon among staff in the closed management ward of the psychiatric department or hospital was severe and widespread, and the leading causes for their fatigue include shiftwork, age, and the high-risk nature of the work itself. Psychiatric staff provide medical and nursing services to patients who have mental illnesses or mental disorders. At any time, they may be wounded or be injured, break facilities, escape from the ward, and even commit suicide. Accidents caused by patients such as lost property, infection, and accidental falls may also cause conflict between staff and the patients or their families. These will directly affect the psychiatric staff and put them under considerable mental pressure. Psychiatric staff were found to have a high level of mental and emotional exhaustion and be prone to negative emotions, which leads to increased fatigue [33], although individual differences such as personality have been suggested to affect the level of their fatigue [30]. It is apparent that there is insufficient research on workload and fatigue of psychiatric staff, and the association between them should be further studied.

1.3 Sleep

Quality of sleep guarantees work efficiency and helps recovery from fatigue. Vice versa, insufficient and inadequate sleep reduces work performance [34], can induce headaches and the feeling of fatigue [35]. Healthcare workers have a high incidence of sleep problems, reduced opportunities for sleep with minimal recuperation time, all of which contribute to their sleep problems and impairments in physical, cognitive, and emotional functioning [36, 37]. Previous studies have also found an association between occupational fatigue and sleep quality in healthcare professionals [37–39]. The sleep of psychiatric healthcare workers has rarely been studied. Li et al. [31] showed that high fatigue and poor sleep quality were frequent among psychiatric staff. Recently, sleep disorders in psychiatric staff were found to be associated with impaired cognitive performance [40].

Sleep quality can be assessed by using subjective measurements, objective outcomes, or both. The subjective measurements include the Pittsburgh Sleep Quality Index scale (PQSI), sleep diary, and Morningness-Eveningness Questionnaire (MEQ). The Pittsburgh Sleep Quality Index scale (PQSI) is a commonly accepted standardised questionnaire developed by Buysse [41], which appraises sleep quality and differentiates "good sleepers" and "poor sleepers". The objective measurements include polysomnography (PSG) and actigraphy. In the current research, the Chinese version of PQSI [42] assessed sleep quality in the occupational setting.

1.4 Rationale of the Present Research

It is necessary to establish a work and sleep quality profile among physicians and nurses working in psychiatric hospitals before further fatigue management. The research described in the current paper aimed to examine the relationships between workload, fatigue, and sleep quality of physicians and nurses in psychiatric hospitals. It also aimed first to investigate the predictors of occupational fatigue among them, using the Demands, Resources, and Individual Effects (DRIVE) model [43] as the framework. The present study contributed to widening the research results in the field of workload analysis by collecting real data in an everyday setting, by translating the research tools into Chinese, by testing that these tools are usable even in a different language and culture.

This research consisted of two studies, a cross-sectional survey and a diary study conducted in Maoming City in China. Study 1 involved a survey of reported mental workload, fatigue and sleep quality among doctors and nurses of the psychiatric hospital, utilising the Smith Wellbeing Questionnaire (SWELL) and the Pittsburgh Sleep Quality Index Scale (PSQI). Study 2 was a diary study that forty-eight psychiatric doctors and nurses completed at the start and end of the first and last day of their working week. The main items included in the diary were sleep duration, sleep quality, alertness before work, workload, and fatigue after work. It should be noted that the COVID-19 cases in that region of China were at zero for three months before and during data collection.

The remainder of this paper is structured as follows. Section 2 describes the methods and materials, the results and a summary of Study 1, while Sect. 3 describes Study 2. Section 4 discusses the results, highlights the contribution of current research and suggests future work. Section 5 summarises the main conclusions of this paper.

2 Study 1

2.1 Methods

Participants. Participants were physicians and nurses recruited from five public psychiatric hospitals in Maoming City, Guangdong Province, China. A total of 360 paper questionnaires were distributed from January to February 2021, and 334 valid questionnaires were returned with a response rate of 92.78%. The criteria for valid questionnaires were those with no obvious errors or omissions of two or more items. These participants were either nurses (N = 216, 64.7%) or physicians (N = 118, 35.3%) in psychiatric hospitals, with a mean age of 36.78 years (SD = 8.29, minimum 19yr, maximum 55yr). 60.18% of them were female (N = 201). The School of Psychology Research Ethics Committee at Shenzhen University reviewed and approved this study.

Materials. The survey included questions about demographics, the SWELL questionnaire, and the PSQI questionnaire. Demographic information included gender, age, years of work, job role, commuting time, and weekly working hours.

The SWELL questionnaire was developed by Smith and Smith [44] and has been used in previous studies in the real-life occupational setting to assess workload, fatigue and wellbeing [3, 13, 14]. It consists of twenty-six single-item questions, some of which were chosen from the Wellbeing Process Questionnaire (WPQ) [45], and took approximately 10 min to complete. Most of the questions were on a 10-point scale, and the remaining were Yes/No answers. Such single-item measures were valid and reliable [13, 46], allowed identification of the overall risks, saved time and brought convenience to this field study [3]. In the current study, workload and fatigue were the main variables of interest.

This survey was translated into Chinese using both forward and backward translations. Two researchers who were proficient in both English and Chinese performed the forward translation that translates the English version of SWELL into Chinese. An independent translator who did not know the assessment then performed the backward translation process. Comparison between the original English and the backward translated English versions were then carried out, and any discrepancies were discussed before any final adjustments were made to the questionnaire. The Chinese version of SWELL was piloted in January 2020 before it was used in the present study.

PSQI is a standardised self-reported questionnaire that assesses sleep quality over a one-month interval. It has been widely used and translated for use with Chinese samples. The PSQI included 19 items that generate seven factors: subjective sleep quality, sleep latency, sleep duration, habitual sleep efficiency, sleep disturbances, use of sleep medication, and daytime dysfunction. The sum of these factors (a global PSQI score), ranging from 0 to 21, indicates good or poor sleep quality. A higher score indicates worse sleep quality. In China, the standard global PSQI threshold is 8 [42], and a global score >8 means poor sleep quality and potential sleep problems in a Chinese adult.

Procedure. The paper information sheet and informed consent form were distributed by researchers with permission and assistance from the hospitals. The purpose, significance and theme of the survey were explained in the information sheet, and participants were informed that they had the right to answer a paper questionnaire voluntarily and withdraw from the survey at any point. The paper survey was handed to participants after they signed the consent form. A pilot study was conducted to revise any potential problems with the Chinese version of these questionnaires before the formal survey started.

Analyses. Data analysis was carried out using SPSS 26. Pearson correlation was used to examine the associations between workload, fatigue and sleep quality, and logistic regression to investigate the predictors of occupational fatigue of psychiatric staff.

2.2 Results

Descriptive. Participants had a mean workload score of 7.40 ± 0.70 and a mean occupational fatigue score of 7.38 ± 0.69, both of which showed a high level according to single-item measurements. The average PQSI global score was 9.51 ± 2.66, and 74.9% of participants had a score above 8, meaning their sleep quality was worse than that of Chinese adults in general.

Associations Between Workload, Fatigue and Sleep Quality. Pearson correlation was used to investigate the association between workload, fatigue and sleep quality (shown in Table 1). Workload showed significant correlations with fatigue ($r = .831$, $p < .01$) and the sleep global score ($r = .213$, $p < .01$), with high levels of workload being associated with high levels of fatigue and poor sleep quality. Fatigue also showed a significant correlation with global sleep scores ($r = .227$, $p < 0.01$), with a higher level of fatigue associated with poorer sleep quality. Both workload and fatigue were significantly correlated with six of the seven PSQI factors, including subjective sleep quality, sleep latency, sleep duration, habitual sleep efficiency, sleep disturbances, and daytime dysfunction, all $p < 0.05$. There was no significant association found between either workload or fatigue and the use of sleep medication.

Predictors of Fatigue. Logistic regressions were run to investigate the predictors of fatigue. Variables scores were categorised into a high/low group using a median split. The dependent variable was categorical fatigue (High/Low). The independent variables included in the model were social-demographic variables (age and gender), individual difference factors (personality and lifestyle) and work-related risk factors (workload, job control and support, being exposed to noise at work, and being exposed to fumes at work), in which age was continuous, and the rest of them were categorical. The OR effect size for each of the IVs is shown in Table 2 below.

Table 1. Correlation between workload, fatigue and sleep variables.

Heading level	(1)	(2)	(3)	(4)	(5)	(6)	(7)	(8)	(9)	(10)
Workload (1)	1									
Fatigue (2)	.831**	1								
Subjective sleep quality (3)	.145**	.155**	1							
Sleep latency (4)	.192**	.244**	.400**	1						
Sleep duration (5)	.114*	.062	.192**	.267**	1					
Habitual sleep efficiency (6)	.108*	.119*	.211**	.356**	.526**	1				
Sleep disturbances (7)	.120*	.143**	.402**	.430**	.201**	.197**	1			
Use of sleep medication (8)	.093	.097	.378**	.334**	.212**	.238**	.414**	1		
Daytime dysfunction (9)	.211**	.207**	.672**	.506**	.274**	.402**	.513**	.473**	1	
Sleep global score (10)	.213**	.227**	.706**	.728**	.547**	.637**	.621**	.615**	.834**	1

*p < 0.05, **p < 0.01.

The results showed that workload was the strongest predictor of reported high fatigue with an odds ratio of 86.234 (p < .001), which indicated that participants who reported a high workload were over eighty times more likely to report a high level of fatigue than those reporting a low workload after controlling social demography and individual difference factors in the model. No significant contribution from other work-related risk factors was found in this model.

2.3 Summary

Fatigue and poor sleep quality were the general problems in physicians and nurses working in psychiatric hospitals. The majority of the participant report high workloads and suffering from fatigue and sleep problem. 74.9% of the participant had their PSQI global score over 8, the standard threshold in China [42], indicating that their sleep quality

Table 2. Odds ratio of IVs on fatigue.

Variables	Odds ratio	95% C. I for Odds Ratio
Social demographics		
Age	1.040	[0.986, 1.098]
Gender	1.216	[0.499, 2.966]
Personal characteristics		
Personality (negative)	1.545	[0.493, 4.842]
Lifestyle (unhealthy)	0.803	[0.260, 2.477]
Work characteristics		
Workload (high)	86.234[**]	[40.235, 184.820]
Job support and control (low)	0.994	[0.451, 2.189]
Noise (high)	0.590	[0.262, 1.327]
Fumes (high)	1.441	[0.610, 3.402]

[*] $p < 0.05$, [**] $p < 0.001$.

was generally worse than that of normal Chinese adults. The present study showed that the associations between workload, fatigue and sleep quality were significant, and with a higher workload, participants reported higher fatigue and more inferior sleep quality.

According to the DRIVE model, the predictors of fatigue were investigated by using logistic regression. The workload was the strongest and the only work-related predictor of occupational fatigue in the psychiatric industry. Participants who reported a high workload were over eighty times more likely to report a high level of fatigue than those reporting a low workload after controlling social demography and individual difference factors.

3 Study 2

3.1 Links Between Studies 1 and 2

Study 1 was a cross-sectional study using a sample of psychiatric staff, which provided an overview of participants' workload, fatigue and sleep quality over recent months. However, the short-term effect of workload on dynamic changes of fatigue and sleep quality was still lacking; thus, a continuous exploration of workload, fatigue, and sleep quality over a working week was needed. Study 2 was a diary study aiming to explore further the relationships between workload, fatigue and sleep quality over a working week. Participants recorded their sleep quality, occupational fatigue, and workload within one working week in the present study. This study aimed to demonstrate a relationship between workload, fatigue, and sleep quality to confirm the results from study 1.

3.2 Methods

Participants. Participants were 48 psychiatric staff, 20 male (41.7%) and 28 female (58.3%). The mean (±SD) age group was 36.21 (±9.49) years with a range of 19–53 years. The participants worked as doctors and nurses in one public psychiatric hospital in Maoming City, China.

Materials. Smith and Smith [3] developed and validated the diary, including five questions in the pre-work diary and five questions in the post-work diary. The pre-work diary was completed immediately before work, and the post-work diary was completed immediately after work, on the first and the last day of a working week (5 uninterrupted working days). The pre-work diary asked about sleep duration, sleep quality, commute time, general wellbeing, and alertness. The post-work diary asked about workload, effort, fatigue, stress, and break time (minutes). There were additional questions in the post-work diary on the last day, which asked participants whether their work task affects their sleep. If yes, participants were asked to provide examples; if not, they were asked to list the primary factors they believed affected their sleep.

Procedure. This study was conducted in March 2021. Participants in Study 1 were informed about this diary study and provided an informed consent form to ask if they would like to participate. If yes, they were asked to provide a start and end date for their usual working week. On the first and the last working day in the agreed testing week, participants were asked to complete a diary questionnaire under the required time frame. This study was reviewed and approved by the Ethics Committee of the School of Psychology, Shenzhen University.

Analysis. Data analysis was carried out using SPSS 26. Data were analysed using paired-samples t-test and Pearson correlation.

3.3 Results

Descriptive. Forty-eight participants fully completed the diary, 41.7% were doctors, and 58.3% were nurses. The range of their commute time was 15 min to 45 min, and the range of their rest time during work was between 120 to 180 min.

Perceived Workload, Fatigue, and Sleep Quality over the Working Week. Table 3 below shows the difference in sleep quality, subjective workload, and fatigue after work between the first and last workdays. As is shown, Sleep quality decreased during the week. Fatigue and subjective workload increased over the week.

A paired-samples t-test analysis was conducted to evaluate the impact of the working week on participants' ratings on perceived workload, fatigue and sleep quality.

There was a statistically significant decrease in sleep quality score from first working day (M = 6.63, SD = .937) to last working day (M = 5.85, SD = .684), t(47) = 6.235, p < 0.001 (two-tail). The mean decrease in sleep quality score was .771 with a 95% confidence interval ranging from .522 to 1.020. The eta squared statistic (.45) indicated a medium effect size.

Table 3. Descriptive statistics for mean of variables.

Variables	First day		Last day	
	Mean	S.D	Mean	S.D
Sleep Quality	6.63	.937	5.85	.684
Subjective Workload	6.71	.852	7.33	.519
Fatigue after Work	6.85	.618	7.58	.647

Both fatigue and subjective workload were found to significantly increase from the first working day to the last working day (fatigue: $t(47) = -8.803$, $p < 0.001$; subjective workload: $t(47) = -7.148$, $p < 0.001$). The eta squared statistics for fatigue (.62), and for subjective workload (.52) indicated large effect size.

Association Between Workload, Fatigue, Sleep Quality and Other Variables. A Pearson correlation was run to investigate the association between workload, fatigue and sleep quality.

On the first day, workload was positively correlated with fatigue ($r = .648$, $p < .001$) and stress ($r = .371$, $p = .010$), and negatively correlated with rest time during work ($r = -.421$, $p = .003$) at a statistically significant level. Fatigue was significantly positively correlated with stress ($r = .547$, $p < .001$) and effort ($r = .440$, $p = .002$), while negatively correlated with break time during work ($r = -.535$, $p < .001$). Sleep quality showed a significant positive correlation with sleep duration ($r = .634$, $p < .001$) and general feeling ($r = .452$, $p < .001$). No significant associations between sleep quality and workload or fatigue were found.

On the last day, fatigue showed a significant positive correlation with stress ($r = .369$, $p = .005$) and effort ($r = .420$, $p = .003$). No other significant associations were found.

The weekly change scores of variables were calculated using the last-day scores minus the first-day work scores. The Pearson correlation result showed that the change of perceived workload was significantly associated with fatigue change ($r = .314$, $p = .030$). The change in sleep quality was not found to be significantly associated with either fatigue or workload.

In the post-work diary, participants were asked if their work tasks affected their sleep on the last day. In this open question, 41 of the 48 participants stated that their work-related factors affected their sleep. For example, they had too many patients each day, spent time receiving patients or their family members' calls, or consulting online during staff breaks, were assigned extra tasks by their supervisor, or had work that needed to be completed during non-working hours. Seven participants believed that work was not the most critical factor affecting their sleep, and the impact of work was less substantial than the impact of family relationships or life stress on their sleep. None of the respondents mentioned that COVID-19 brought them more mental workload or impacted their sleep.

3.4 Summary

The present diary study aimed to explore the relationships between fatigue, workload and sleep quality in realistic situations over a working week. The results showed that within the working week, as the number of working days increased, the perceived workload and fatigue increased, while the sleep quality deteriorated. These effects of the working week were found to be significant. Similarly to study 1, workload and fatigue showed a significant positive correlation in the present study. However, no significant correlation was found between sleep quality and workload or between it and fatigue.

4 Discussion

Occupational fatigue and poor sleep quality were common occupational issues among working people, especially medical workers. Psychiatric medical staff, like other workers in this industry, work under a high mental workload. However, there is very little relevant literature focused on psychiatric staff. This research aimed to examine the association between workload, occupational fatigue, and sleep quality of the psychiatric medical staff. The present research included two studies: Study 1 was a cross-sessional study using SWELL and PSQI, and study 2 was a diary study conducted in Maoming City in China. Both two studies showed the associations between workload, fatigue and sleep quality, supporting the hypothesis that workload affects fatigue and sleep quality among psychiatric staff.

The finding of study 1 suggested that the majority of the psychiatric staff report a high mental workload, which was in line with the previous studies of other healthcare staff, either inside or outside China [16, 28, 29]. It is also in line with previous studies using NASA-TLX to measure workload [18–20]. Meanwhile, they suffered from fatigue and sleep problem with high self-reported ratings. It was not surprising that the fatigue and poor sleep quality were frequent among psychiatric staff, with a higher fatigue score and severe sleep problems, just as Li et al. [31] suggested. However, it should be noticed that 74.9% of the participant in the present study had their PSQI global score above the number 8, the standard threshold in China [42], indicating that most of their sleep quality was generally worse than that of normal Chinese adults.

The findings showed clear associations between workload, fatigue and sleep quality so that those with a higher workload reported higher fatigue and worse sleep quality. In study 1, such correlations were significant. Although in study 2, the associations between workload and sleep quality did not reach statistical significance, the effect of workload was found to be significant for sleep quality, with self-reported sleep quality scores significantly decreasing over the working week with a medium effect size.

The qualitative data also supported the effect of workload on sleep. 41 of the 48 participants stated that work-related factors were affecting their sleep. The examples they provided in the open question gave a detailed picture of the nature of their daily work. These work-related factors influenced their sleep quality and included too many patients each day, receiving patients or their family members' calls or consulting online during staff breaks, and being assigned extra tasks by their supervisor. Further research needs to investigate their non-working hours, as other participants believed that work was not the most crucial factor affecting their sleep, and it was family relationships or life stress that was affecting their sleep quality.

This research also aimed to investigate the main predictors of the occupational fatigue of psychiatric staff, as there was limited literature concerned with fatigue in this particular job. In study 1, workload was the strongest and only work-related predictor of occupational fatigue in the psychiatric staff, partially supporting the DRIVE model [43]. Participants who reported a high workload were over eighty times more likely to report a high level of fatigue than those reporting a low workload after controlling social demography and individual difference factors. In study 2, the diary result showed a large effect size of weekly work on fatigue. Both studies supported the hypothesis that workload affects fatigue and sleep quality among psychiatric staff. These results bring more insight in understanding the relationship between workload, fatigue and sleep quality among psychiatric staff and can be used to back up initiatives to detect work-related fatigue quickly in order to provide adequate support to the medical and psychiatric staff suffering from the workload and take action to reduce the risks of ill-health and accidents.

An essential feature of the study was the use of single-item measures of workload and fatigue. We translated the SWELL questionnaire [3] from its original English version to the Chinese version by forward-translation and back-translation. Such measurements are acceptable, manageable, can be further applied in field studies of real-life settings, particularly in the medical workplace, as it allows us to identify risk factors conveniently in a short time compared to multi-item measures. Detecting work-related fatigue quickly will allow individuals to self-manage fatigue and allow organisations to provide adequate support to the medical and psychiatric staff and to take action to reduce the risks of ill-health and accidents.

4.1 Limitations

The unexpected results led to reflections on the limitations of this research. The single-item measurement of sleep quality currently used in the diary study may have its limitation. When the PSQI was used as a multi-item measurement in study 1, the associations between sleep quality (its seven factors and the global score) and fatigue was apparent. However, when a single-item measurement of sleep quality was used in the diary study, no such associations were found. In the future, one could integrate the objective measurement of sleep quality (e.g., actigraphy) and the single-item measurement of sleep quality to further examine any potential bias. Furthermore, the sample used in the present study was from psychiatric hospitals in one medium city in China, which may limit the generalisation of the results to psychiatry staff working in general hospitals or those with other cultural backgrounds.

5 Conclusion

Overall, the studies described in this article have shown that psychiatric staff have a high workload, leading to high fatigue and poor sleep quality. Associations between workload and fatigue were found in both studies, probably due to using the same measuring instruments. The sleep quality associations seen in study 1 with the PQSI were not observed when single sleep items were used in the diary study. Further research must determine whether this reflected the different measuring instruments or the focus on specific days. The influence of non-work confounders also needs to be addressed, as does the extent to which effects of workload may persist outside of the workplace.

References

1. Smith, A.P., Smith, K.: Effects of workload and time of day on performance and mood. In: Megaw, E.D. (ed.) Contemporary Ergonomics, pp. 497–502. Taylor & Francis, London (1988)
2. Smith, A.P., Clayton, H.: The effects of chewing gum on perceived stress and wellbeing in students under a high and low workload. In: Longo, L., Leva, M.C. (eds.) H-WORKLOAD 2020. CCIS, vol. 1318, pp. 124–137. Springer, Cham (2020). https://doi.org/10.1007/978-3-030-62302-9_8
3. Smith, A.P., Smith, H.N.: Workload, fatigue and performance in the rail industry. In: Longo, L., Leva, M.C. (eds.) H-WORKLOAD 2017. CCIS, vol. 726, pp. 251–263. Springer, Cham (2017). https://doi.org/10.1007/978-3-319-61061-0_17
4. Fan, J., Smith, A.P.: Mental workload and other causes of different types of fatigue in rail staff. In: Longo, L., Leva, M.C. (eds.) H-WORKLOAD 2018. CCIS, vol. 1012, pp. 147–159. Springer, Cham (2019). https://doi.org/10.1007/978-3-030-14273-5_9
5. Fan, J., Smith, A.P.: Causes of rail staff fatigue: results of qualitative analysis and a diary study. In: Longo, L., Leva, M.C. (eds.) H-WORKLOAD 2020. CCIS, vol. 1318, pp. 227–249. Springer, Cham (2020). https://doi.org/10.1007/978-3-030-62302-9_14
6. Jahns, D.W.: A concept of operator workload in manual vehicle operations (1973)
7. Wickens, C.D.: Measures of workload, stress and secondary tasks. In: Moray, N. (ed.) Mental Workload. NATO Conference Series, vol. 8. Springer, Boston (1979). https://doi.org/10.1007/978-1-4757-0884-4_6
8. Gopher, D., Donchin, E.: Workload: An examination of the concept. In: Boff, K.R., Kaufman, L., Thomas, J.P. (eds.) Handbook of Perception and Human Performance, vol. 2, pp. 1–49. Wiley (1986)
9. Cain, B.: A review of the mental workload literature. Defence Research and Development Toronto, Canada (2007)
10. Longo, L.: A defeasible reasoning framework for human mental workload representation and assessment. Behav. Inf. Technol. 34(8), 758–786 (2015)
11. Rizzo, L., Dondio, P., Delany, S.J., Longo, L.: Modeling mental workload via rule-based expert system: a comparison with NASA-TLX and workload profile. In: Iliadis, L., Maglogiannis, I. (eds.) AIAI 2016. IAICT, vol. 475, pp. 215–229. Springer, Cham (2016). https://doi.org/10.1007/978-3-319-44944-9_19
12. Orru, G., Longo, L.: Direct and constructivist instructional design: a comparison of efficiency using mental workload and task performance. In: Longo, L., Leva, M.C. (eds.) H-WORKLOAD 2020. CCIS, vol. 1318, pp. 99–123. Springer, Cham (2020). https://doi.org/10.1007/978-3-030-62302-9_7
13. Fan, J., Smith, A.P.: The impact of workload and fatigue on performance. In: Longo, L., Leva, M.C. (eds.) H-WORKLOAD 2017. CCIS, vol. 726, pp. 90–105. Springer, Cham (2017). https://doi.org/10.1007/978-3-319-61061-0_6
14. Fan, J., Smith, A.: The mediating effect of fatigue on work-life balance and positive wellbeing in railway staff. Open J. Soc. Sci. 6(6), 1 (2018). https://doi.org/10.4236/jss.2018.66001
15. Alhenieidi, H., Smith, A.P.: Effects of perceptions of information overload, noise and environmental demands on wellbeing and academic attainment. In: Longo, L., Leva, M.C. (eds.) H-WORKLOAD 2020. CCIS, vol. 1318, pp. 87–96. Springer, Cham (2020). https://doi.org/10.1007/978-3-030-62302-9_6

16. Williams, J., Smith, A.P.: Stress, job satisfaction and mental health of NHS nurses. In: Anderson, M. (ed.) Contemporary Ergonomics and Human Factors 2013: Proceedings of the international conference on Ergonomics & Human Factors 2013, pp. 95–102. Taylor & Francis, Cambridge (2013)

17. Hsiao, W.C., Braun, P., Yntema, D., Becker, E.R.: Estimating physicians' work for a resource-based relative-value scale. N. Engl. J. Med. **319**(13), 835–841 (1988). https://doi.org/10.1056/NEJM198809293191305

18. Hoonakker, P., et al.: Measuring workload of ICU nurses with a questionnaire survey: the NASA Task Load Index (TLX). IIE Trans. Healthc. Syst. Eng. **1**(2), 131–143 (2011). https://doi.org/10.1080/19488300.2011.609524

19. Van Bogaert, P., Clarke, S., Willems, R., Mondelaers, M.: Nurse practice environment, workload, burnout, job outcomes, and quality of care in psychiatric hospitals: a structural equation model approach. J. Adv. Nurs. **69**(7), 1515–1524 (2013). https://doi.org/10.1111/jan.12010

20. Lowndes, B.R., et al.: NASA-TLX assessment of surgeon workload variation across specialties. Ann. Surg. **271**(4), 686–692 (2020). https://doi.org/10.1097/SLA.0000000000003058

21. Frone, M.R., Tidwell, M.C.O.: The meaning and measurement of work fatigue: development and evaluation of the three-dimensional work fatigue inventory (3D-WFI). J. Occup. Health Psychol. **20**(3), 273–288 (2015). https://doi.org/10.1037/a0038700

22. Smith, A.P., McNamara, R.L., Wellens, B.T.: Combined Effects of Occupational Health Hazards. HSE Books, Sudbury (2004)

23. Barker, L.M., Nussbaum, M.A.: Fatigue, performance and the work environment: a survey of registered nurses. J. Adv. Nurs. **67**(6), 1370–1382 (2011). https://doi.org/10.1111/j.1365-2648.2010.05597.x

24. Motowidlo, S.J., Packard, J.S., Manning, M.R.: Occupational stress: its causes and consequences for job performance. J. Appl. Psychol. **71**(4), 618 (1986). https://doi.org/10.1037/0021-9010.71.4.618

25. Geiger-Brown, J., Rogers, V.E., Trinkoff, A.M., Kane, R.L., Bausell, R.B., Scharf, S.M.: Sleep, sleepiness, fatigue, and performance of 12-hour-shift nurses. Chronobiol. Int. **29**(2), 211–219 (2012). https://doi.org/10.3109/07420528.2011.645752

26. Fan, J., Smith, A.P.: Effects of occupational fatigue on cognitive performance of staff from a train operating company: a field study. Front. Psychol. **11**, 558520 (2020). https://doi.org/10.3389/fpsyg.2020.558520

27. Wang, L.L.: Moushi Sanji Jiadeng Yiyuan Yihu Renyuan Pilao Xianzhuang Ji Cuoshi Yanjiu [Fatigue and Its Intervention Study of Medical Staff in 3A Hospitals]. Master's thesis. Dalian Medical University (2012)

28. Jiang, D.L.: Neike Hushi Gongzuo Manyidu Yu Pilao Zhuangkuang De Xiangguanxing Fenxi [The Correlation of job satisfaction and fatigue of internal medicine nurses]. Forum Prim. Med. **20**(34), 4894–4896 (2016)

29. Niu, L., Zhang, L., Mei, S., He, B., Guo, J.: Fatigue, sources of stress and perception of control of operating room nurses. J. Changchun Univ. Chin. Med. **32**(4), 813–815. (2016). https://doi.org/10.13463/j.cnki.cczyy.2016.04.056

30. Zhang, Q., Ni, Y., Chen, A.: Jingshenke Hushi Zhiye Juandai Shuiping Diaocha Ji Yingxiangyinsu Fenxi [Investigation and analysis on job burnout level and its influencing factors of psychiatric nurse]. In: Zhejiang Province Annual Conference of Psychiatry 2005 (2005)

31. Li, L., Jiang, F., Li, J., Han, H.: Guangzhoushi Huiai Hospital Yihurenyuan Pilao Zhuangtai Ji Shuimian Zhiliang Xiangguan Yanjiu [Correlation between fatigue status and sleep quality of medical staff in Huiai Hospital of Guangzhou City]. Chin. J. Nerv. Mental Dis. **43**(12), 756–759 (2017). https://doi.org/10.3969/j.issn.1002-0152.2017.12.012

32. Dong, R., Hu, Q., Li, H., Zhang, X., Gu, W., Zhao, S.: Jingshenke Fengbiguanli Bingqu Hushi Pilao Ji Yali Zhuangkuang De Diaocha Fenxi [Investigation and analysis of the fatigue and stress status of nurses in closed management wards of psychiatric department]. In: Conference of Psychiatric Nursing Risk Management 2012 (2012)

33. Xu, D., Song, L., Wang, L.: Comparative study of psychiatric nurses' life quality. Chin. J. Mod. Nurs. **9**(12), 905–908 (2003). https://doi.org/10.3760/cma.j.issn.1674-2907.2003.12.002

34. Poulton, E.C., Hunt, G.M., Carpenter, A., Edwards, R.S.: The performance of junior hospital doctors following reduced sleep and long hours of work. Ergonomics **21**(4), 279–295 (1978). https://doi.org/10.1080/00140137808931725

35. Kjellberg, A.: Sleep deprivation and some aspects of performance. Waking Sleeping **1**(2), 139–143 (1977)

36. Estryn-Behar, M., et al.: Stress at work and mental health status among female hospital workers. Occup. Environ. Med. **47**(1), 20–28 (1990). https://doi.org/10.1136/oem.47.1.20

37. Owens, J.A.: Sleep loss and fatigue in healthcare professionals. J. Perinat. neonatal Nursing **21**(2), 92–100 (2007). https://doi.org/10.1097/01.JPN.0000270624.64584.9d

38. Ghasemi, F., Samavat, P., Soleimani, F.: The links among workload, sleep quality, and fatigue in nurses: a structural equation modeling approach. Fatigue: Biomedicine, Health Behav. **7**(3), 141–152 (2019). https://doi.org/10.1080/21641846.2019.1652422

39. Wang, U., Nie, J., Liu, L.: Correlation between occupational fatigue status and sleep quality of obstetrics and gynecology physicians in Nanchang City. Occup. Health **2018**(20), 2789–2793 (2018)

40. Hu, W., Li, L., Hui, L., Ye, G., Jia, Q.: Study on the relationship between sleep disorder and cognitive function in psychiatric medical staff. Manage. Observer **9**, 182–183 (2019). https://doi.org/10.3969/j.issn.1674-2877.2019.09.072

41. Buysse, D.J., Reynolds, C.F., III., Monk, T.H., Berman, S.R., Kupfer, D.J.: The Pittsburgh Sleep Quality Index: a new instrument for psychiatric practice and research. Psychiatr. Res. **28**(2), 193–213 (1989). https://doi.org/10.1016/0165-1781(89)90047-4

42. Liu, X., Tang, M., Hu, L.: Pittsburgh Sleep Quality Index De Xindu He Xiaodu. [Reliability and Validity of the Pittsburgh Sleep Quality Index]. Chin. J. Psychiatr. **29**(02), 105–107 (1996)

43. Mark, G.M., Smith, A.P.: Stress models: a review and suggested new direction. In: Houdmont, J., Leka, S. (eds.) Occupational Health Psychology: European Perspectives on research, education and practice, pp. 111–144. Nottingham University Press, Nottingham (2008)

44. Smith, A.P., Smith, H.: An international survey of the wellbeing of employees in the business process outsourcing industry. Psychology **8**(01), 160–167 (2017). https://doi.org/10.4236/psych.2017.81010

45. Williams, G.M., Smith, A.P.: A holistic approach to stress and wellbeing. Part 6: the wellbeing process questionnaire (WPQ short form). Occup. Health (At Work) **9**(1), 29–31 (2012)

46. Williams, G.M., Smith, A.P.: Using single-item measures to examine the relationships between work, personality, and wellbeing in the workplace. Psychol. Spec. Ed. Posit. Psychol. **7**, 753–767 (2016)

Author Index

Printed in the United States
by Baker & Taylor Publisher Services